ILLUSTRATOR'S REFERENCE MANUAL

ILLUSTRATOR'S
REFERENCE MANUAL

angus

A QUANTUM BOOK

Produced by
Quantum Publishing Ltd
6 Blundell Street
London N7 9BH

This edition printed 2003

Published by Angus Books Ltd
Unit 16, Northfields Prospect Business Centre
Northfields
London
SW18 1PE

ISBN 1-904594-22-0

QUMSIF

Printed in China by
Leefung-Asco Printers Ltd

Contents

3·32 Gymnastics – crab
3·33 Keep fit
3·34 Keep fit
3·35 Keep fit
3·36 Keep fit
3·37 Yoga
3·38 Yoga
3·39 Yoga
3·40 Skateboarding
3·41 Walking the dog
3·42 Walking with walking stick
3·43 Couple playing chess
3·44 Playing cards
3·45 Artist painting

Sitting

4·01 Backwards on a chair
4·02 In a chair doing the crossword
4·03 In a chair looking through filofax
4·04 Sideways in a chair
4·05 Kneeling on a chair talking on the phone
4·06 On a bar stool
4·07 Vicar asleep in rocking chair
4·08 On the floor thinking
4·09 On a table talking on the phone
4·10 Relaxing in an armchair
4·11 Reclining on a sofa
4·12 Couple sitting side by side
4·13 On the floor

Person to person

5·01 Couple kissing
5·02 Kissing goodbye
5·03 Waving goodbye
5·04 Crying into handkerchief
5·05 Macho man
5·06 Gent kissing lady's hand
5·07 Couple talking at dinner table
5·08 GI greeting his girl
5·09 Couple at the races
5·10 Bully threatening a small guy
5·11 Cowering on the ground
5·12 Curtseying
5·13 Greeting a friend
5·14 Taking the lady home
5·15 Couple at the beach

Religion

6·01 Genuflecting
6·02 Vicar preaching
6·03 Vicar blessing girl
6·04 Girl praying

Law and order

7·01 New York policeman – stop!
7·02 New York policeman directing traffic
7·03 Cowgirl shooting
7·04 British policeman saluting
7·05 Gangster with violin case

The working day

8·01 Businessman holding briefcase hailing taxi
8·02 Secretary running looking at watch
8·03 Businessman opening umbrella
8·04 Standing under an umbrella
8·05 Secretary taking dictation
8·06 Businessman talking on phone looking at watch
8·07 Secretary at typewriter
8·08 Secretary at desk talking on phone
8·09 Commuting

Carrying

9·01 Heavy suitcase
9·02 Stack of boxes
9·03 Large potted plant
9·04 Step-ladder
9·05 "Smelly socks"
9·06 Shoulder bag and carrier bag

Domestic

10·01 Sewing
10·02 Washing-up
10·03 French maid dusting
10·04 Sweeping up
10·05 Vacuuming
10·06 Knitting in rocking chair
10·07 Painting with a roller
10·08 Leaning on broom
10·09 Sawing

10'10 Hammering in a nail
10'11 Hitting thumb with hammer
10'12 Ironing
10'13 Painting with a brush

Eating and drinking

11'01 Eating sandwiches and drinking tea
11'02 Drinking from a can
11'03 Eating pizza with hands
11'04 Eating with chopsticks
11'05 Secretary drinking from teacup and saucer
11'06 Vicar drinking tea and biscuits
11'07 Drinking wine and smoking
11'08 Drinking wine at cocktail party
11'09 Waiter serving wine
11'10 Waitress with tray

Music and entertainment

12'01 Disco dancing
12'02 Rock and roll dancing
12'03 Ballroom dancing – quickstep
12'04 Ballroom dancing – waltz
12'05 Ballroom dancing – tango
12'06 Conducting – vivace
12'07 Conducting – adagio
12'08 Playing the clarinet
12'09 Playing the violin
12'10 Playing the double bass
12'11 Opera singer
12'12 Country and western singer
12'13 Rock singer
12'14 Playing an acoustic guitar
12'15 Playing an electric guitar
12'16 Playing an electric piano
12'17 Jazz trumpeter

Dressing and undressing

13'01 Putting hat on
13'02 Putting jacket on
13'03 Clipping suspenders
13'04 Putting skirt on
13'05 Putting trousers on
13'06 Putting socks on
13'07 Putting shoes on
13'08 Taking boots off
13'09 Taking jumper off
13'10 Clipping brassiere
13'11 Putting shirt on

Washing

14'01 Drying hair with towel
14'02 Brushing hair
14'03 Brushing teeth
14'04 Filing nails
14'05 Touching up lipstick
14'06 Shaving

Cheesecake

15'01 Cheesecake
15'02 Cheesecake
15'03 Cheesecake
15'04 Cheesecake
15'05 Cheesecake
15'06 Cheesecake
15'07 Cheesecake
15'08 Cheesecake
15'09 Cheesecake
15'10 Cheesecake
15'11 Cheesecake
15'12 Cheesecake

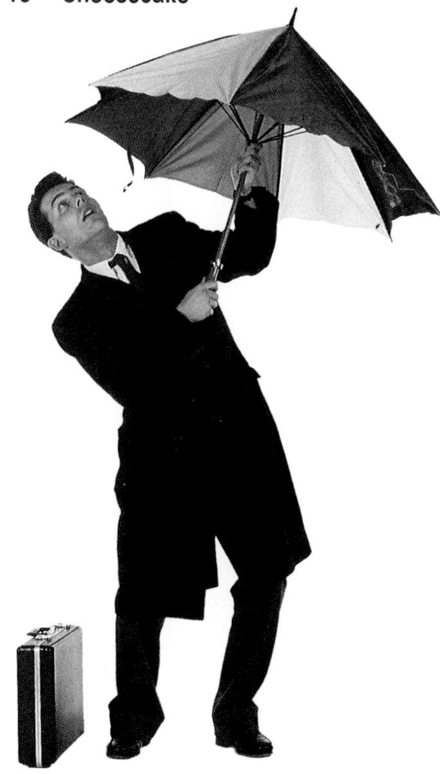

Using the figure reference manual

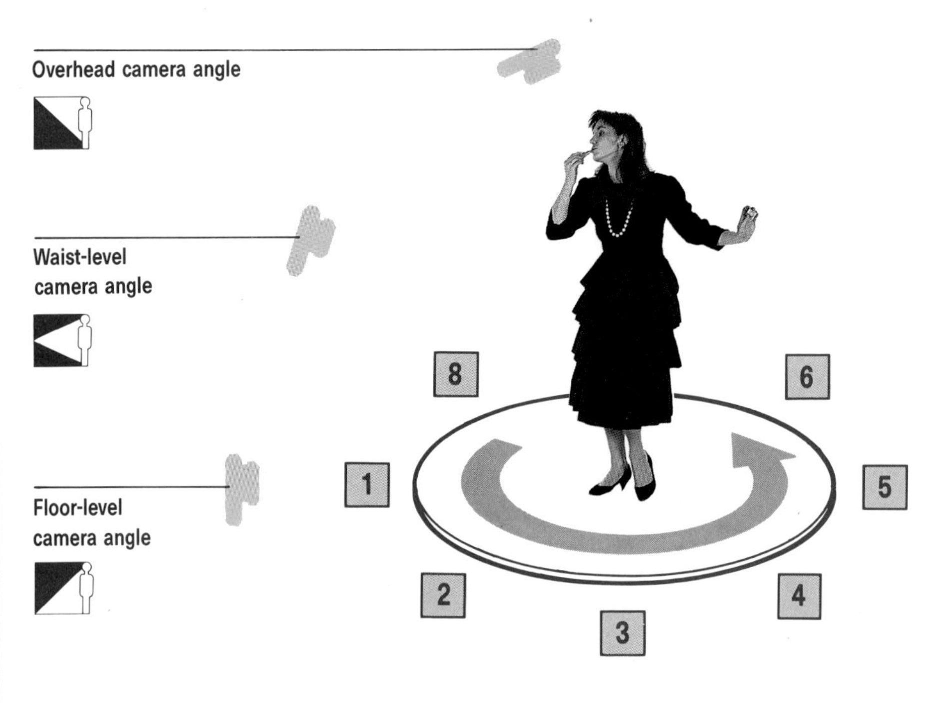

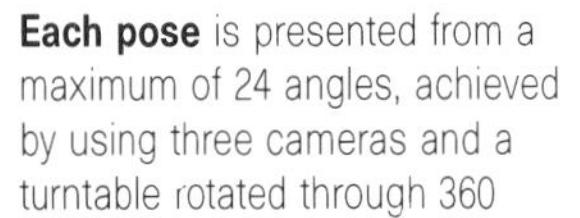

Each pose is presented from a maximum of 24 angles, achieved by using three cameras and a turntable rotated through 360 degrees (above). A simple camera angle symbol (above left) accompanies the relevant group of images within a pose.

The ILLUSTRATOR'S FIGURE REFERENCE MANUAL comprises 250 "poses" categorized under 10 general headings. Each category has an "index code", and within each category each pose has a further "sub-index code" for ease of reference.

Each pose is presented from a maximum of 24 angles. In order to provide images of a size sufficiently large enough to be of use as a reference, some poses are presented in a different scale to others (although all images within a pose are presented in the same scale). In order to facilitate the drawing of composite poses a simple calibrated bar accompanies each pose. To draw a composite pose using elements from poses presented in different scales, simply use a visualizing camera to enlarge or reduce the calibrated bar on the relevant poses until a precise match is achieved. This will then ensure that the elements you require from different poses appear in the same scale.

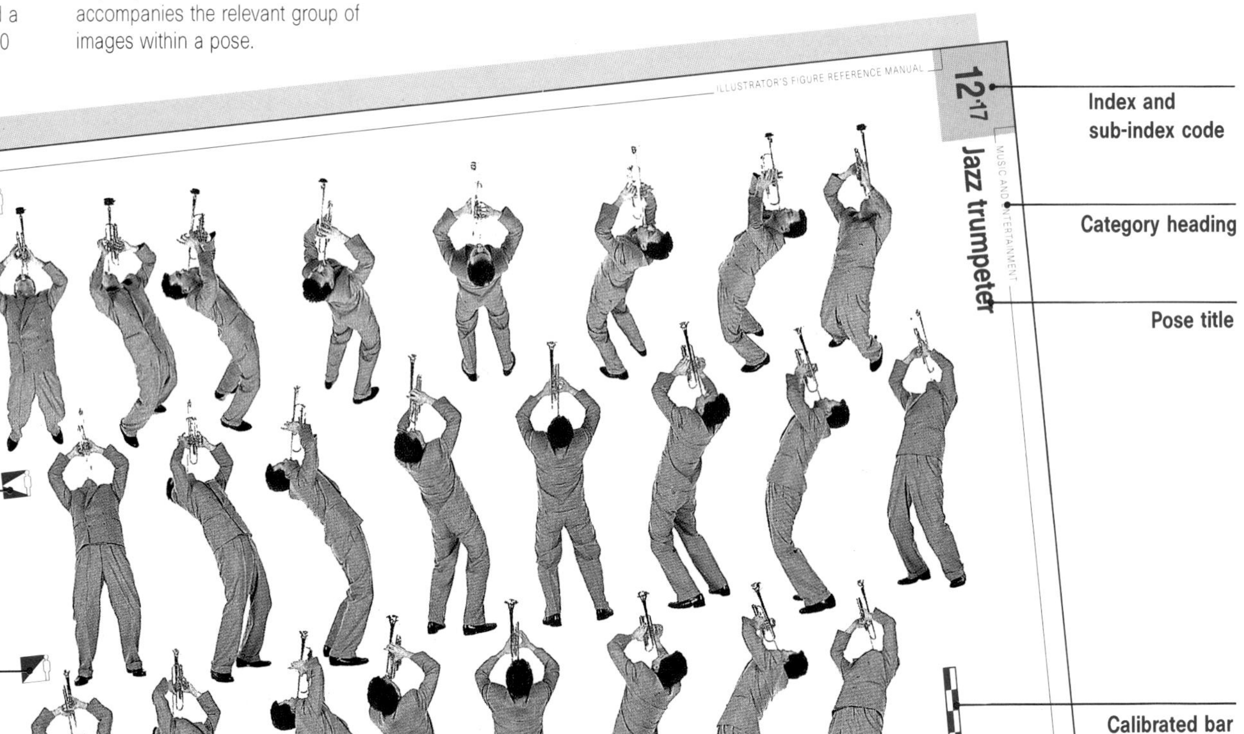

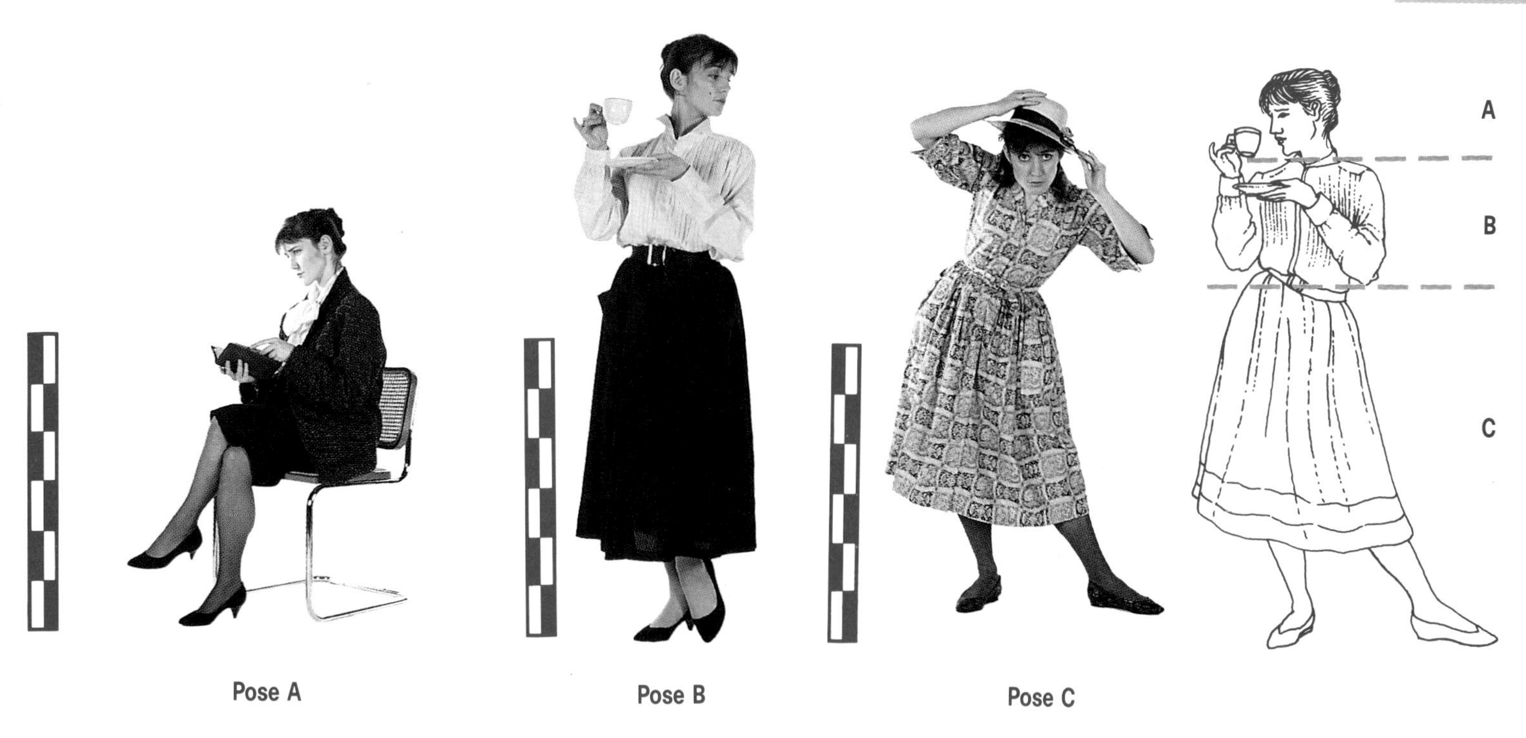

Pose A

Pose B

Pose C

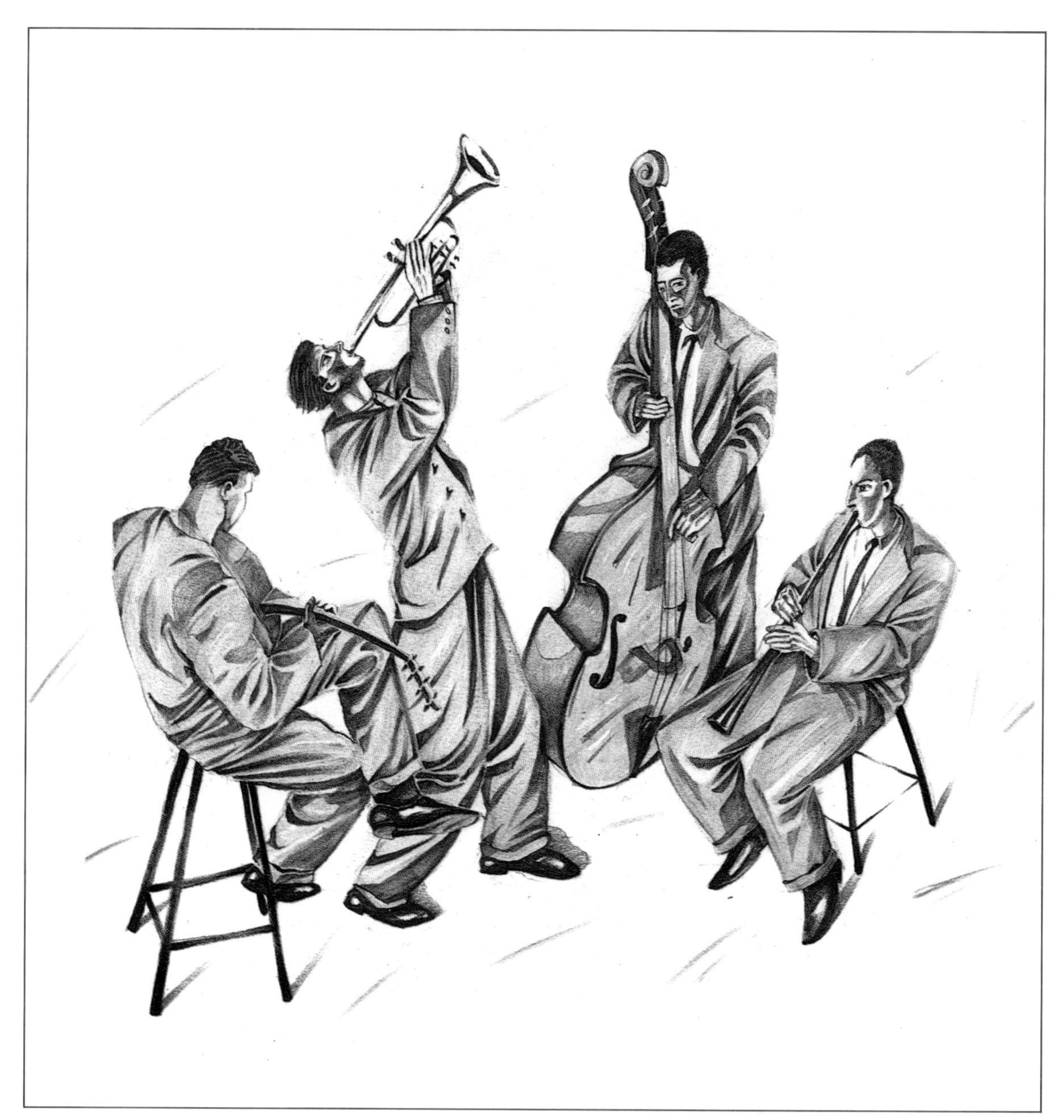

Composite figures (above) can be drawn using elements from different poses. The calibrated bar allows elements from poses presented in different scales to be combined.

Group illustrations (left) can easily be drawn. The calibrated bar accompanying each pose can be used to standardize the scales.

Arms stretched up

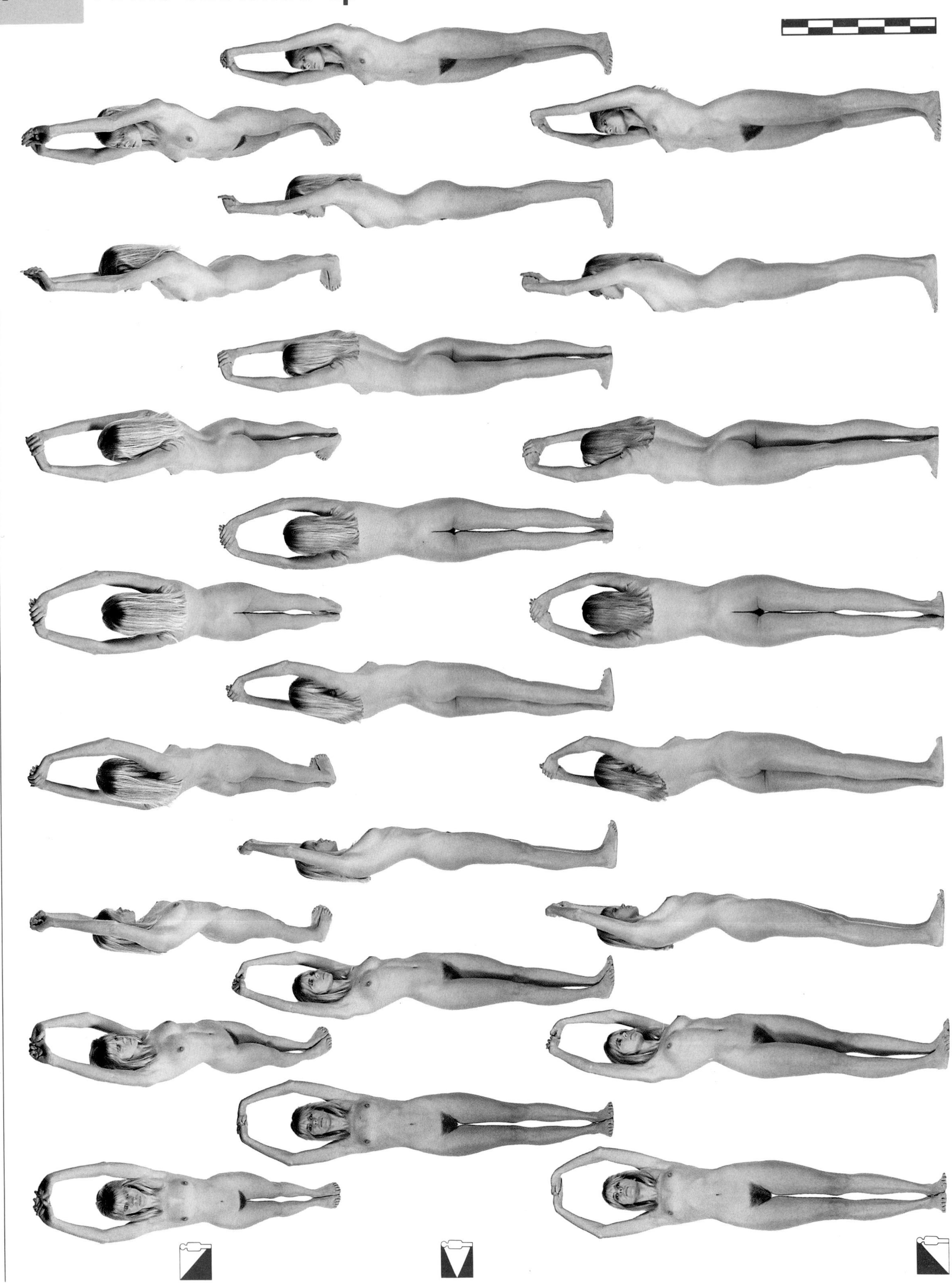

Hands behind head

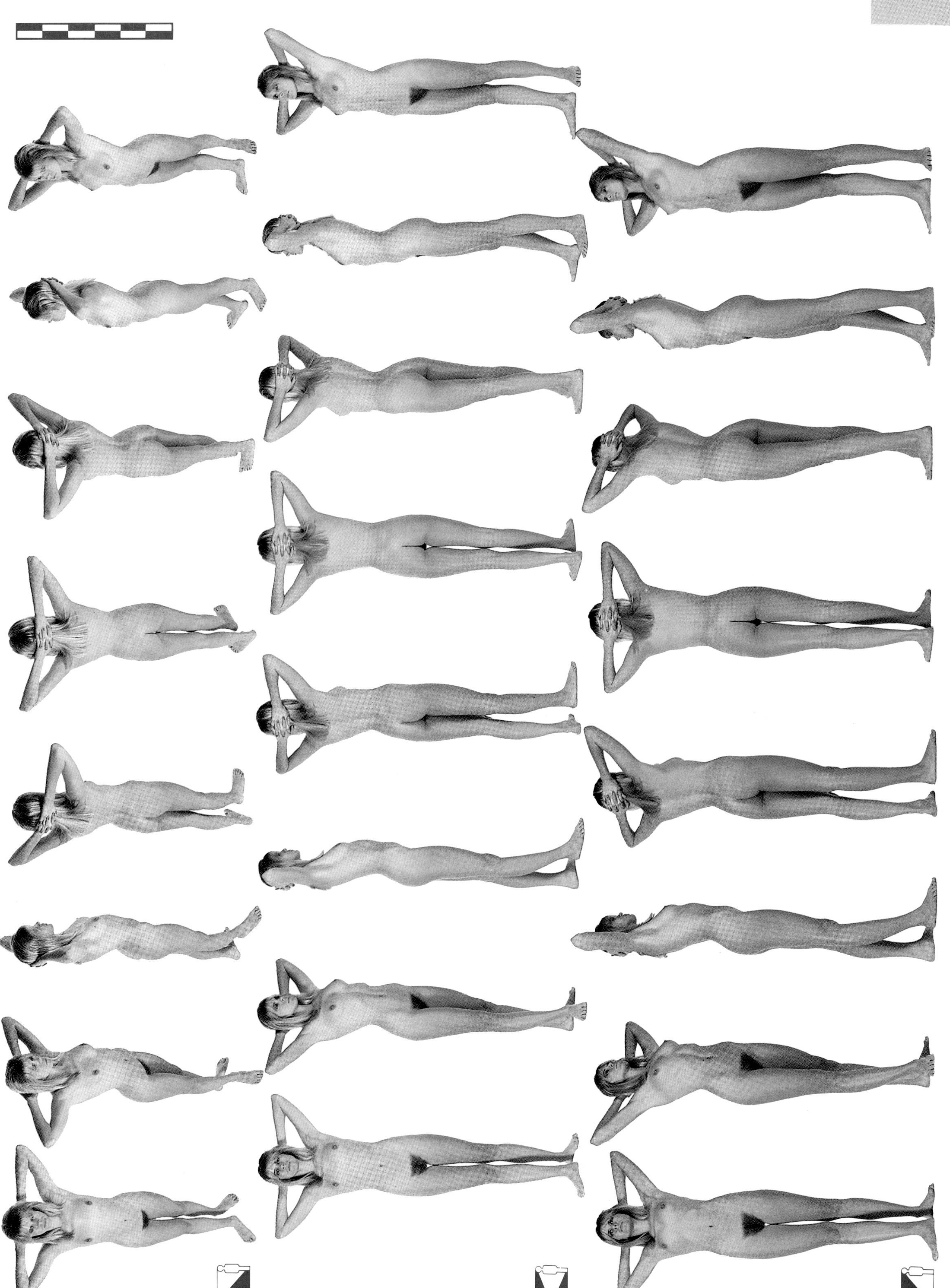

1·03 Arms stretched to side

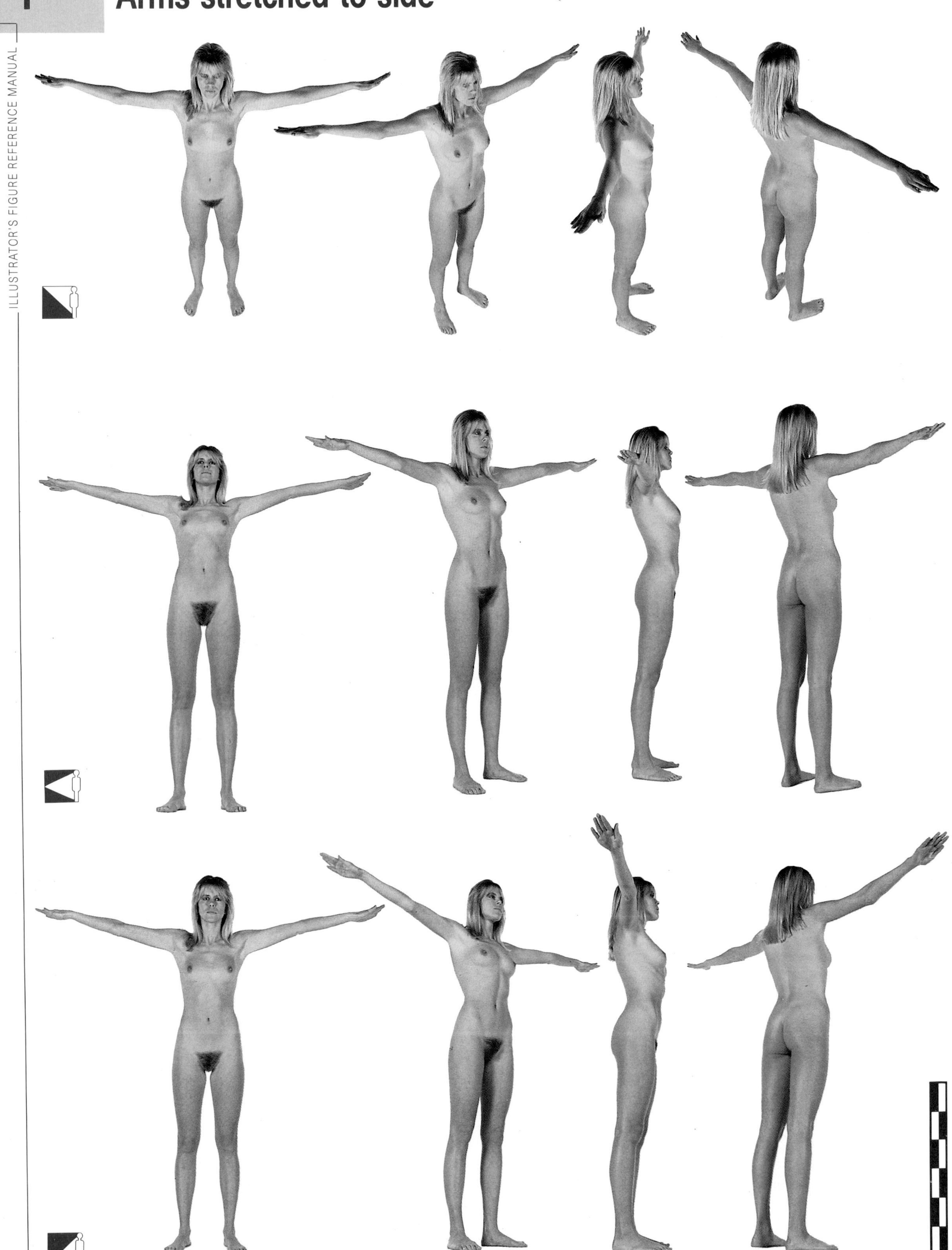

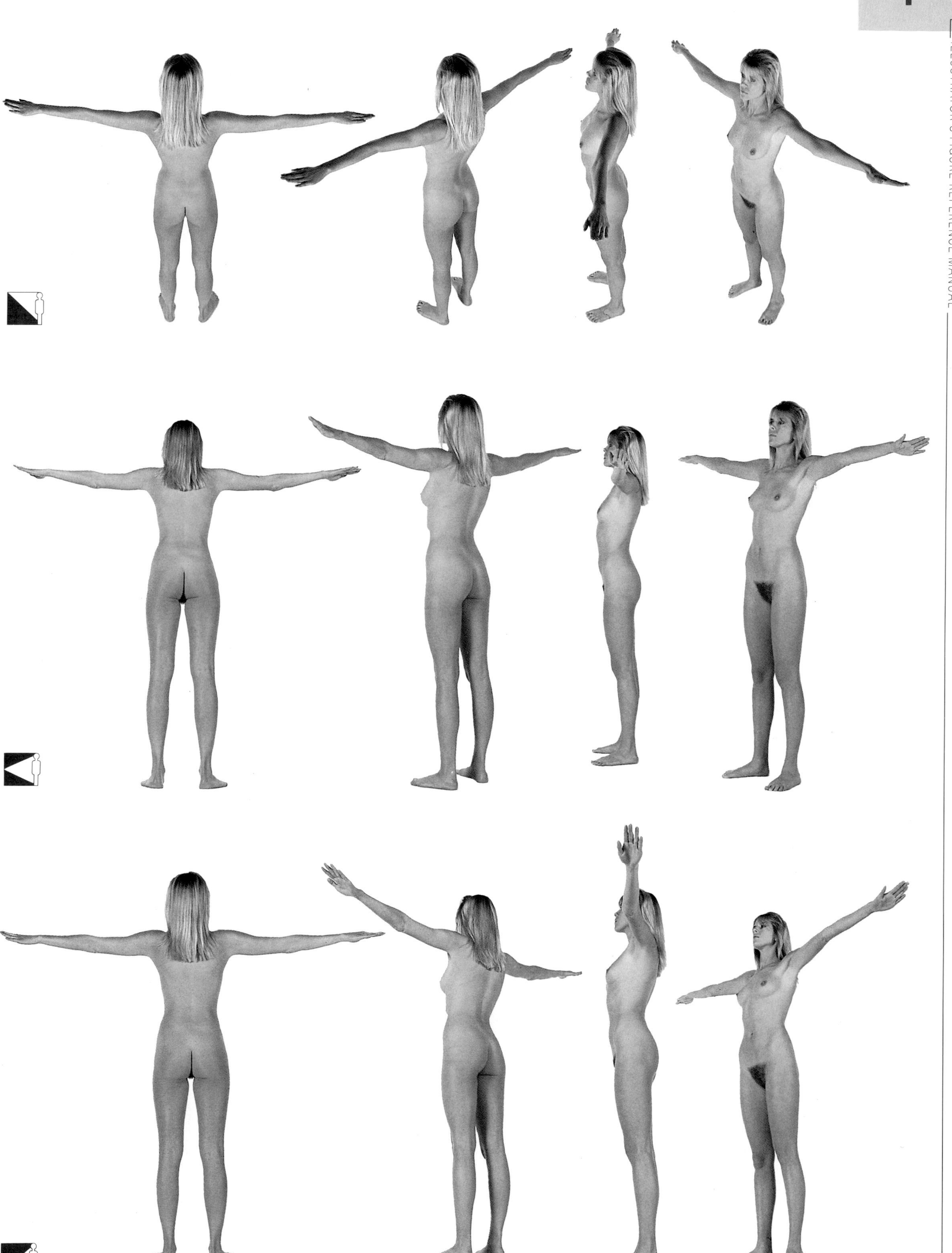

1·04 Hands on hips

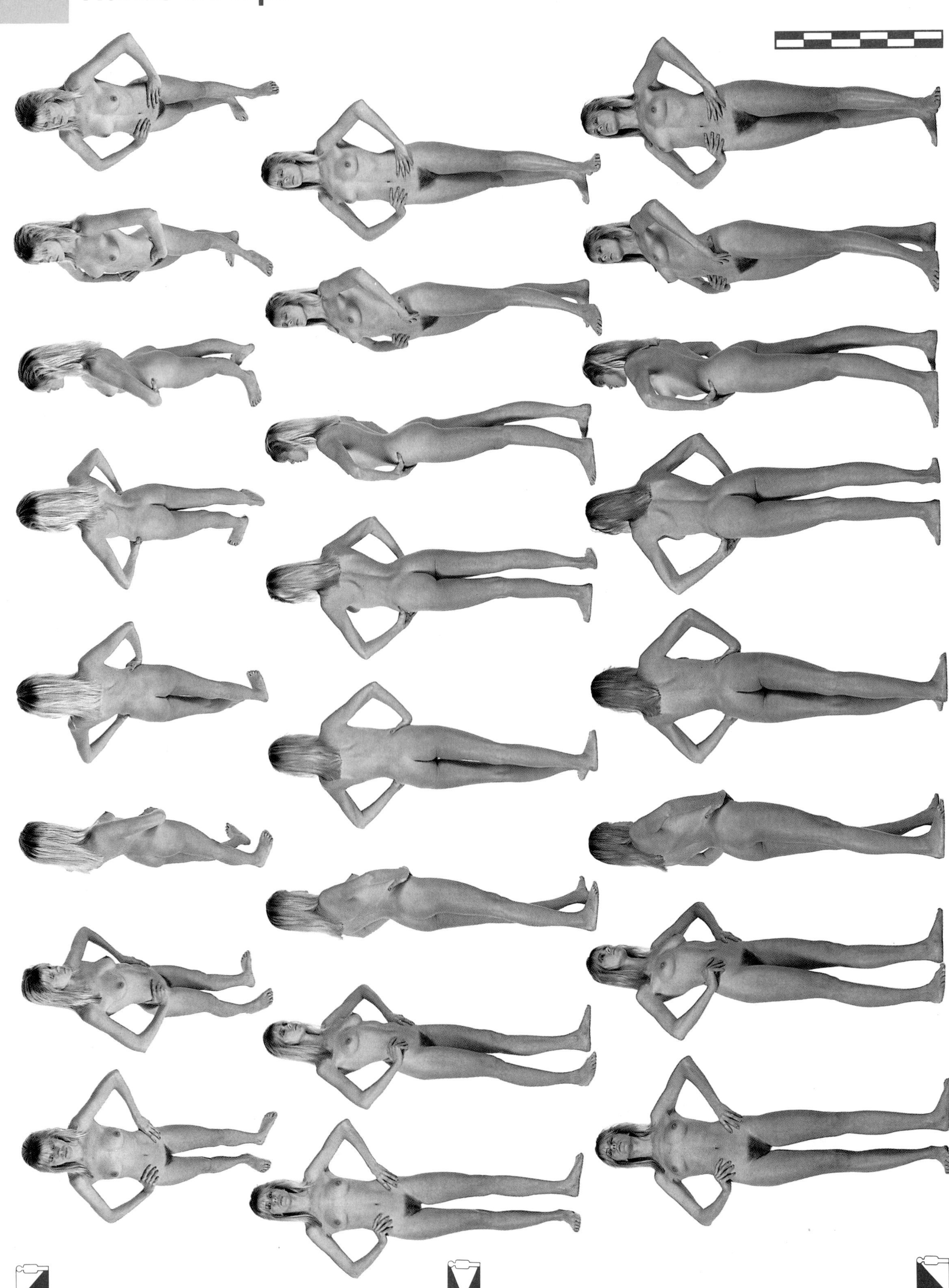

Upper trunk twisted round

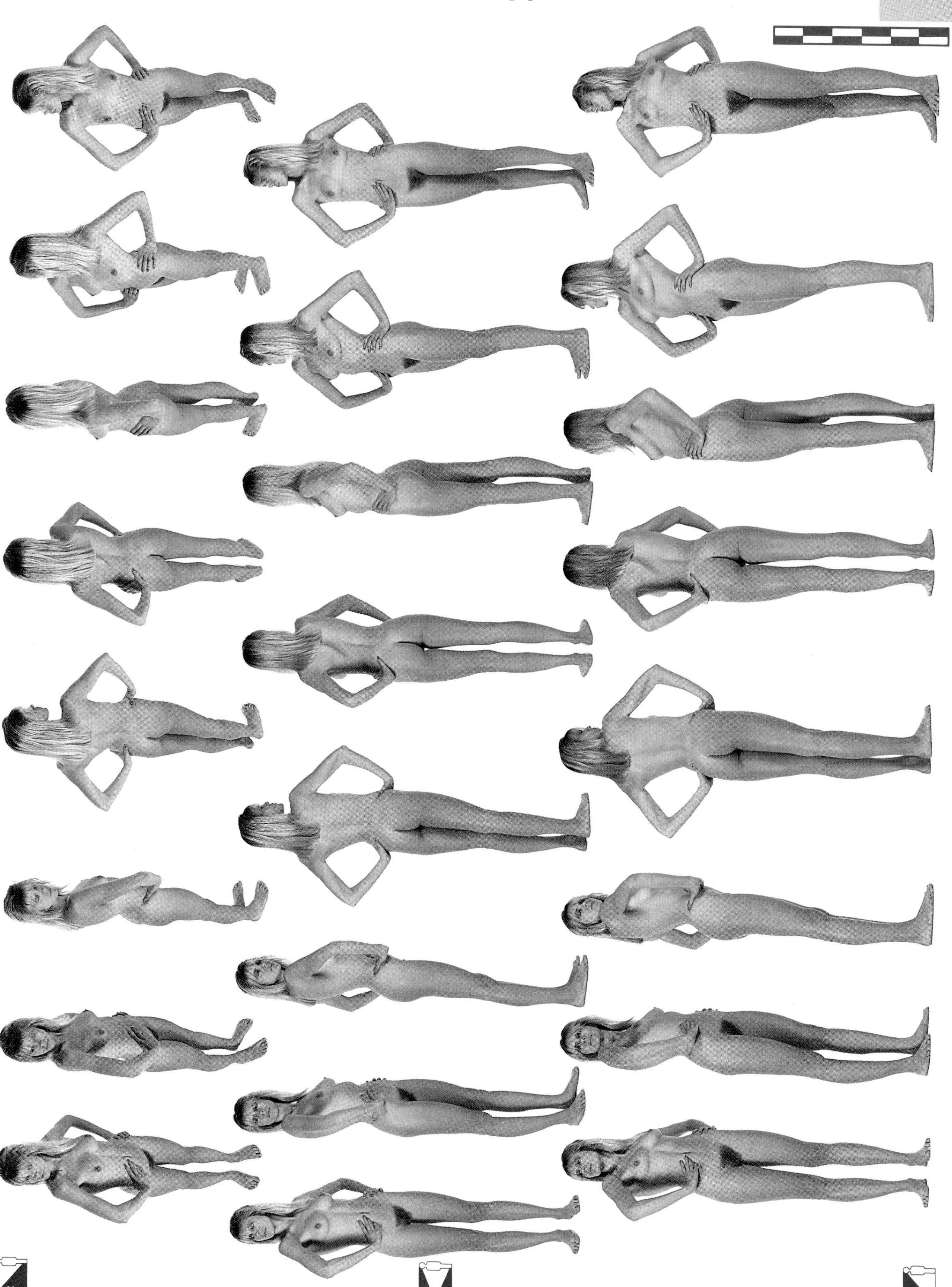

Arms folded

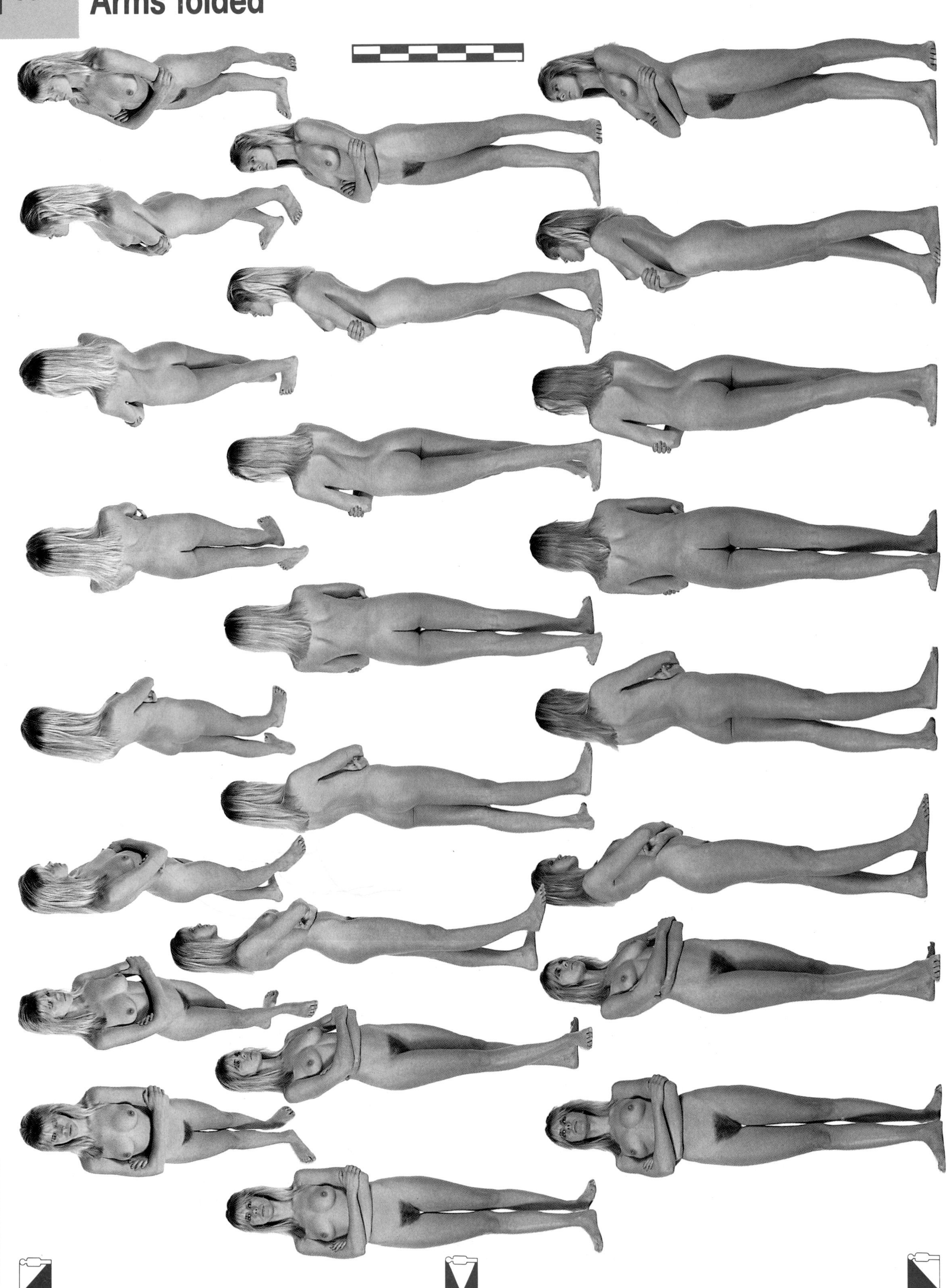

Leaning against wall with shoulders

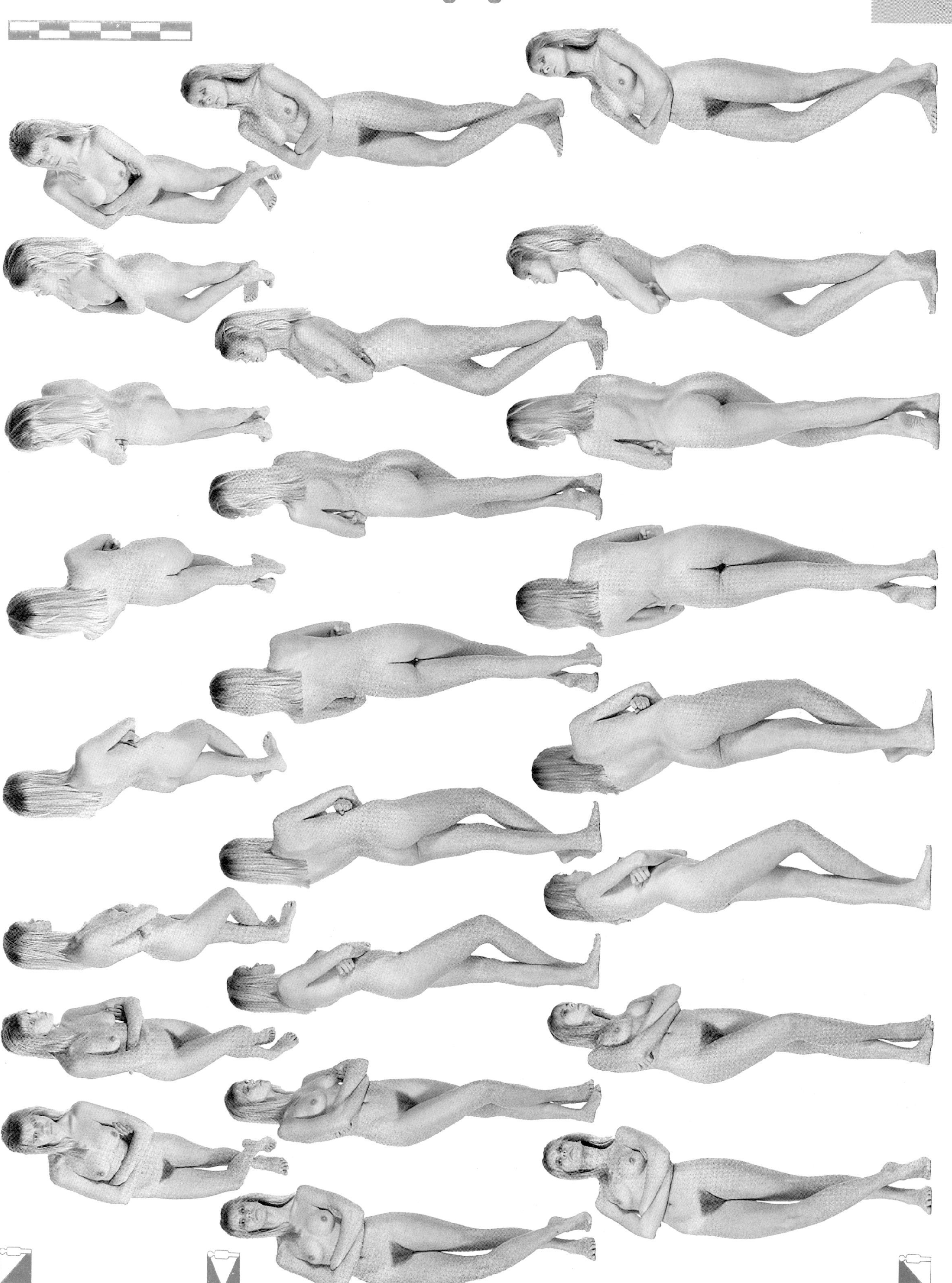

Hands behind back

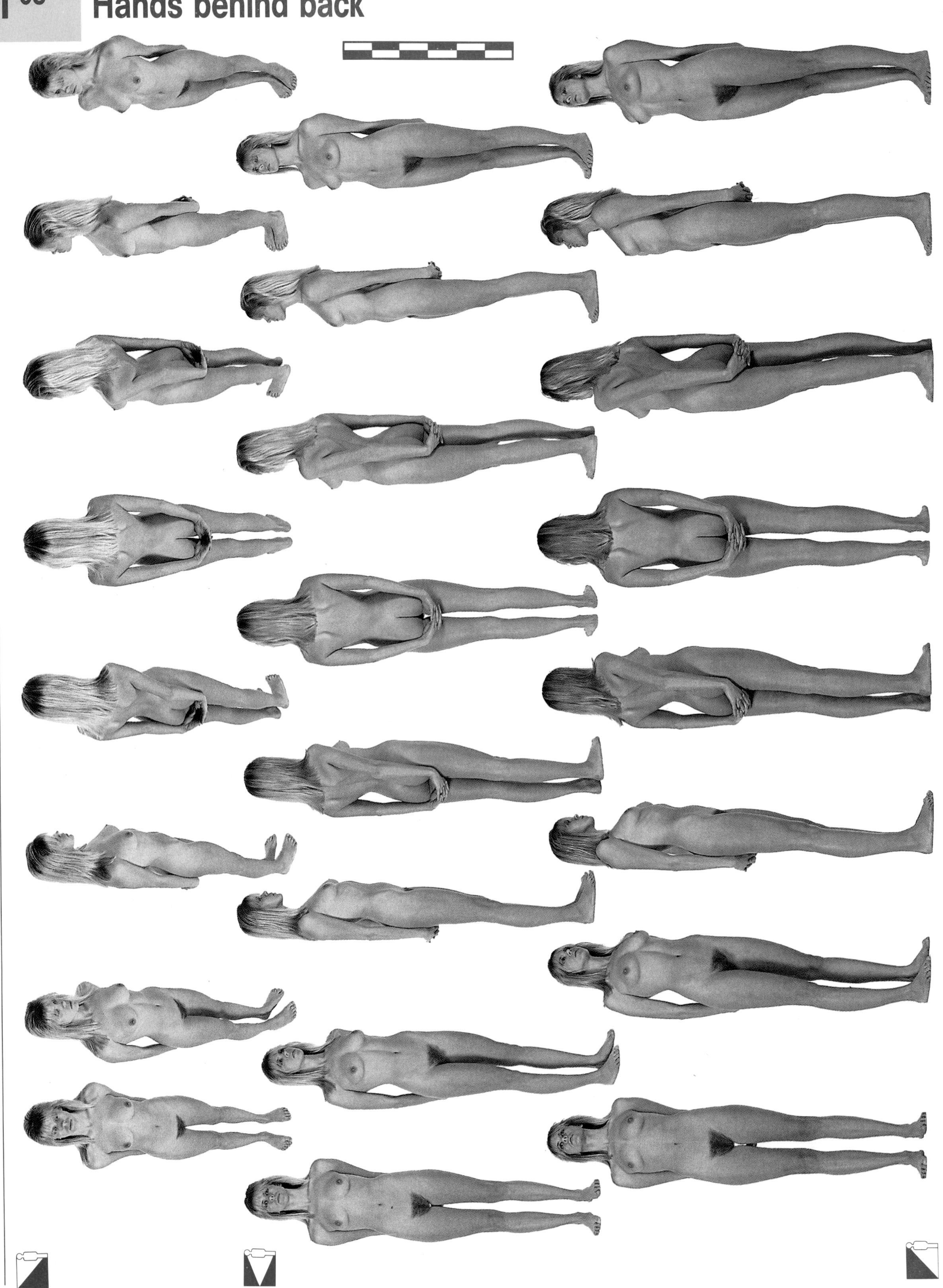

Climbing a step

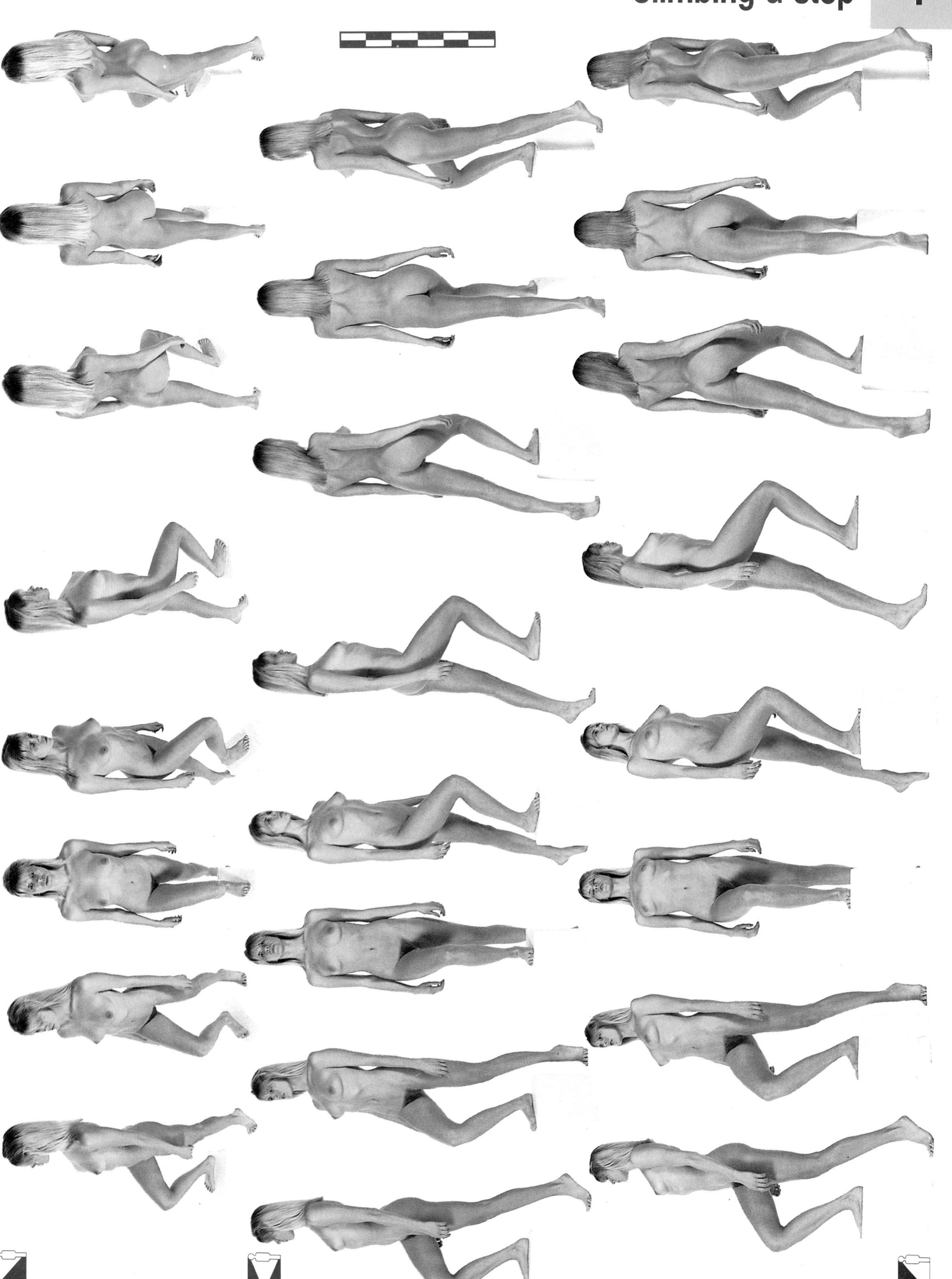

1·10 Marching

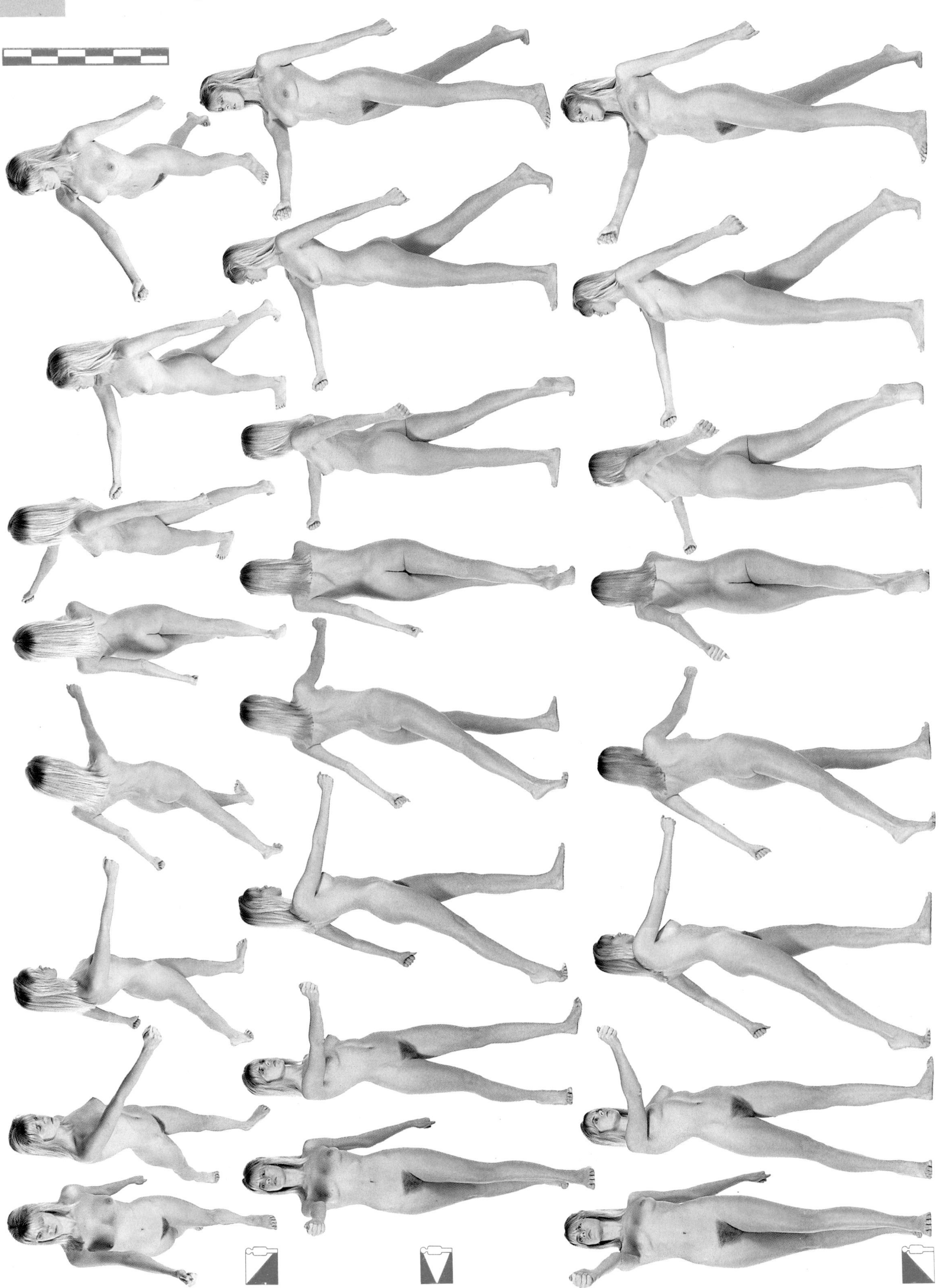

Upper trunk bending down

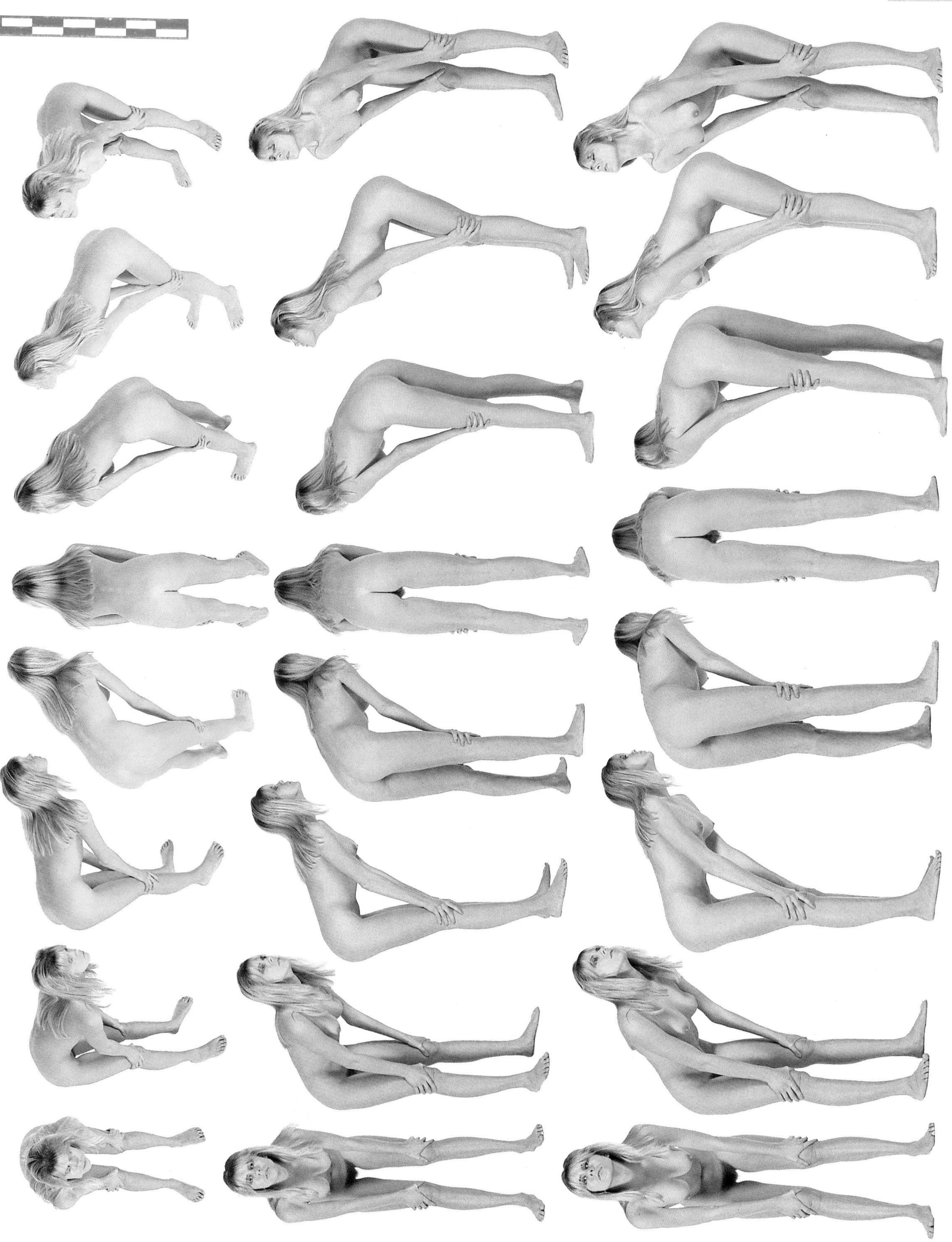

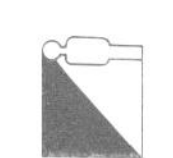

Crouching

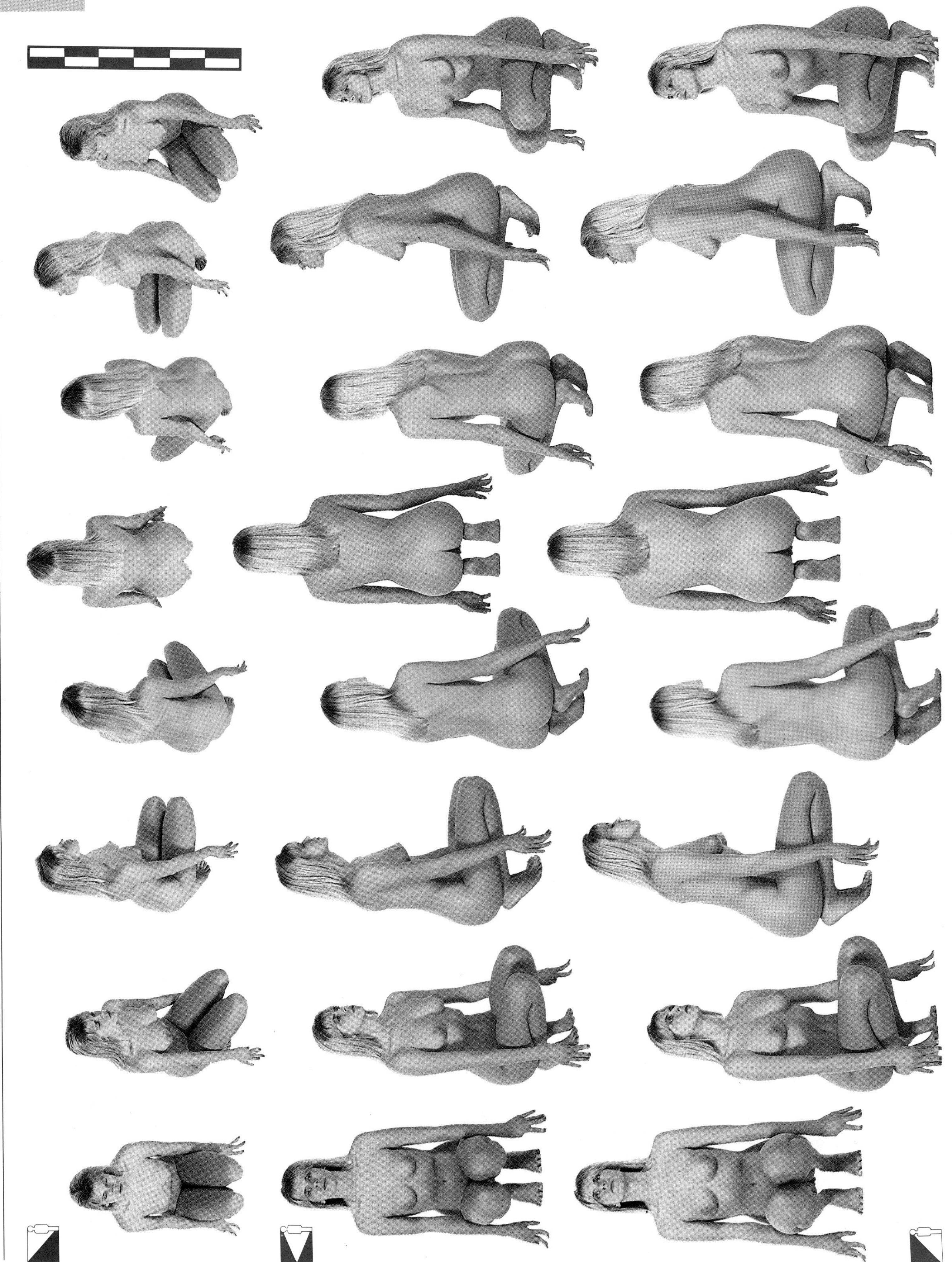

Crouching, one leg raised

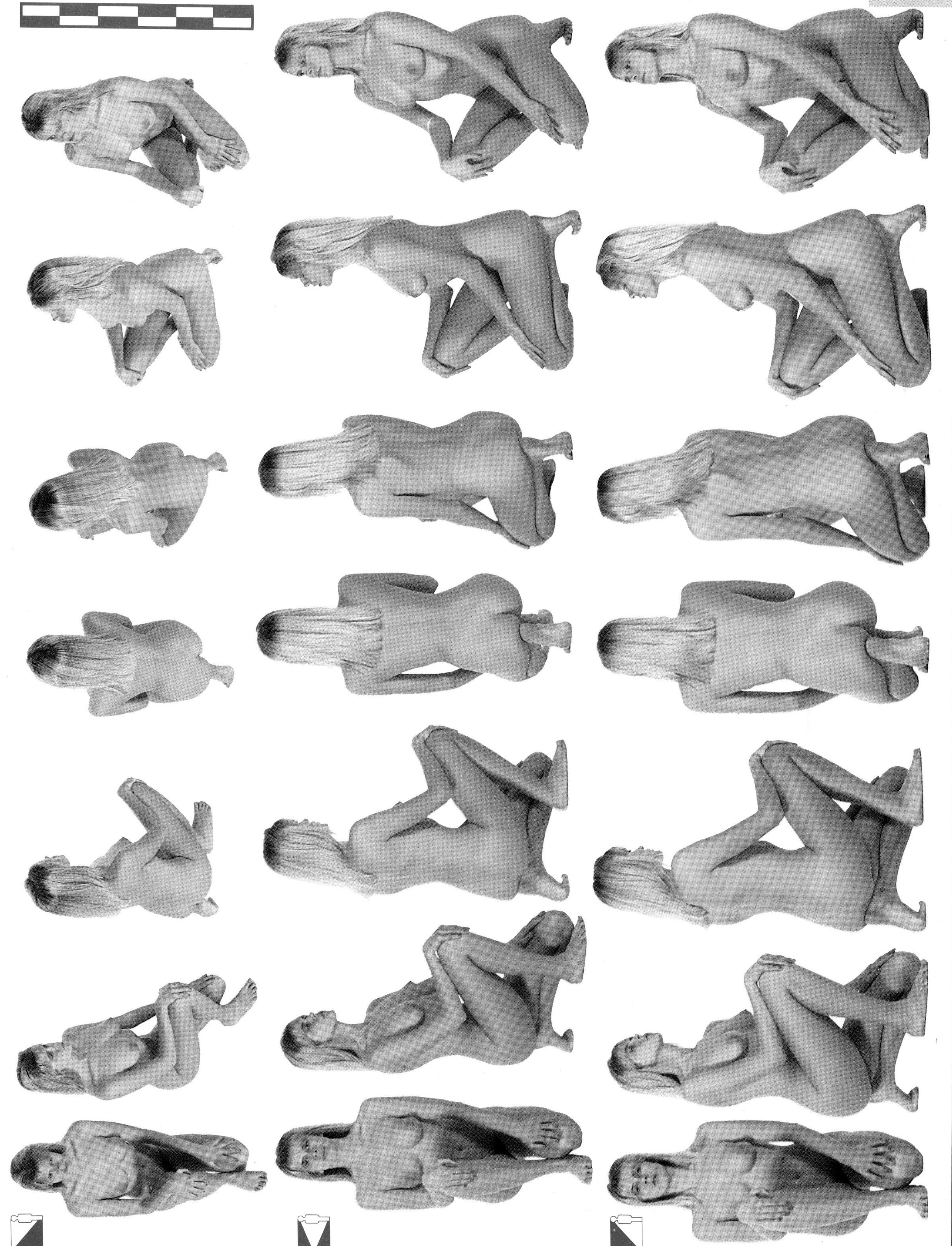

Kneeling

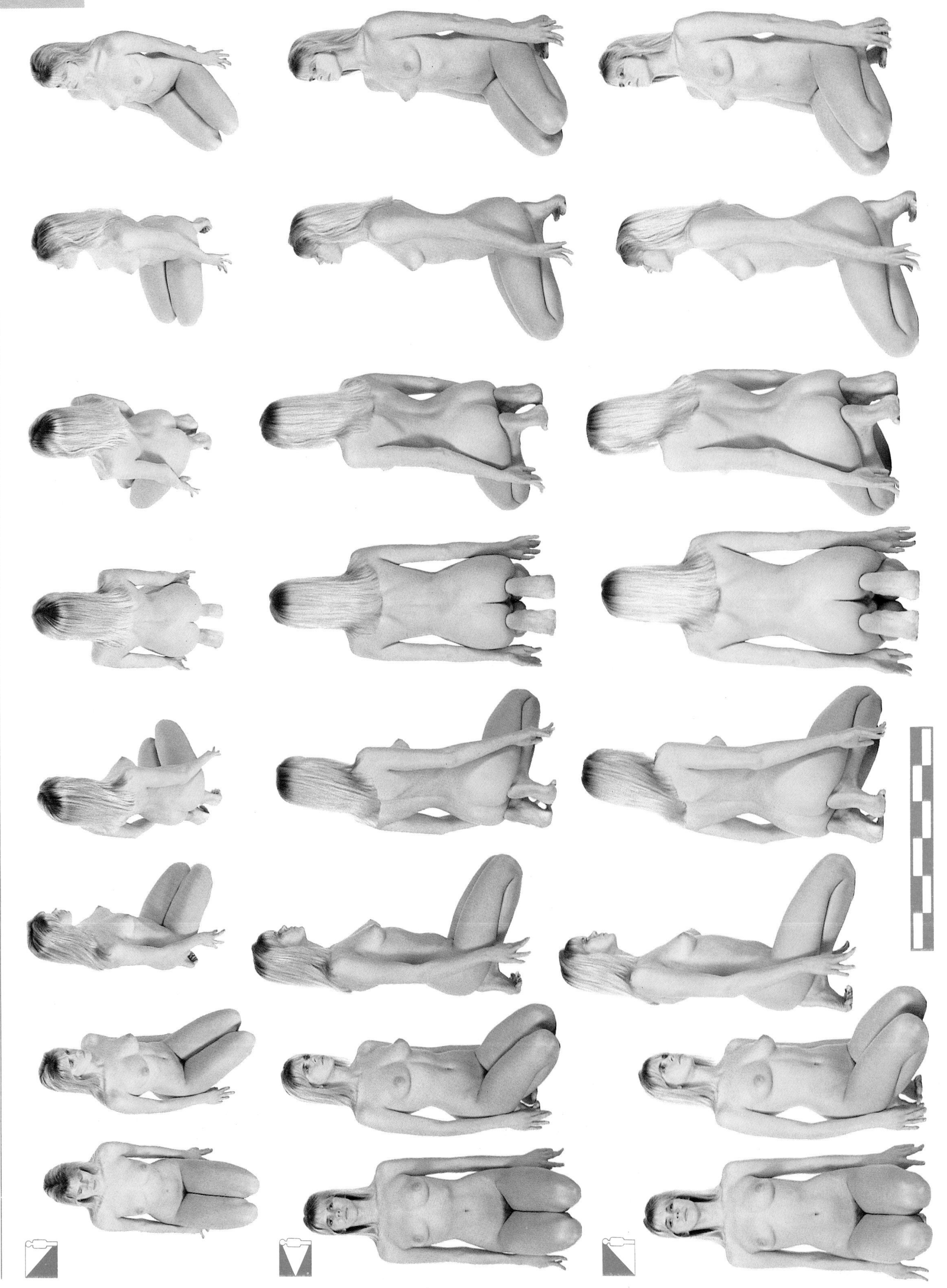

Sitting with arms round knees

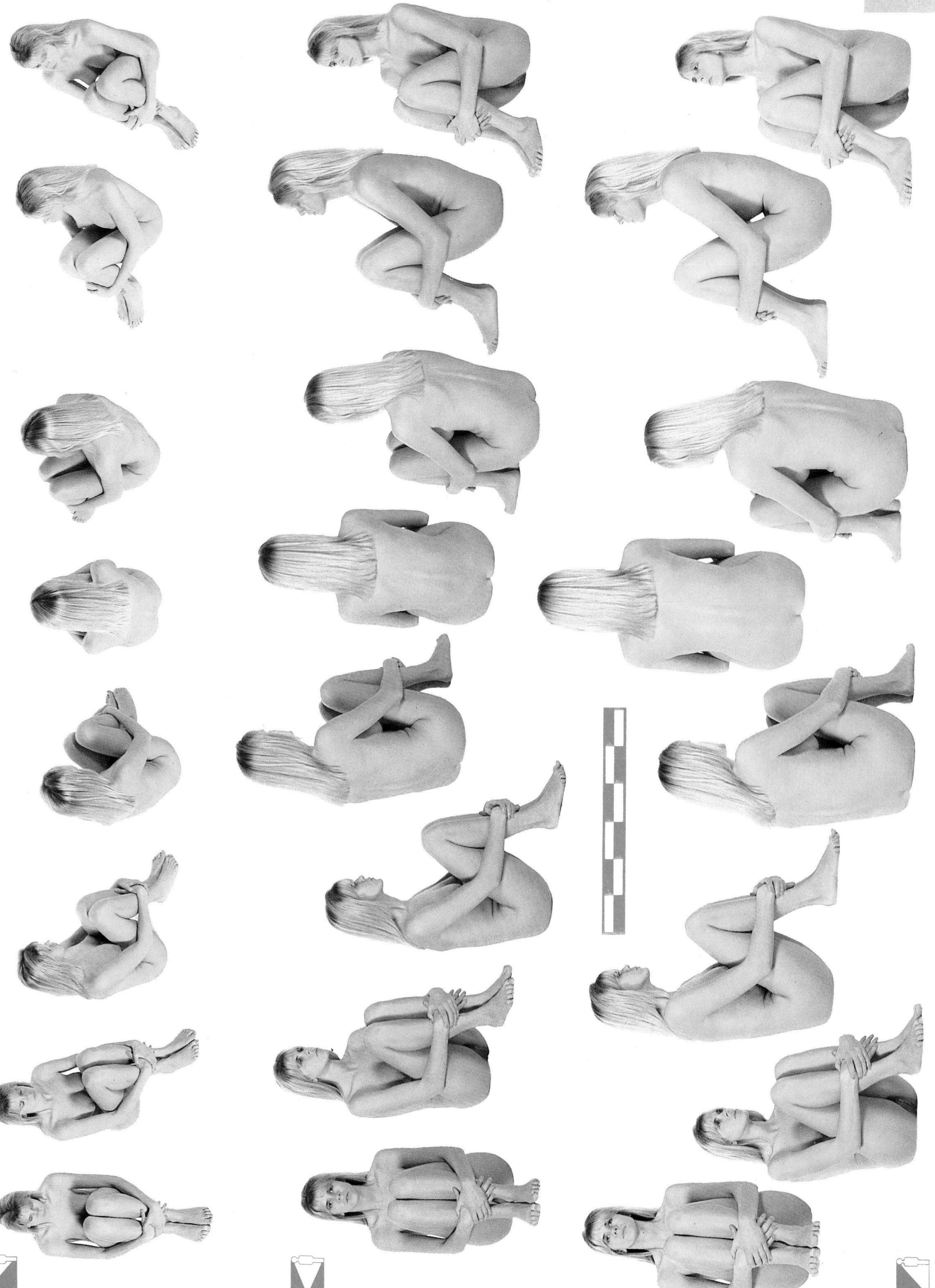

Sitting with arms by sides

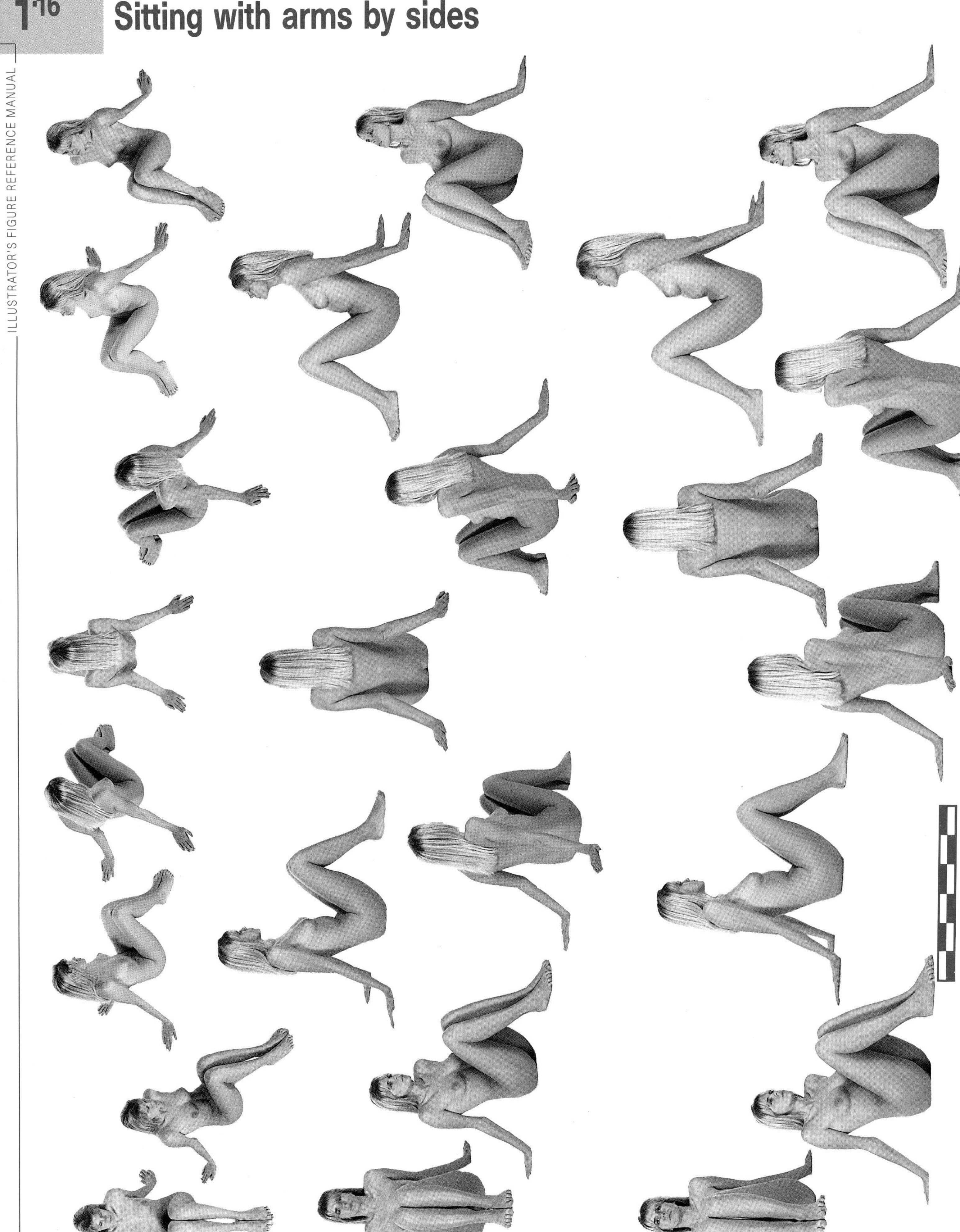

Sitting with one leg outstretched

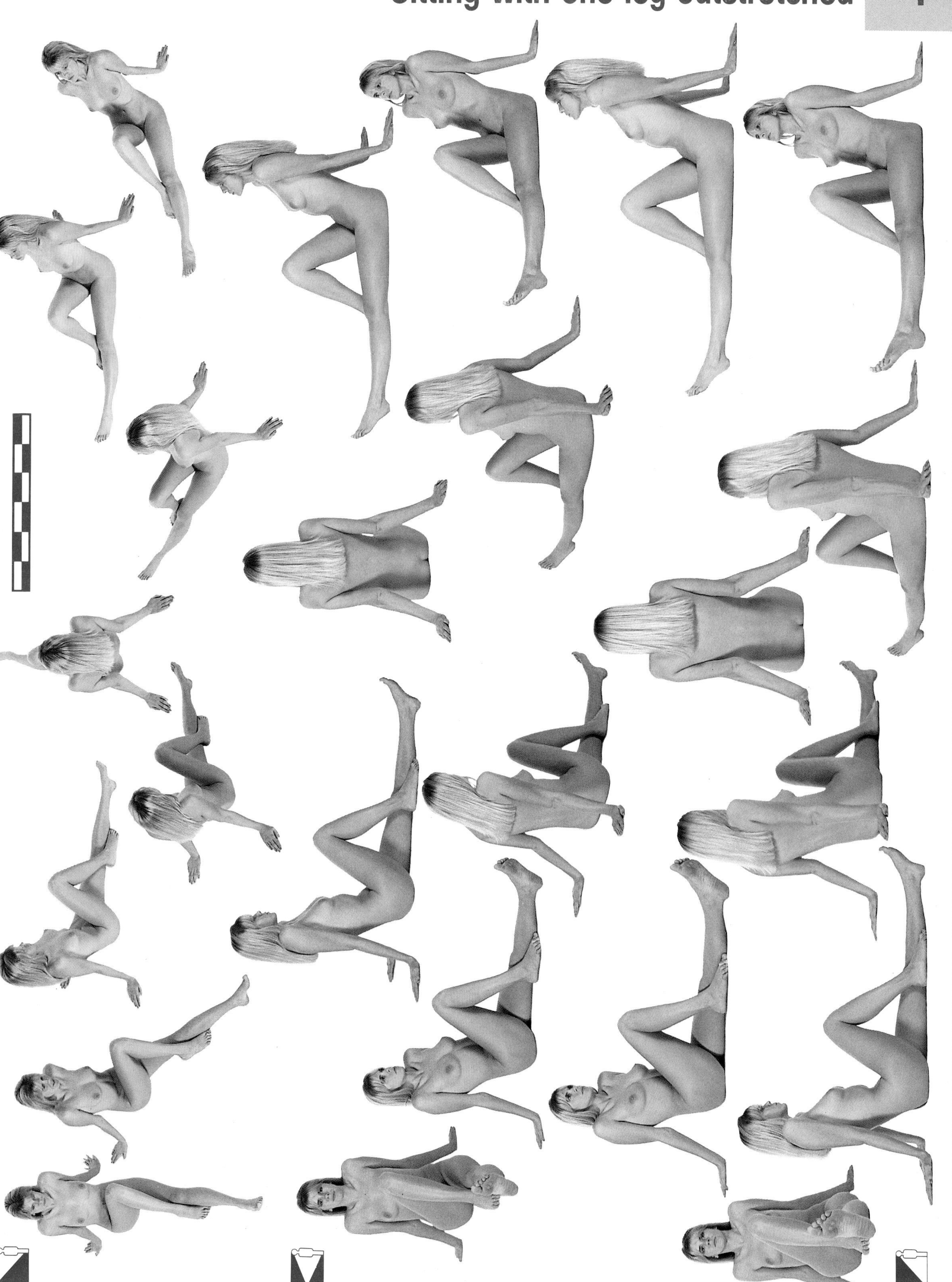

Sitting propped up by one arm

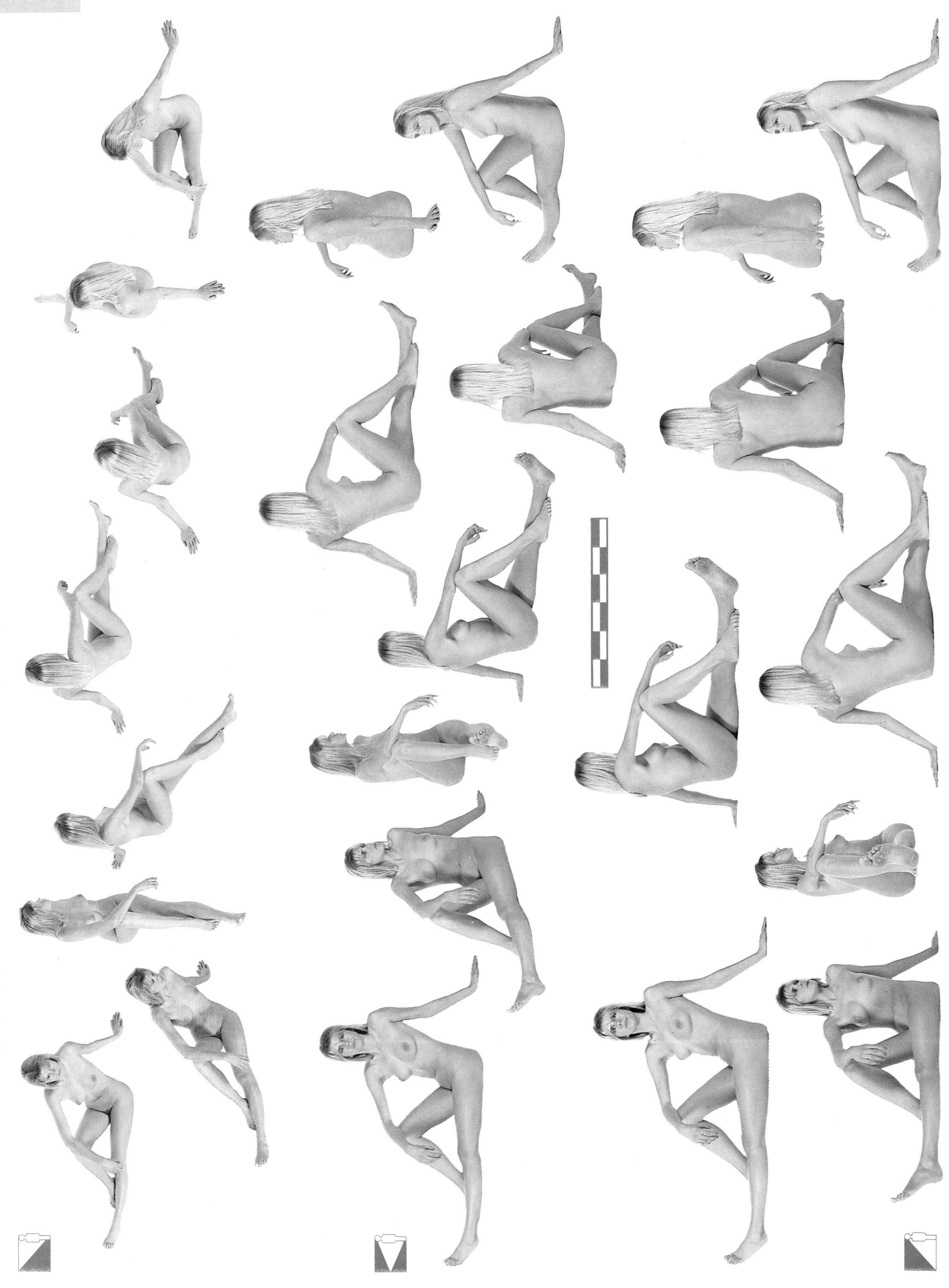

Sitting with legs outstretched

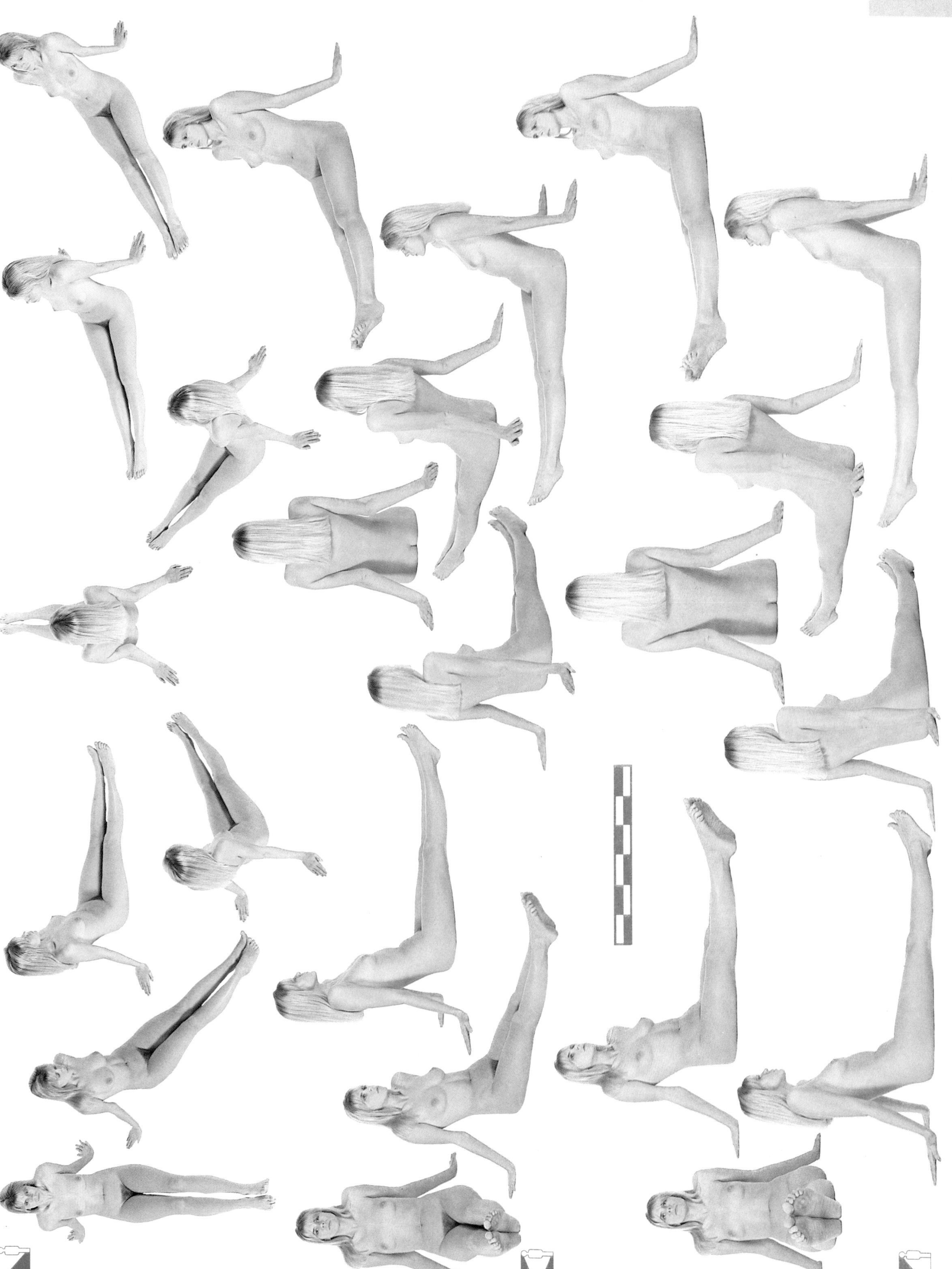

1·20 On back, hands behind head, one knee raised

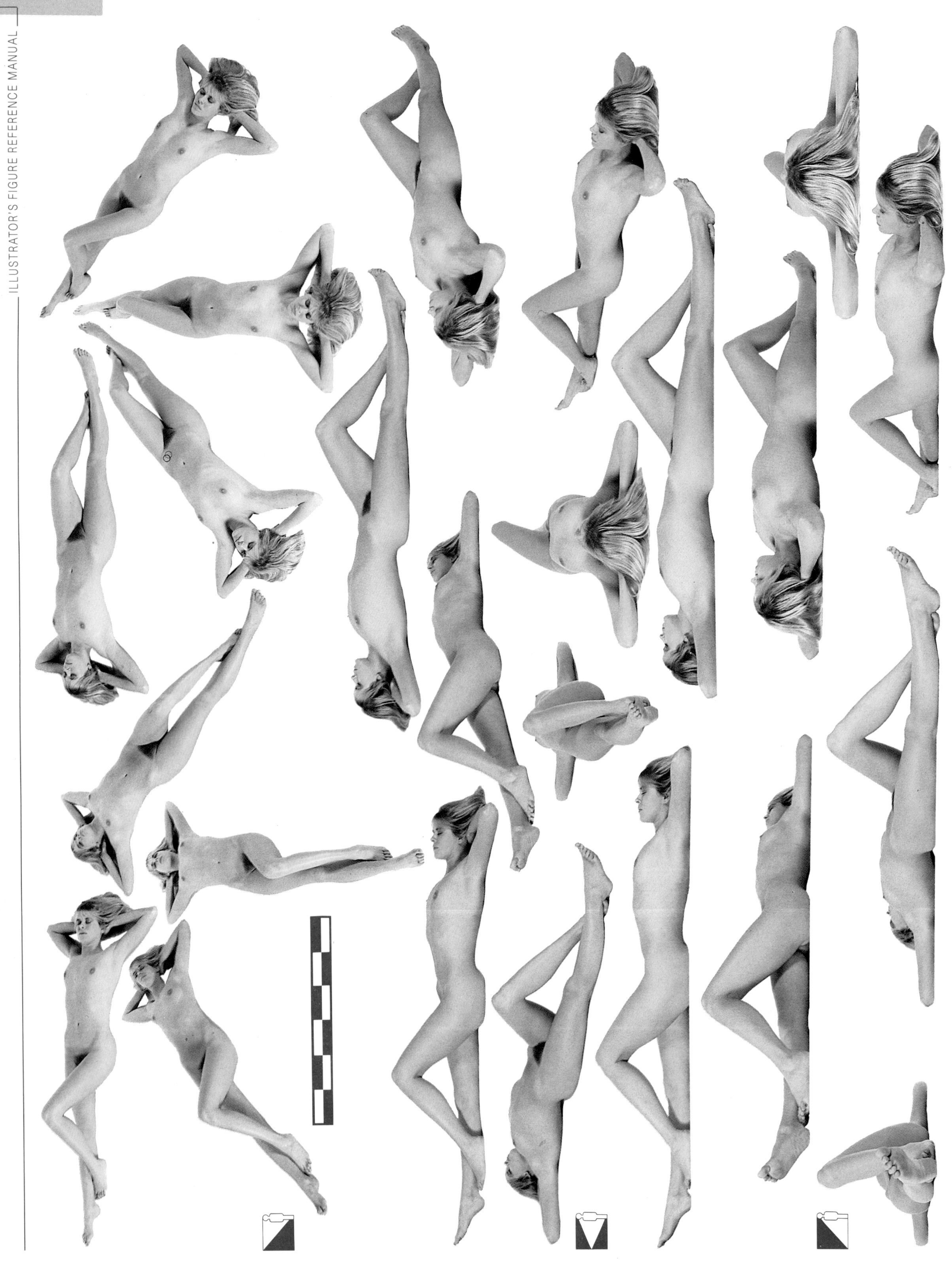

On back, hands behind head

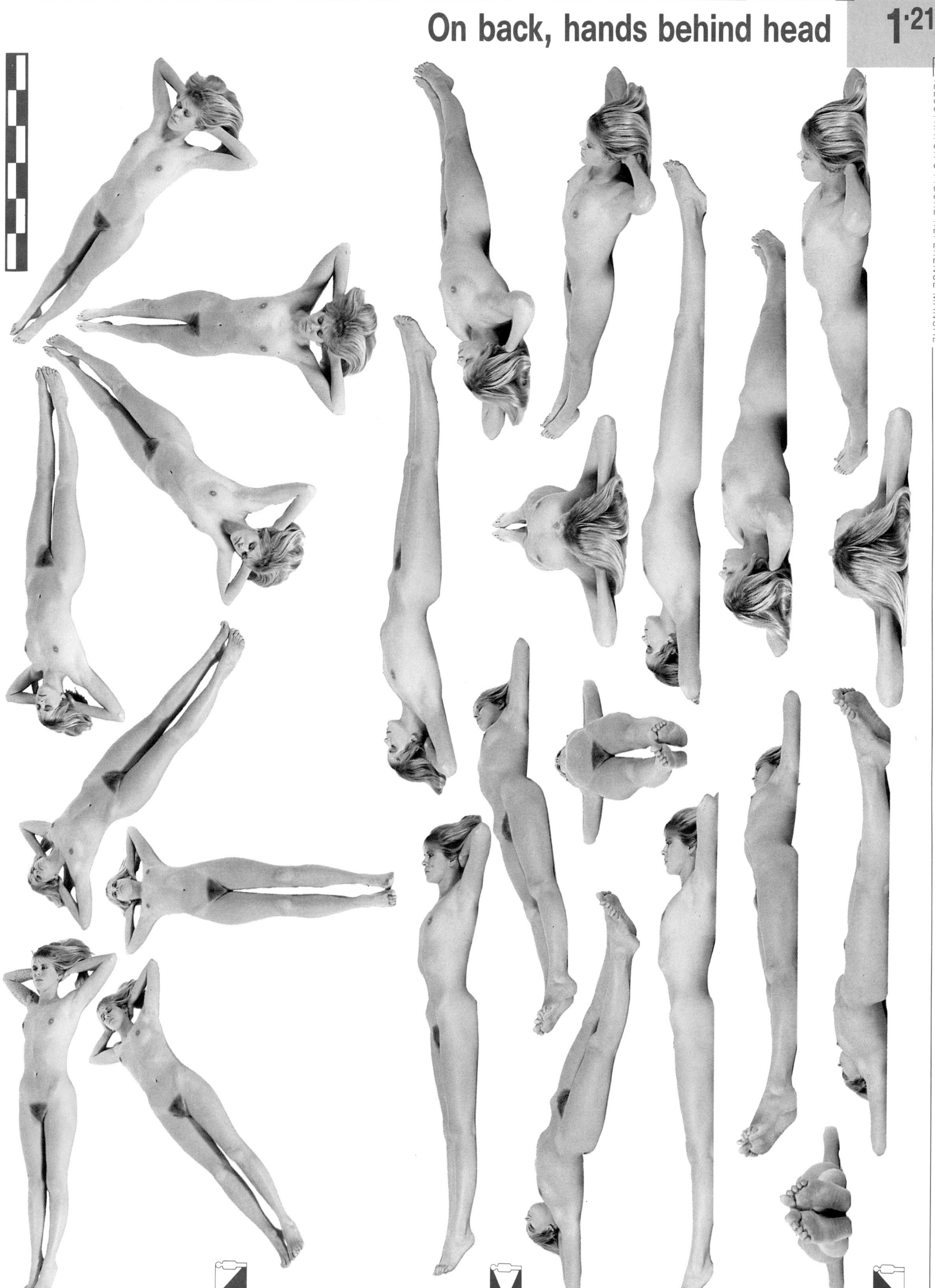

On back, limbs outstretched

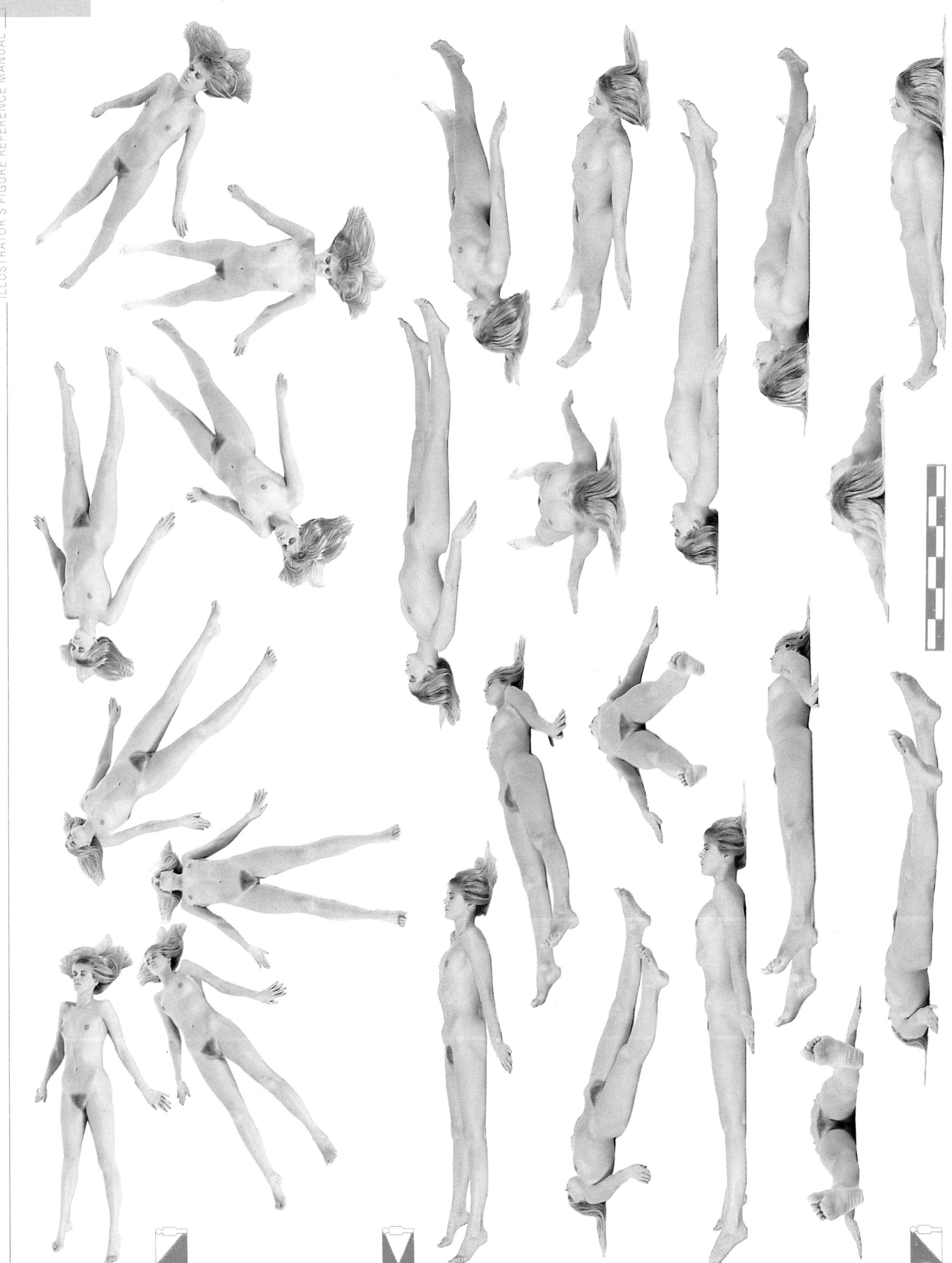

On side, limbs by the side

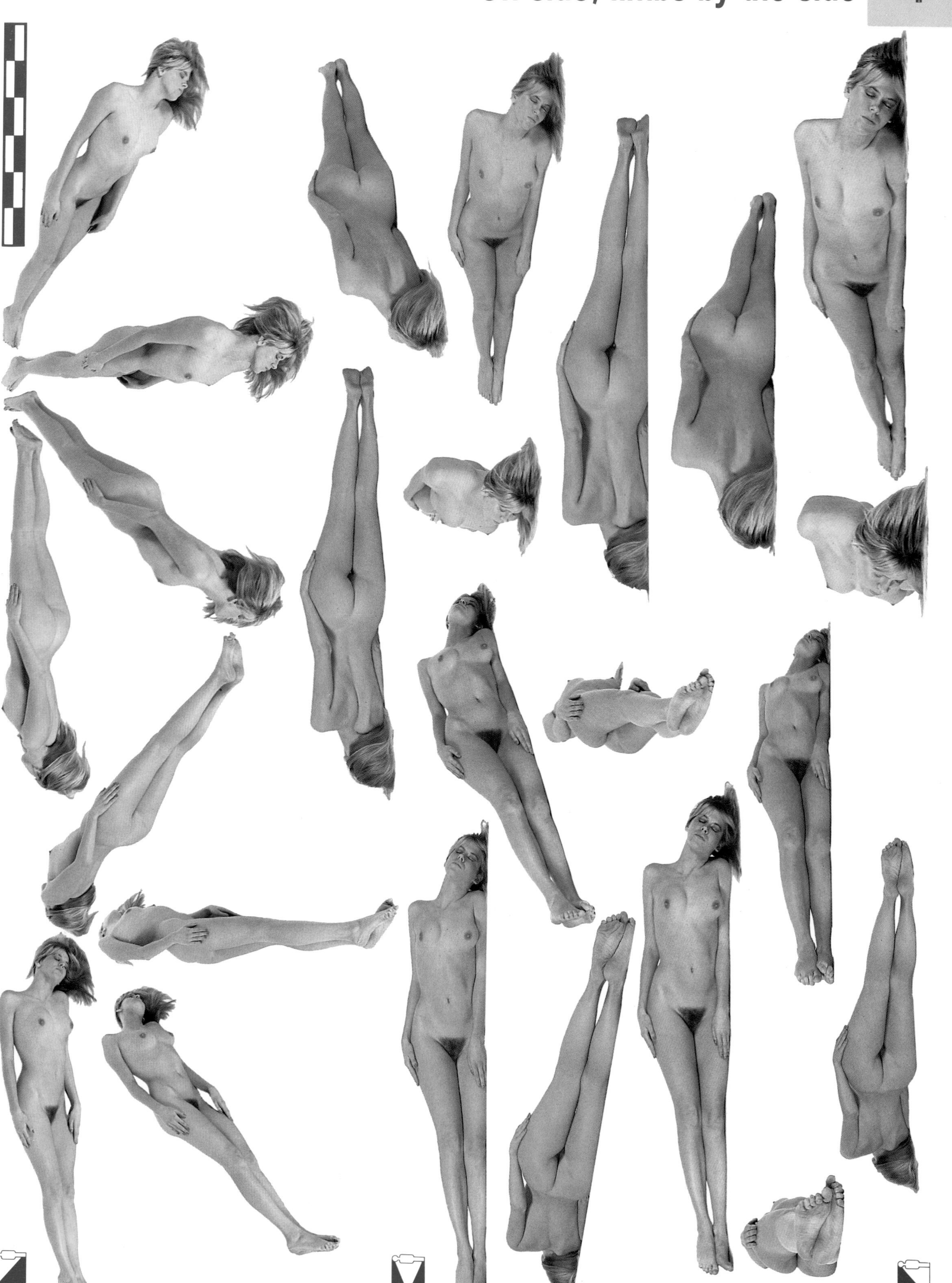

On side, limbs outstretched

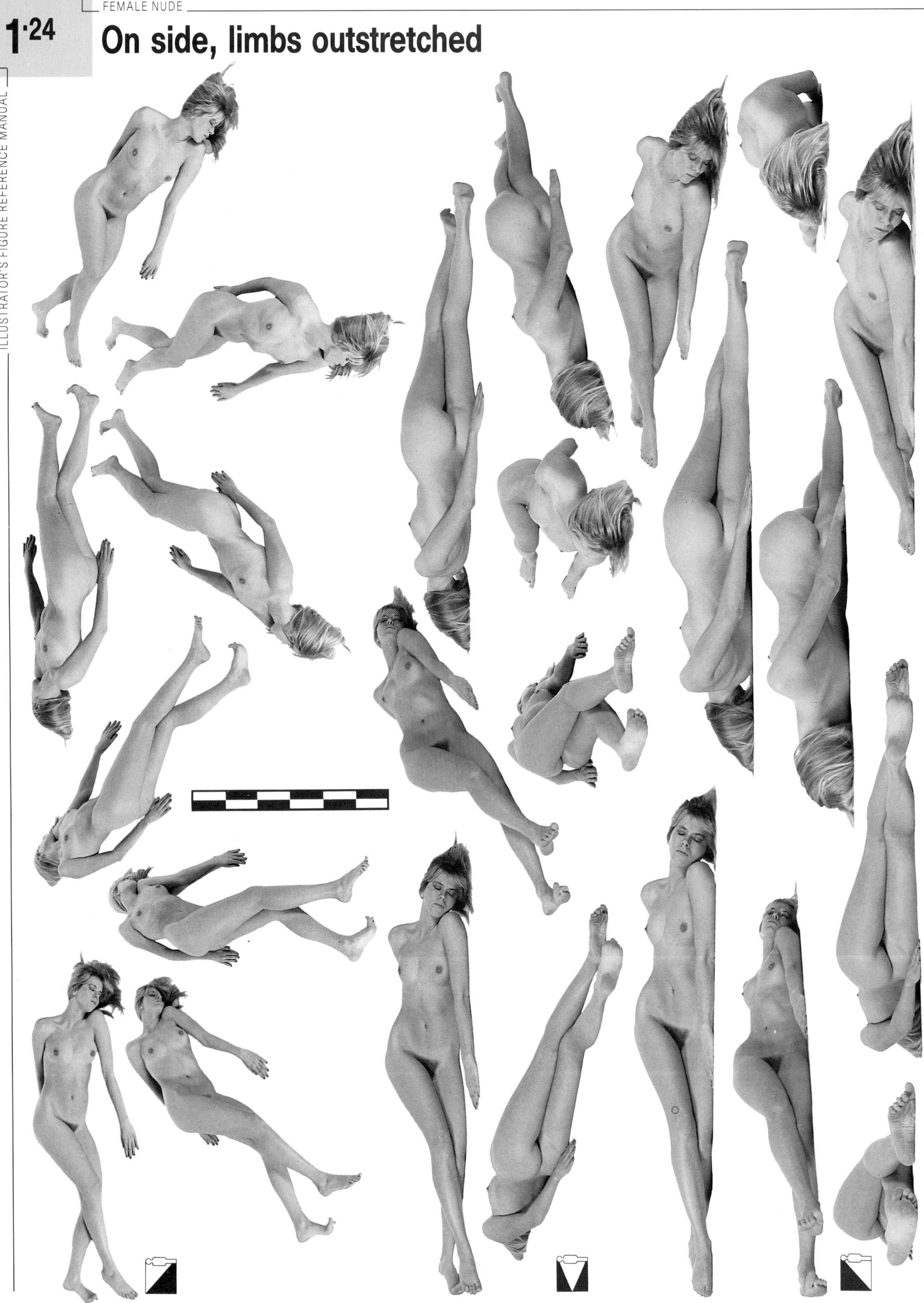

Face down, limbs outstretched

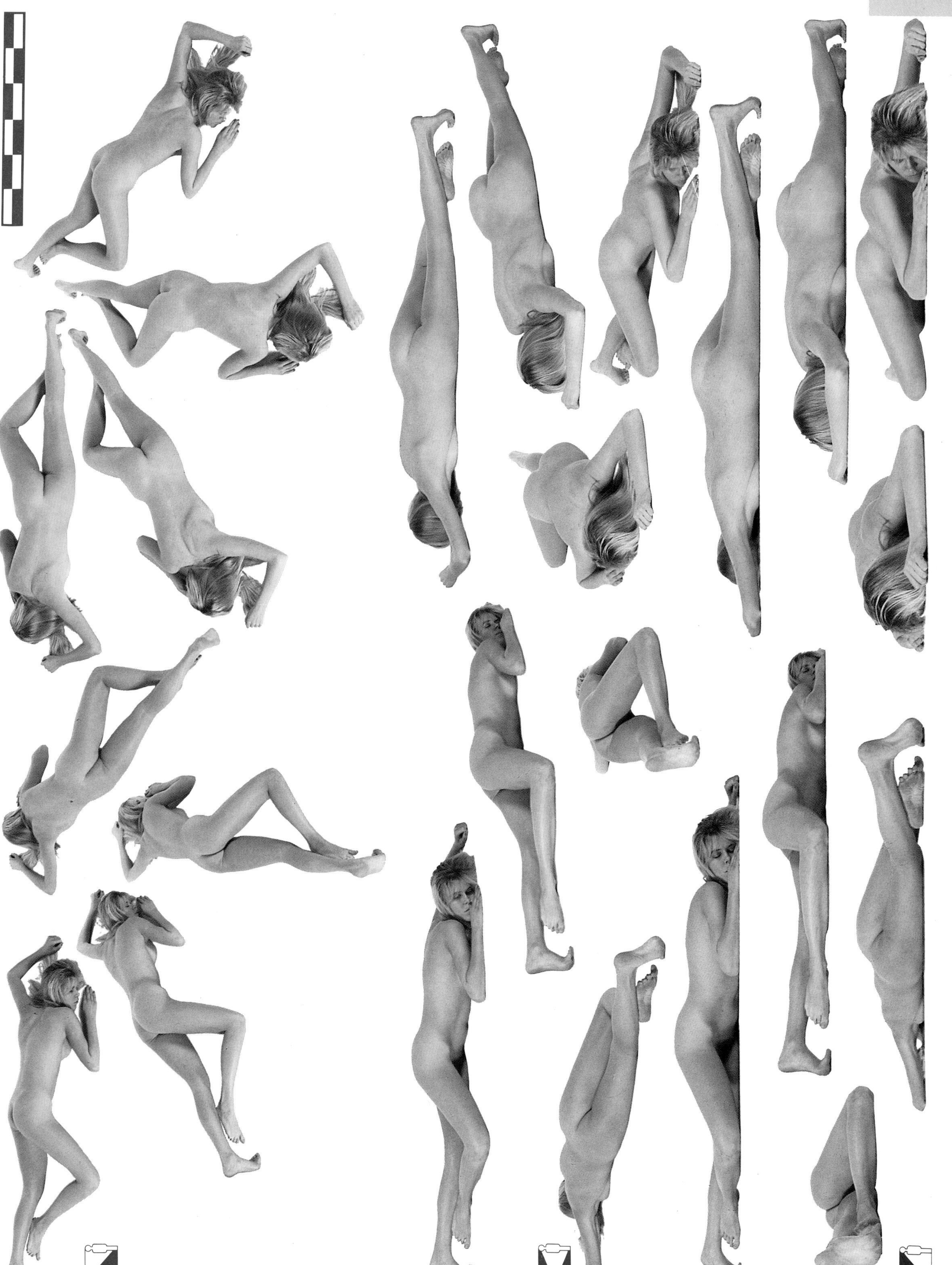

Face down, limbs by the side

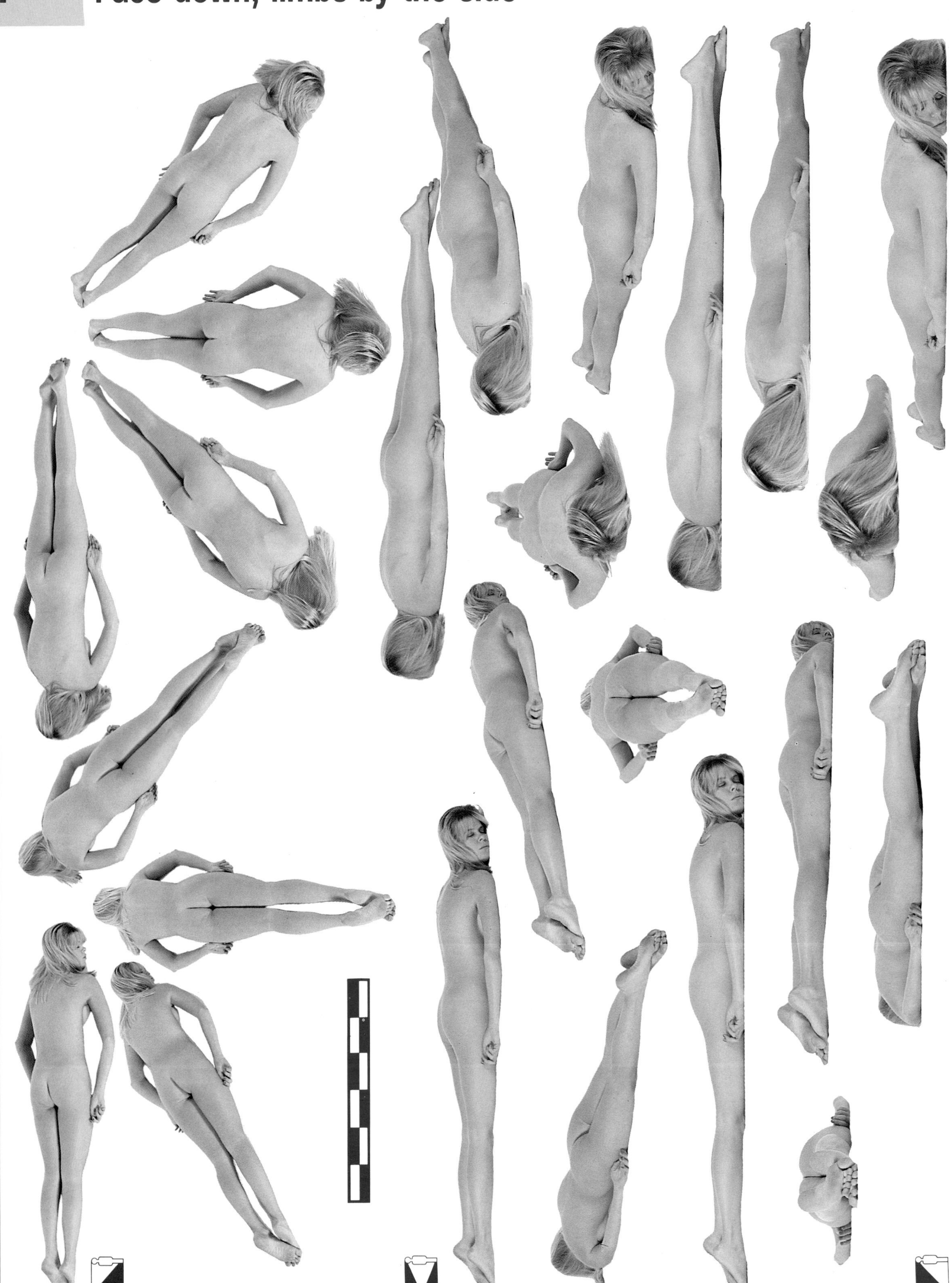

Arms stretched up

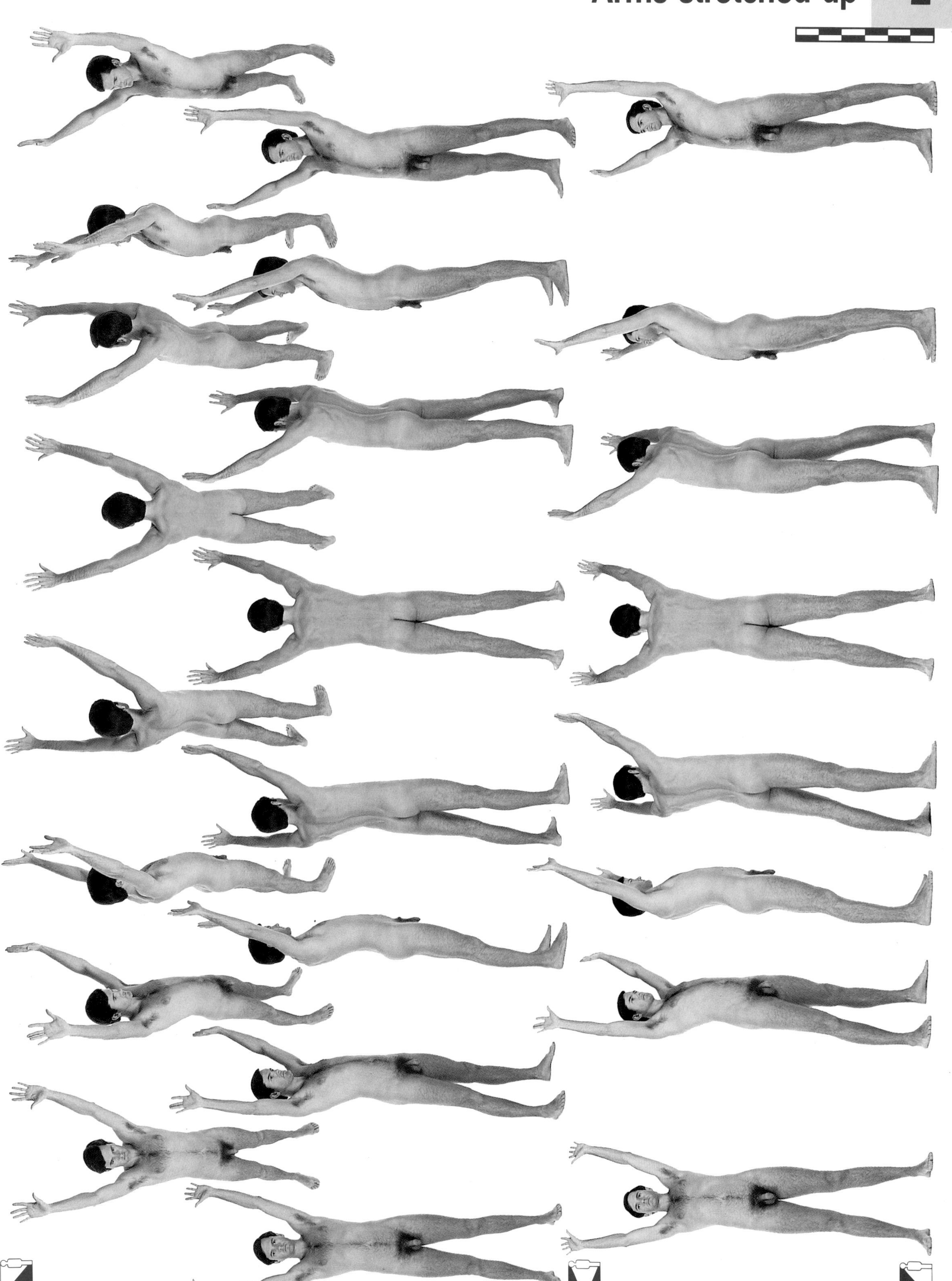

Hands behind head

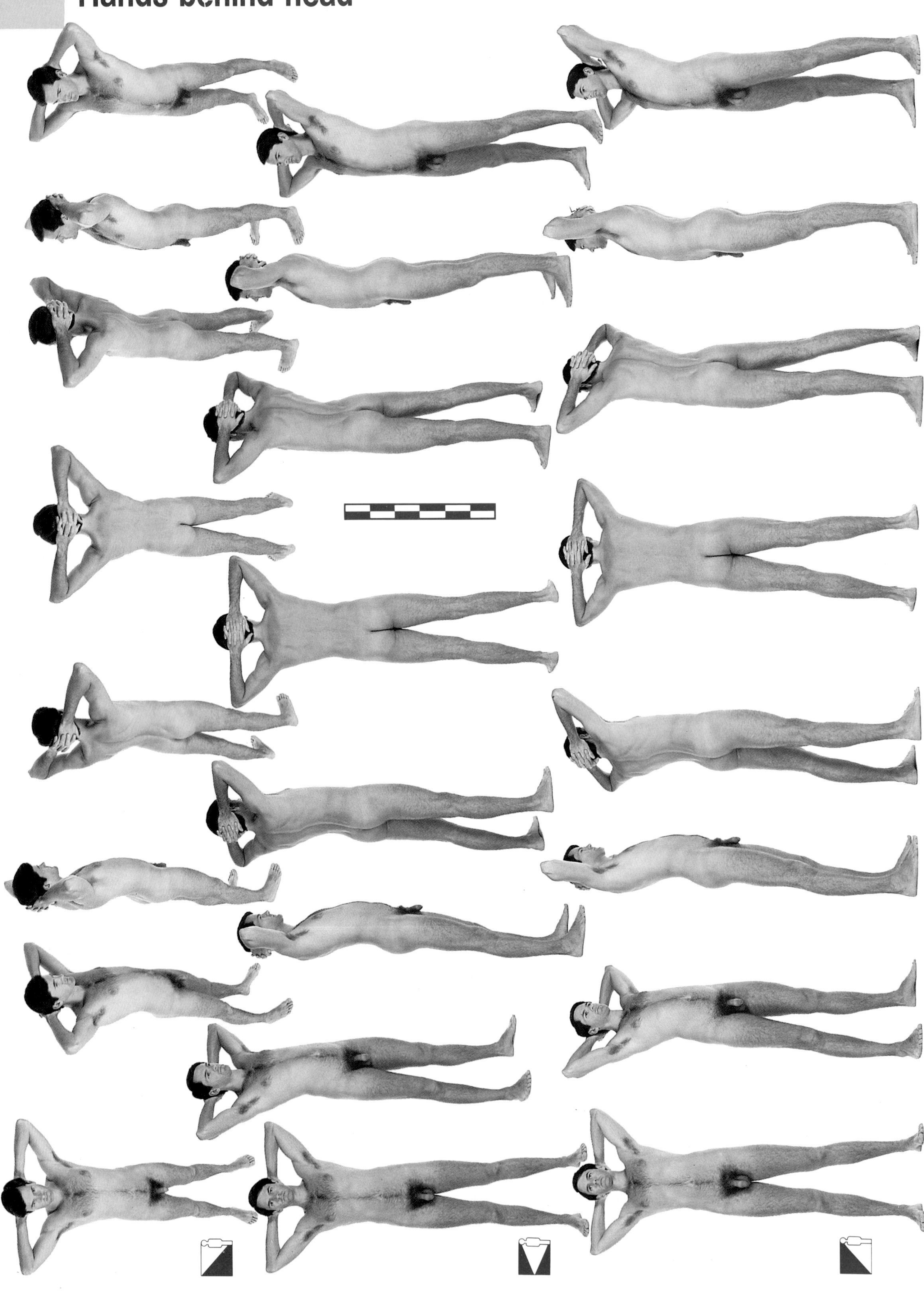

Arms folded

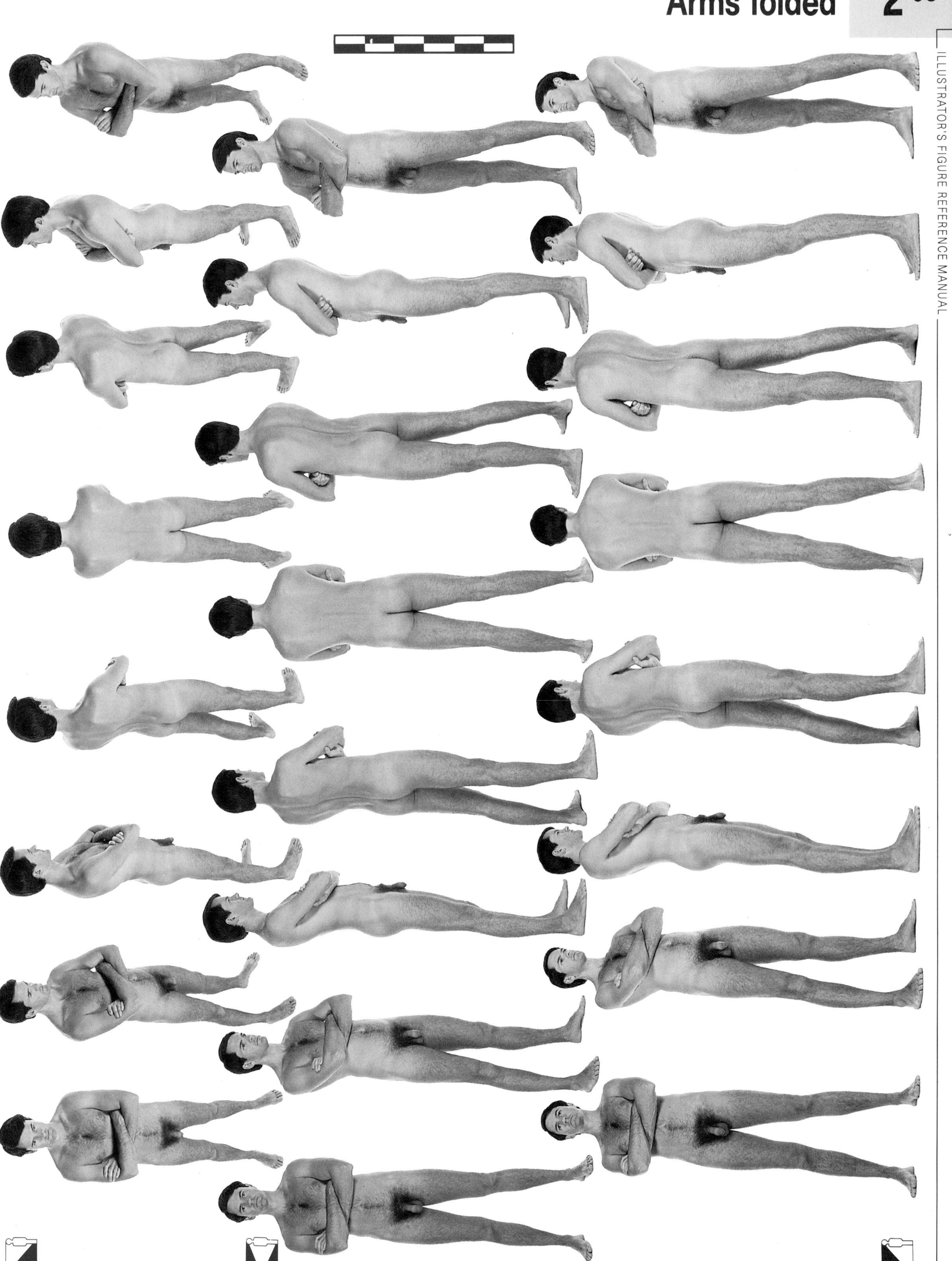

Arms stretched to side

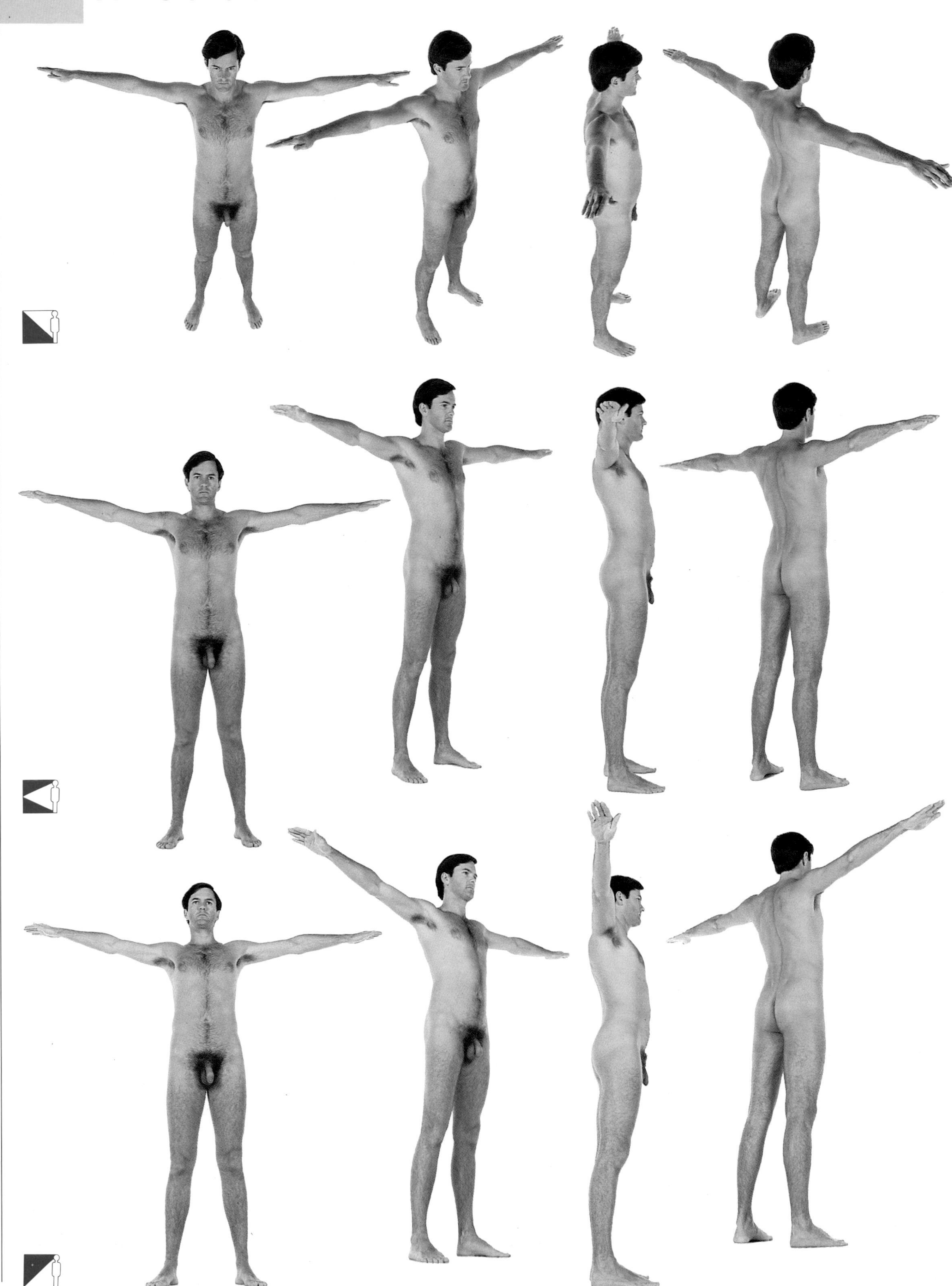

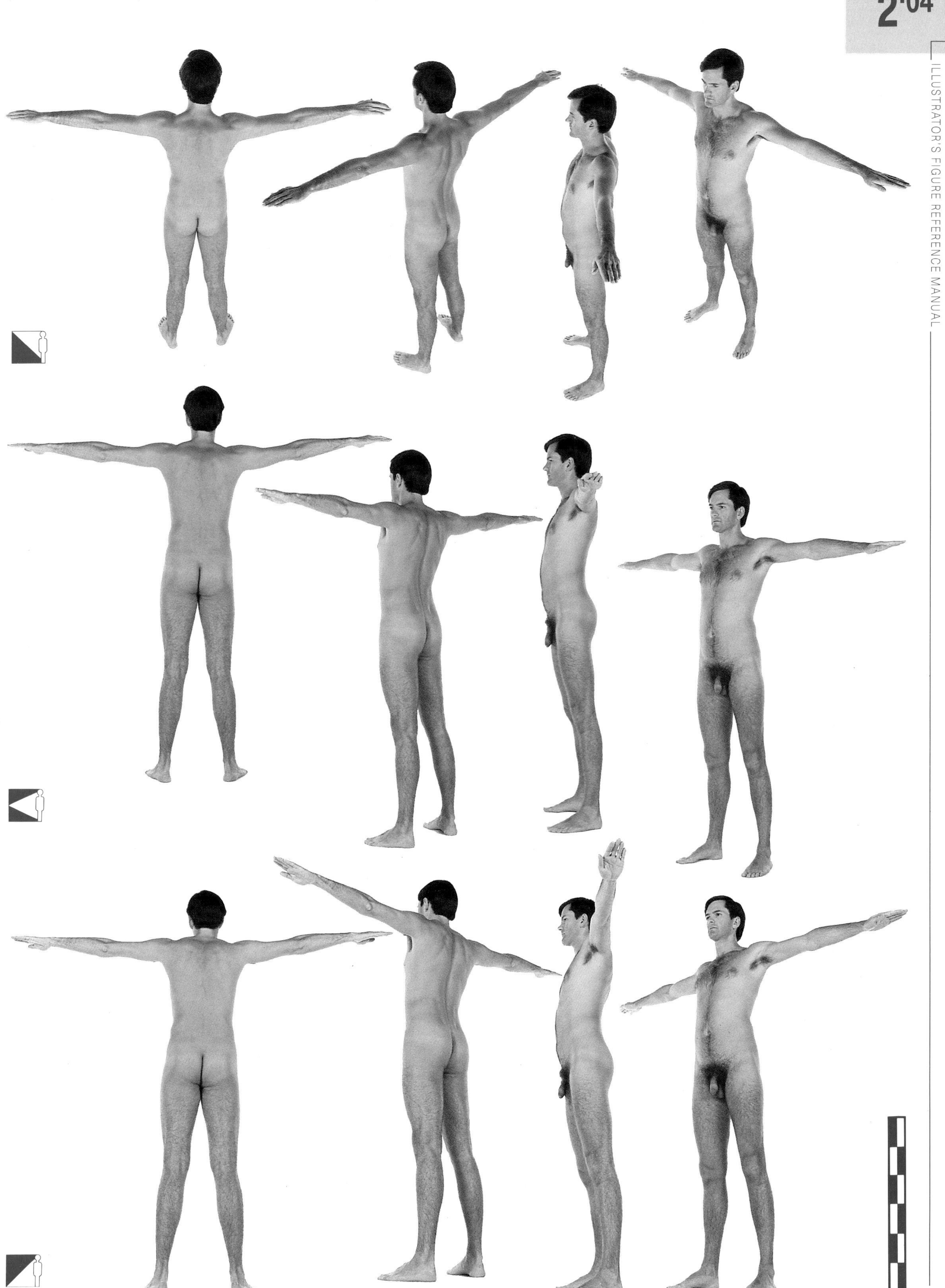

Leaning against wall with back

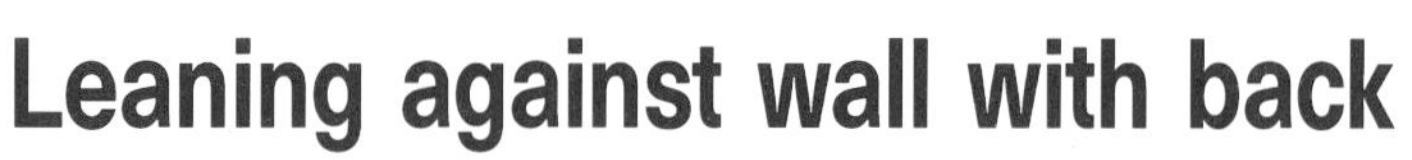

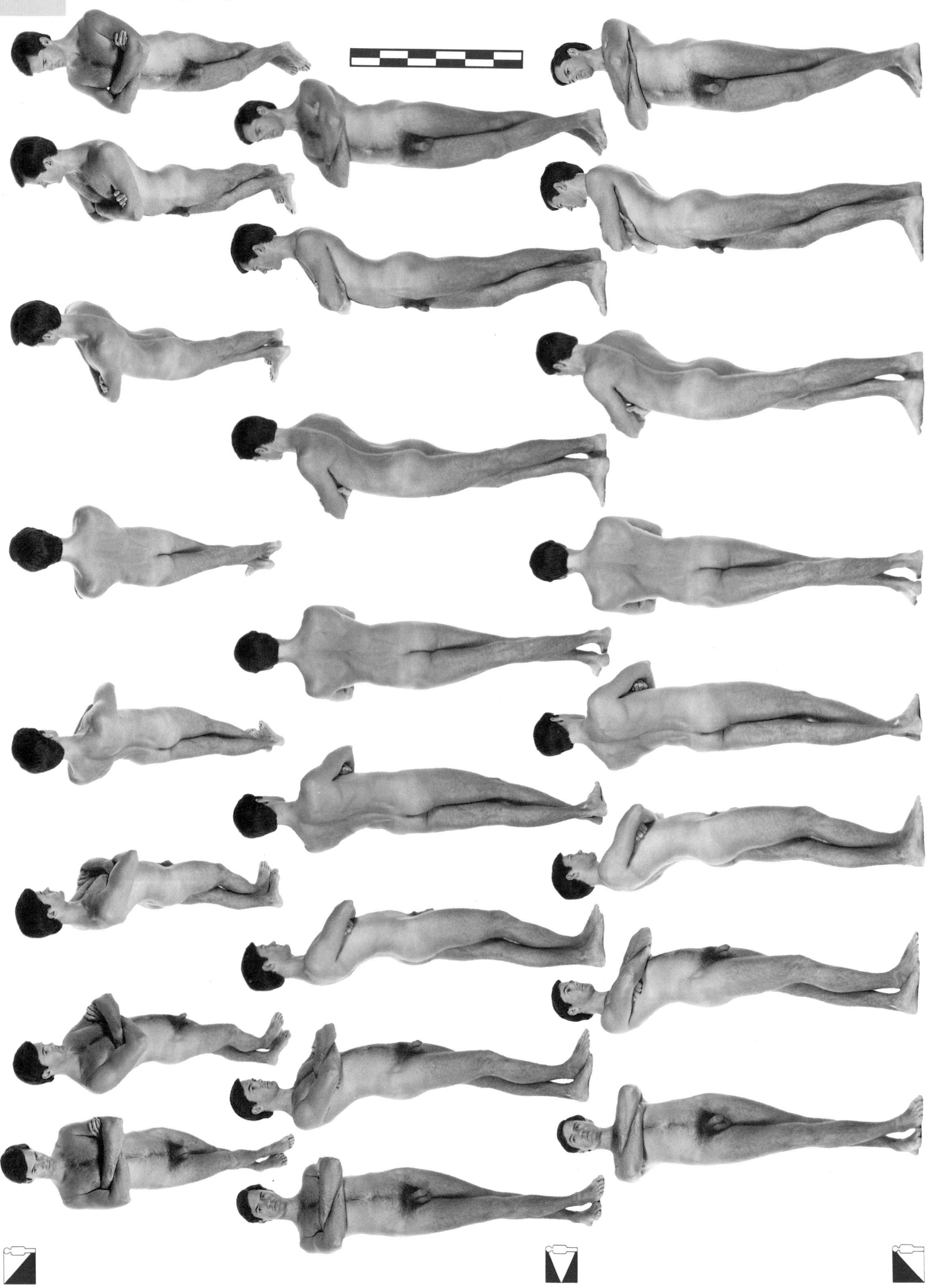

Leaning against wall with shoulders

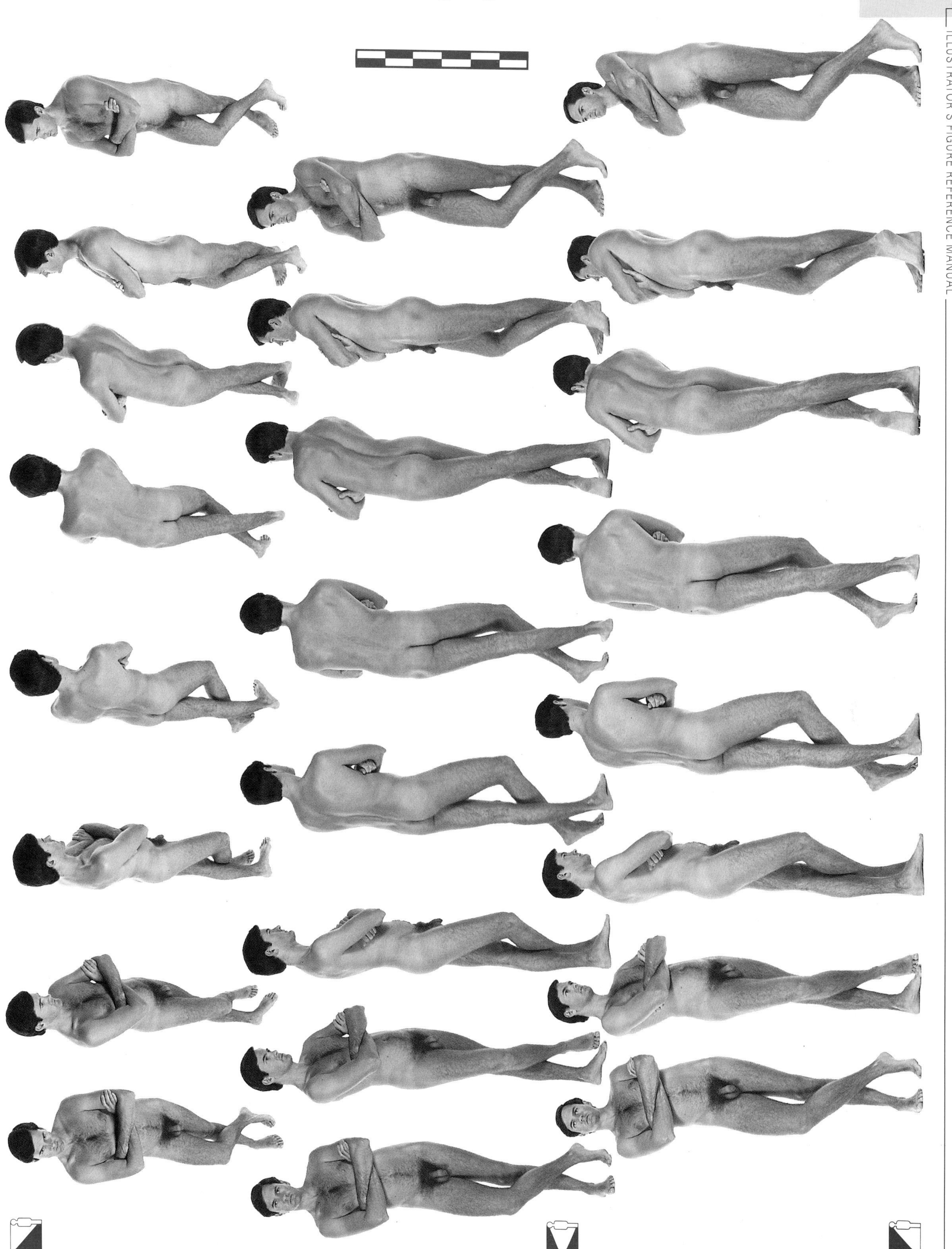

2·07 Climbing a step

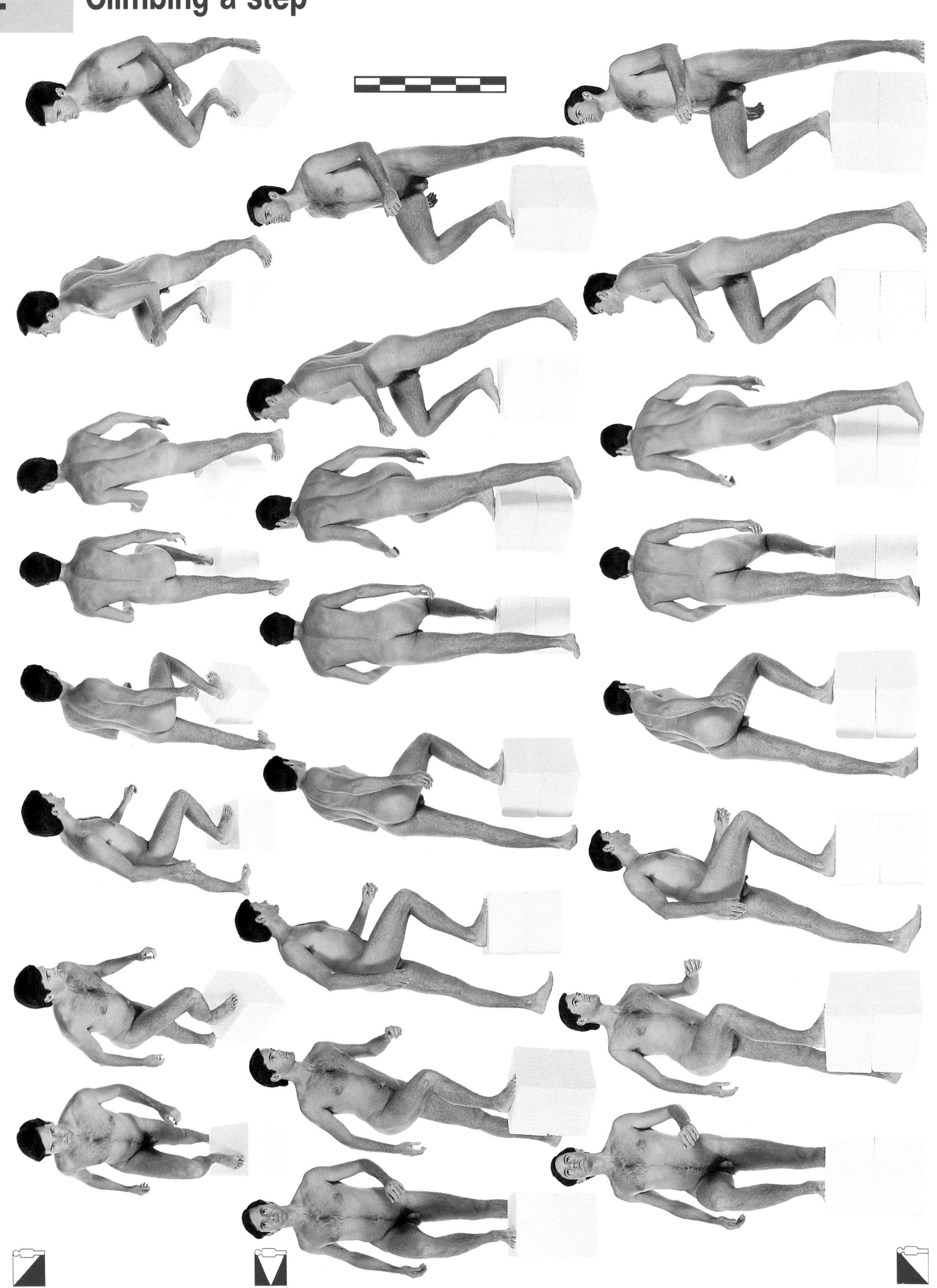

Walking

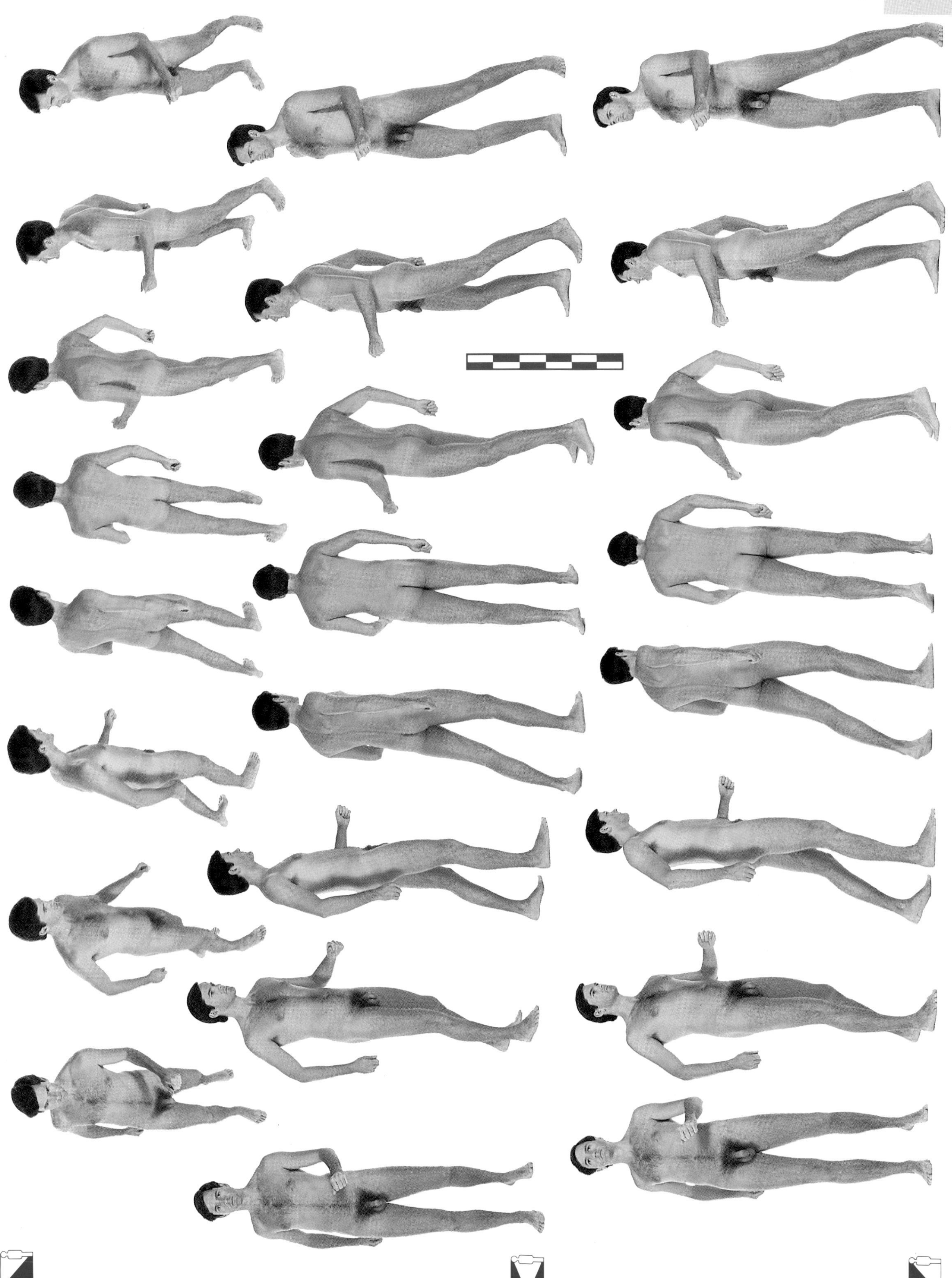

Marching

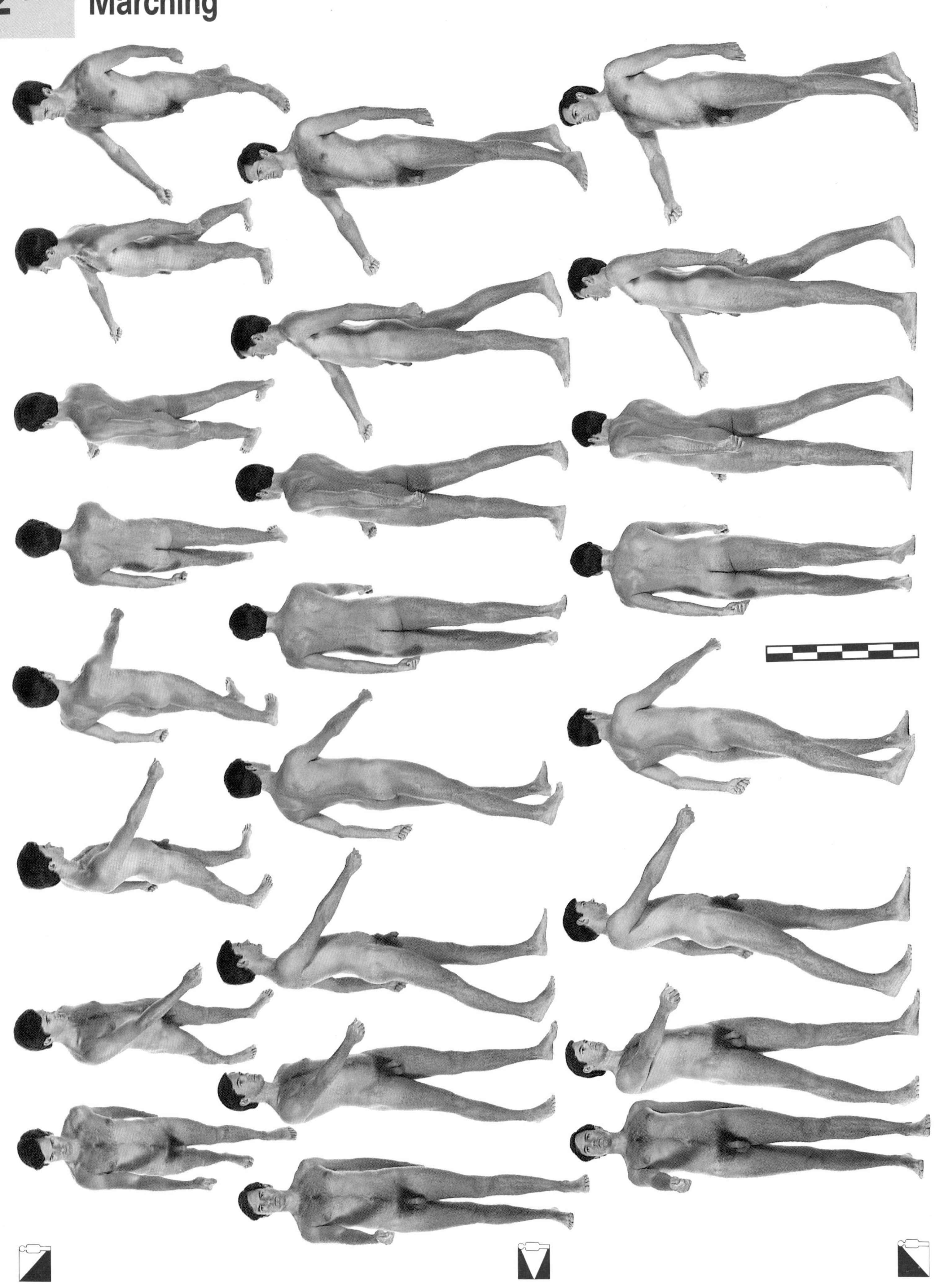

Running

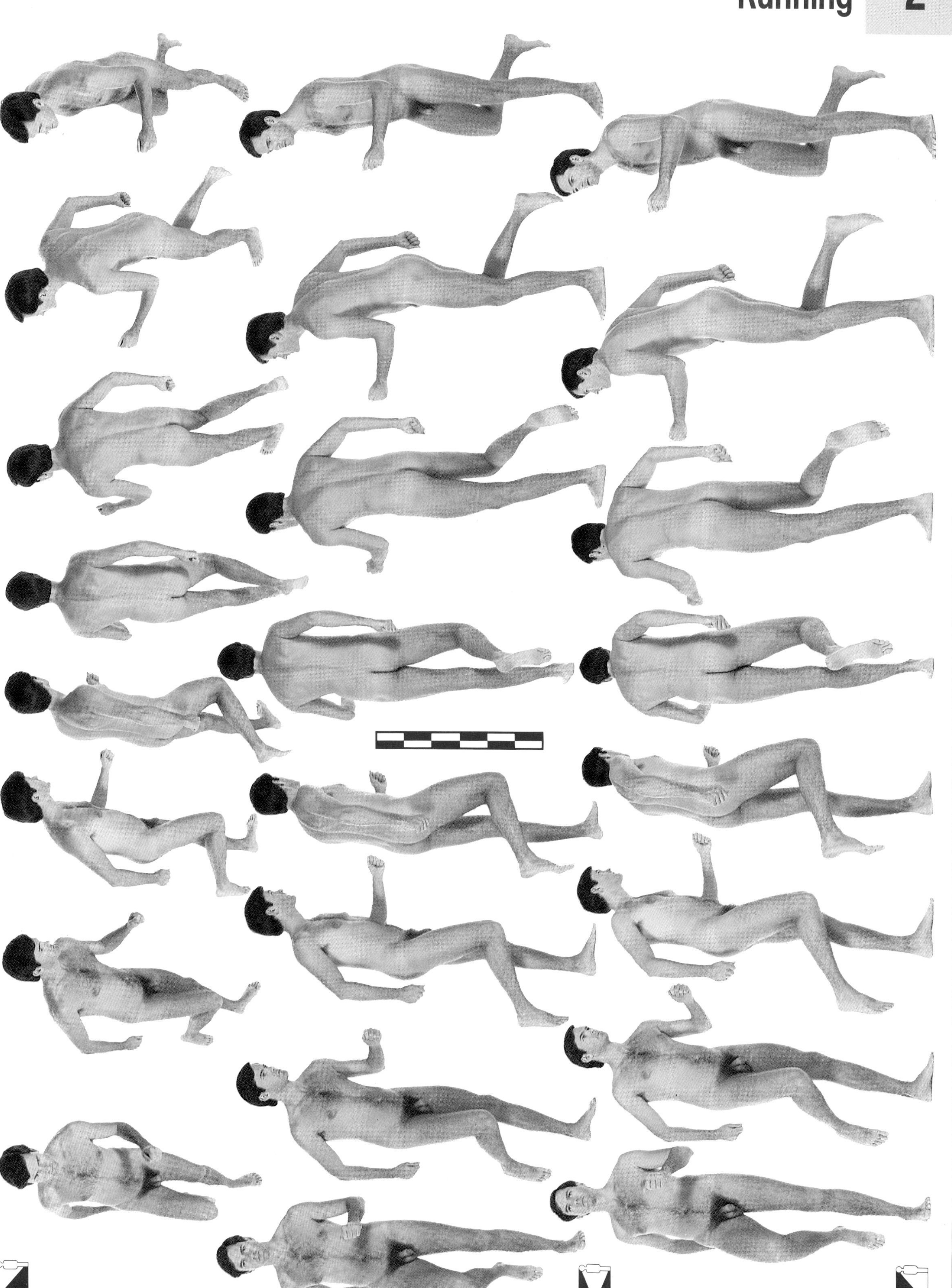

Upper trunk bending down

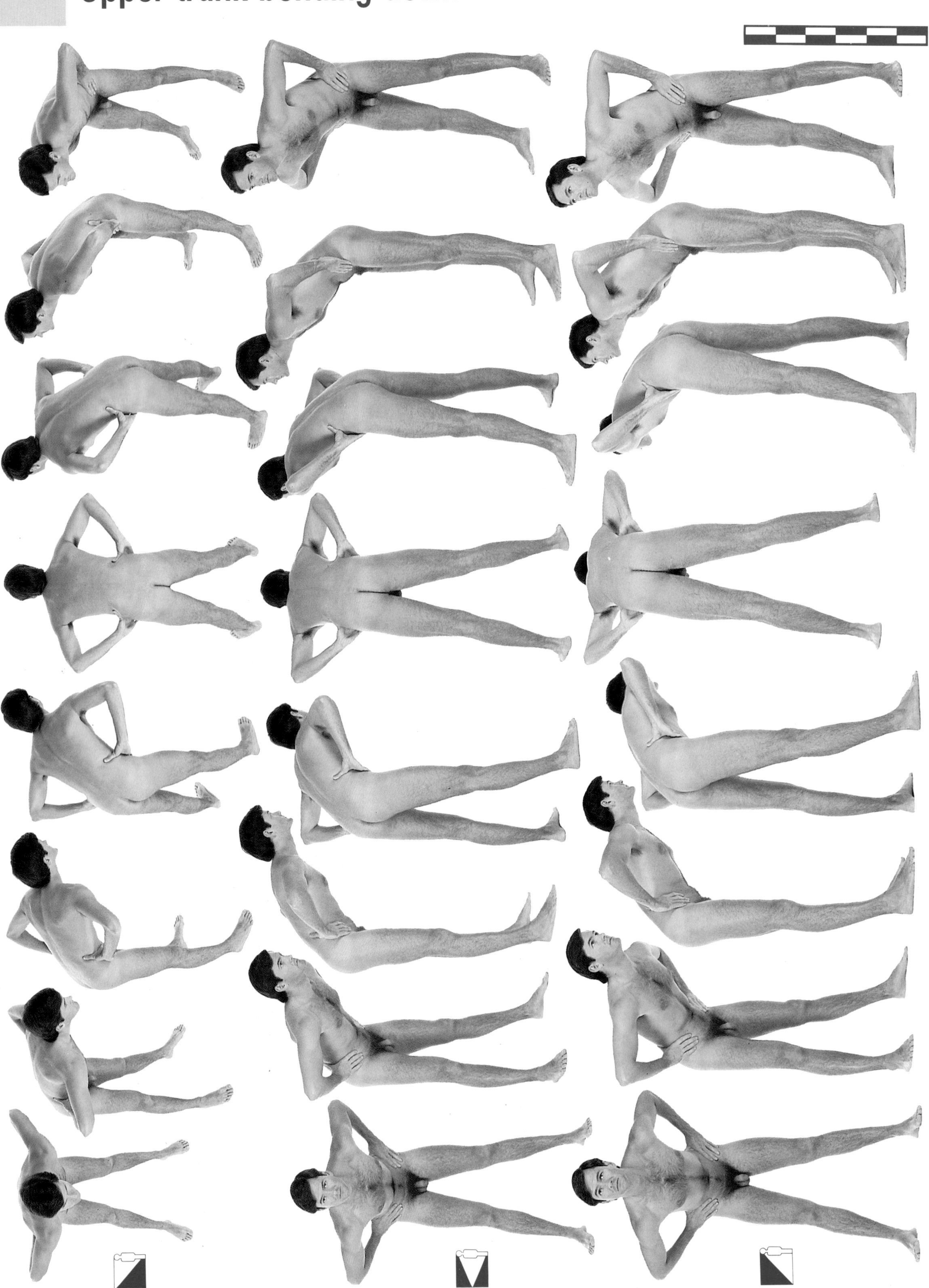

Crouching

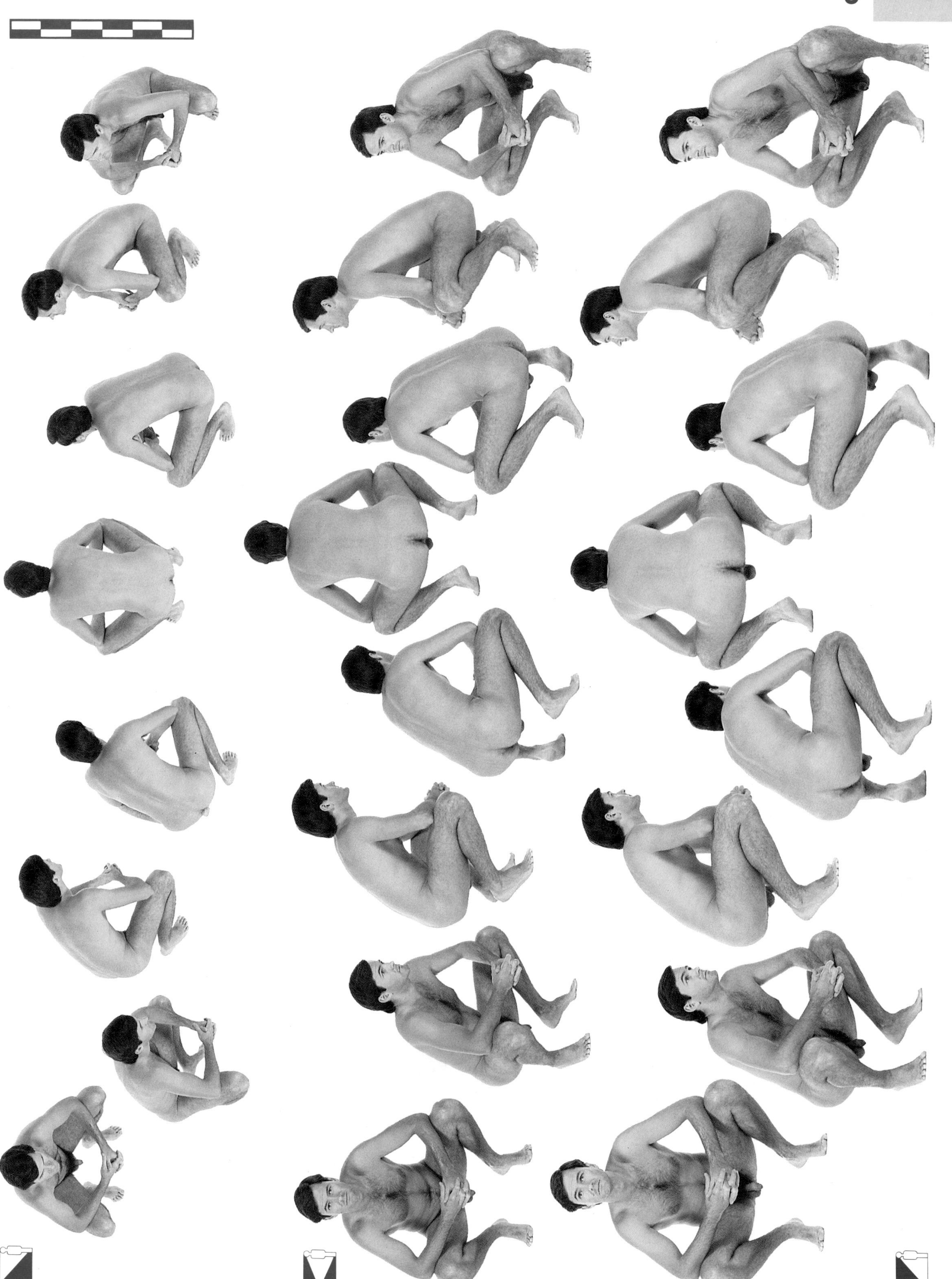

Kneeling

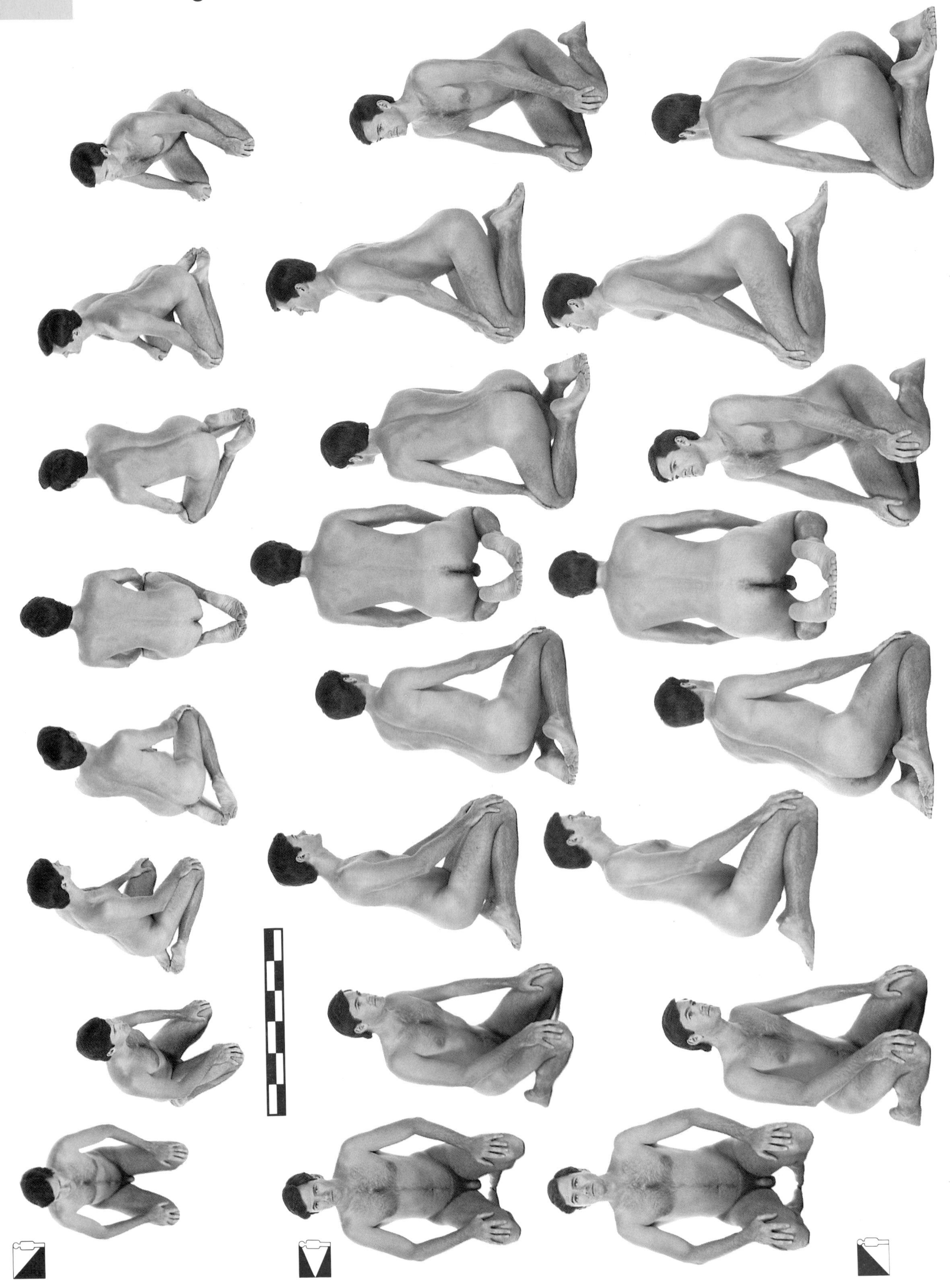

Crouching, one leg raised

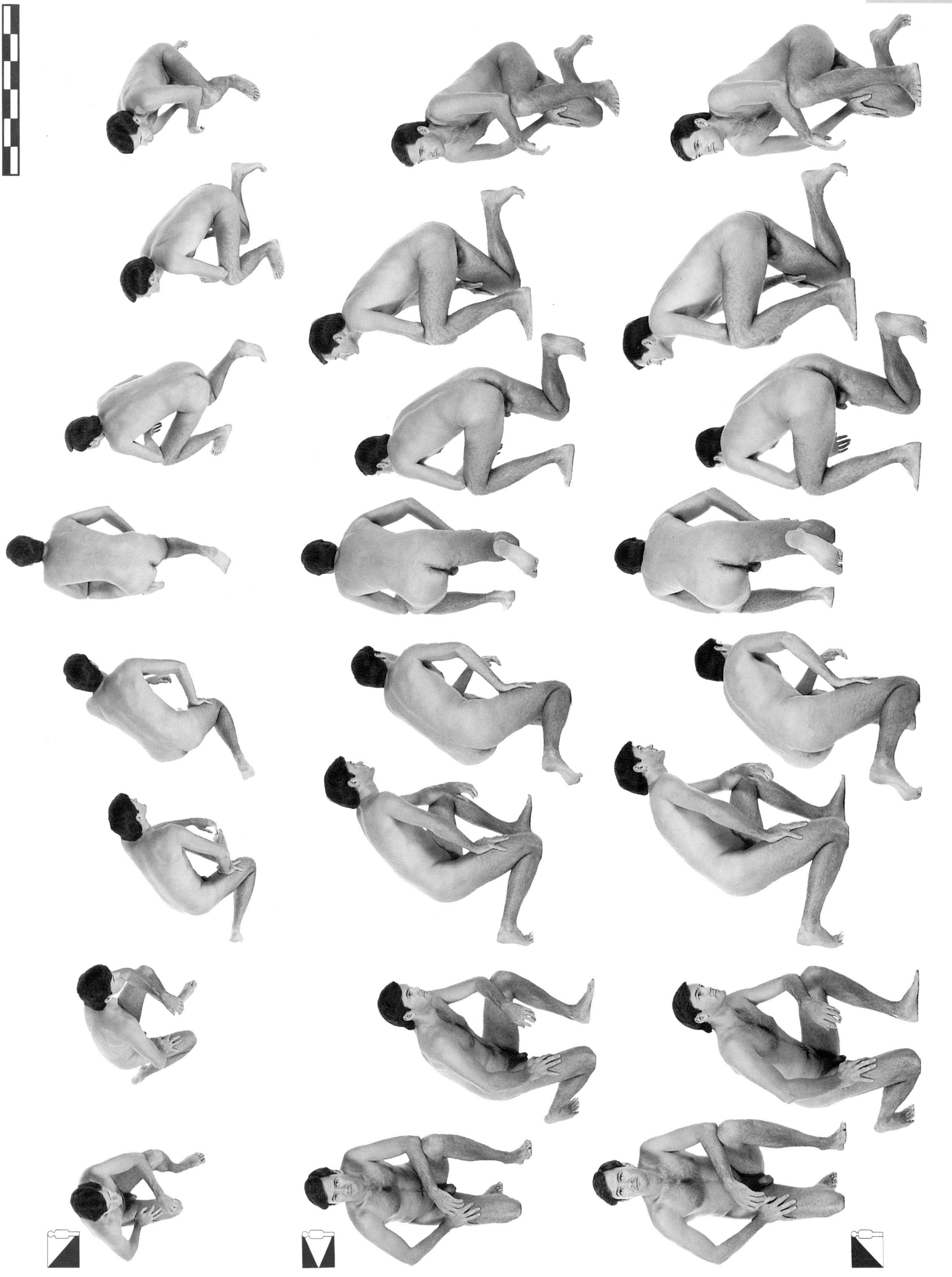

2·15 Sitting with arms by sides

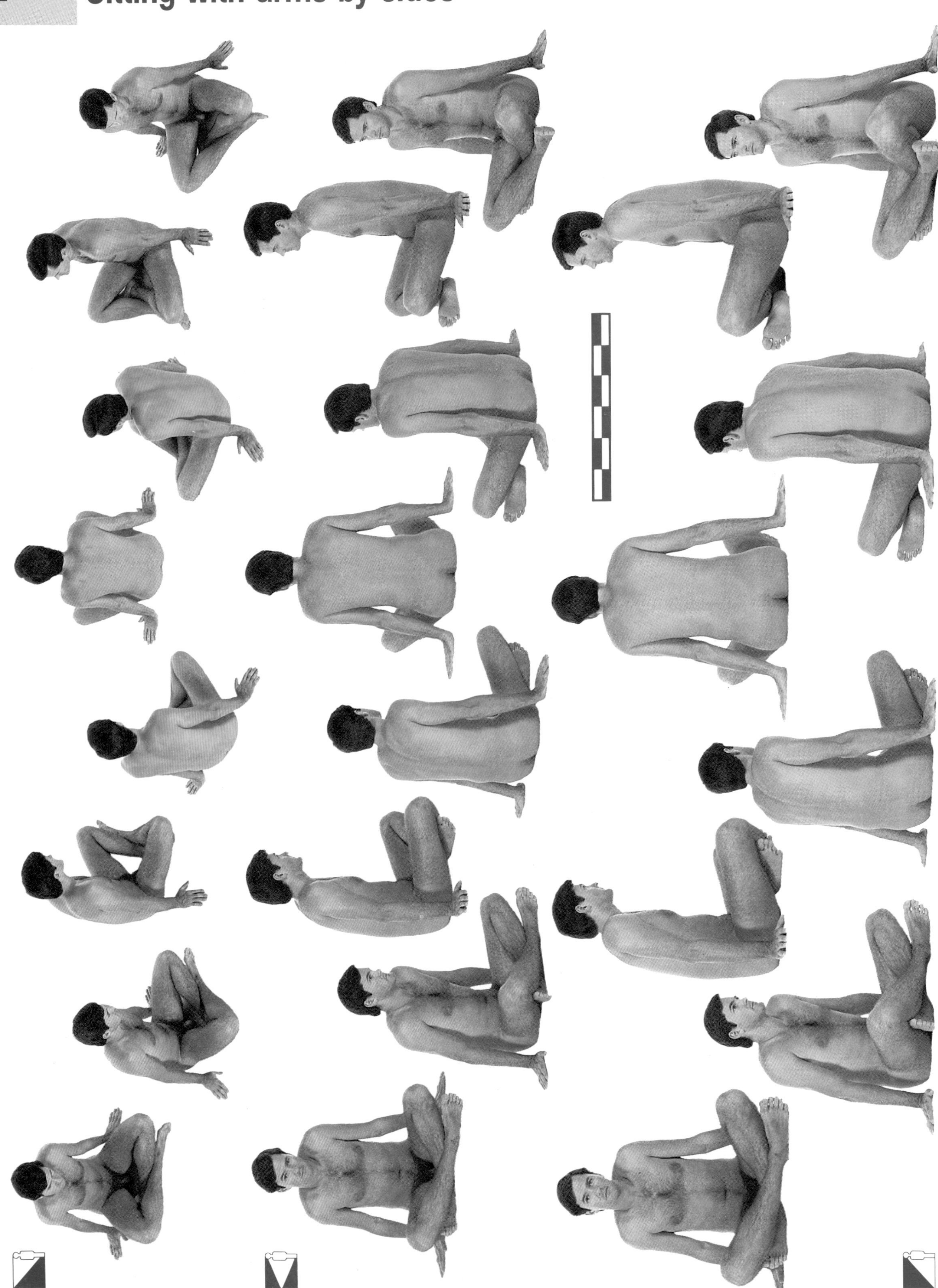

Sitting propped up by one arm

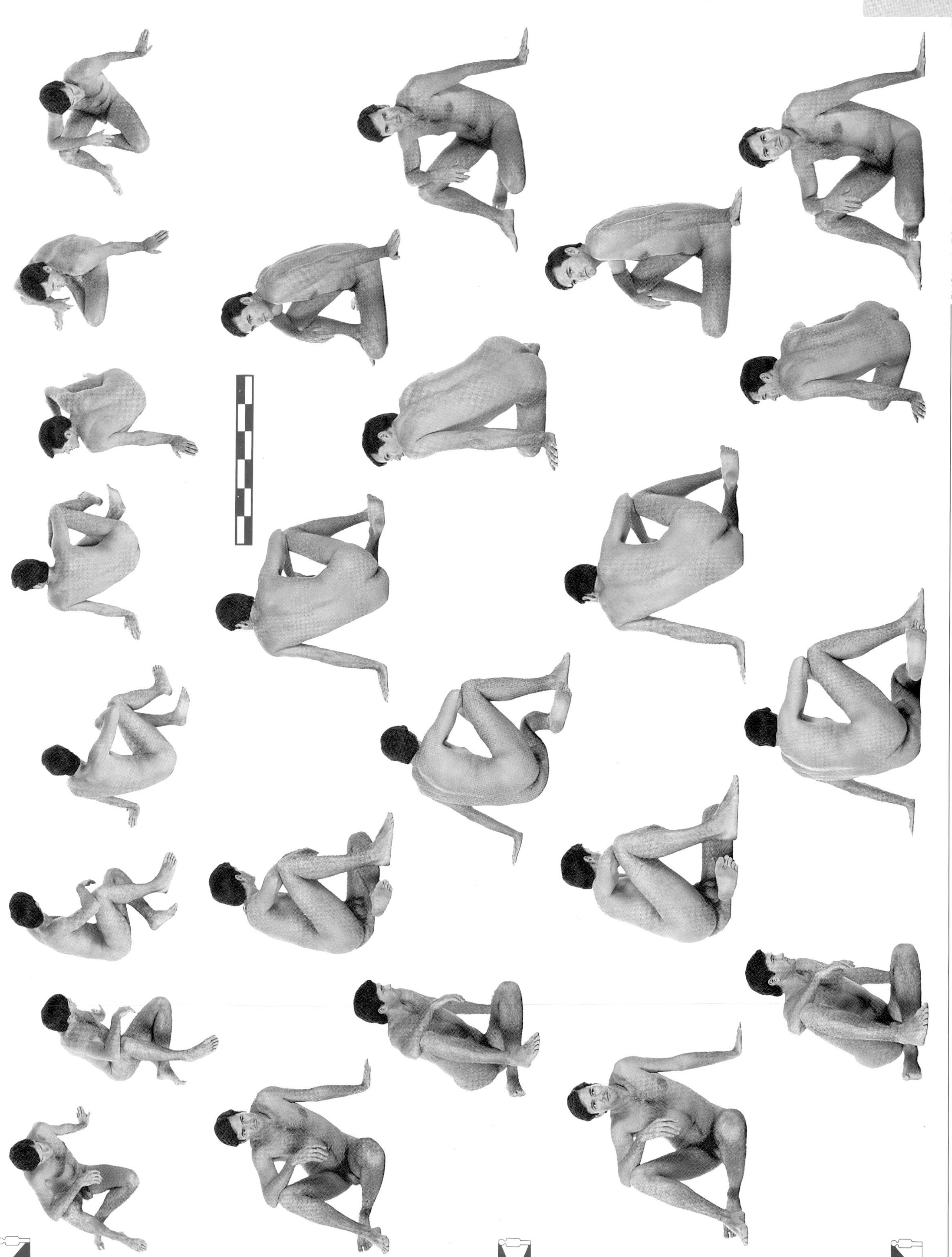

Sitting with one leg outstretched

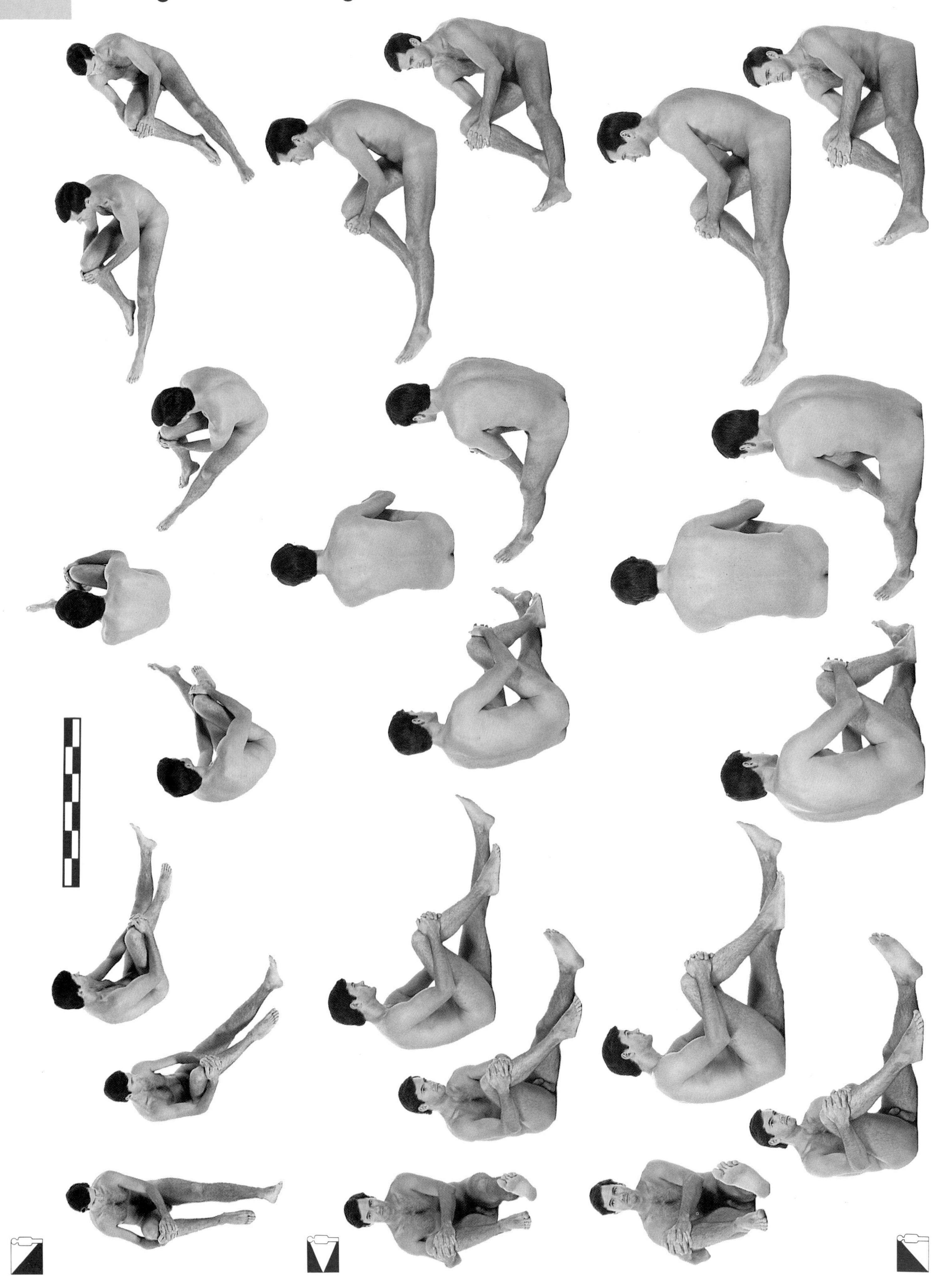

Sitting with arms round knees

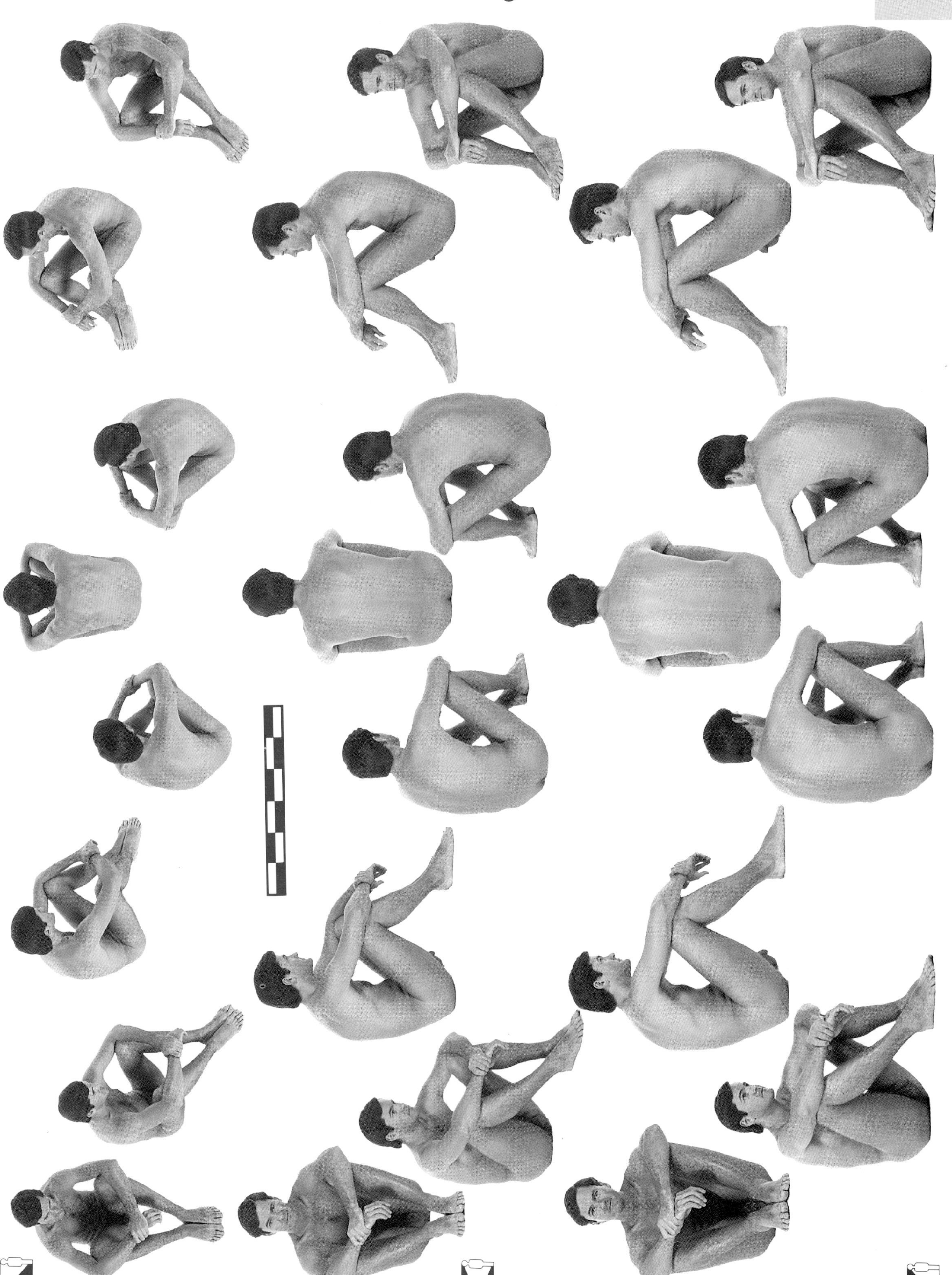

2·19 Sitting with legs outstretched

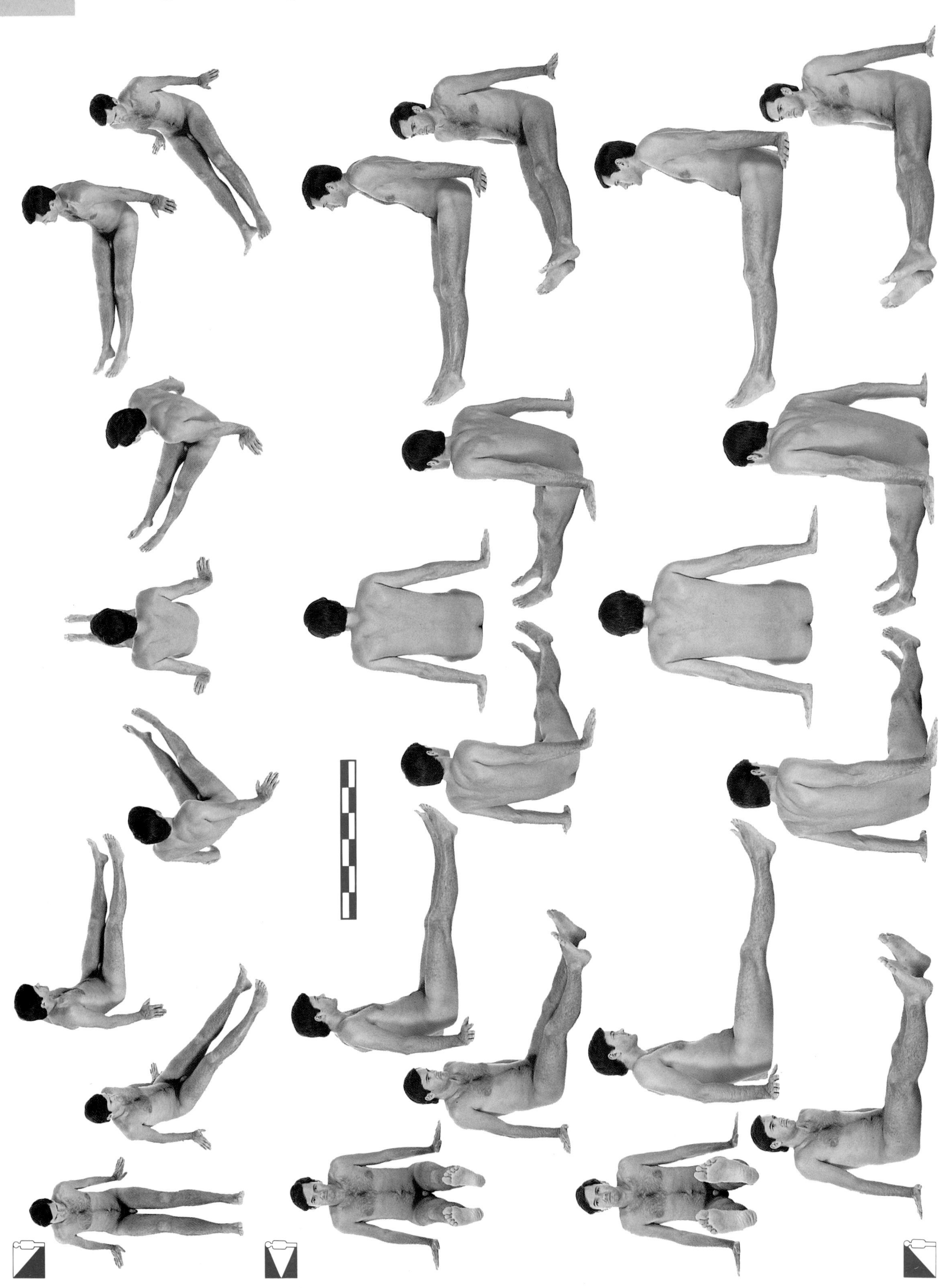

On back, hands behind head, one knee raised

On back, hands behind head

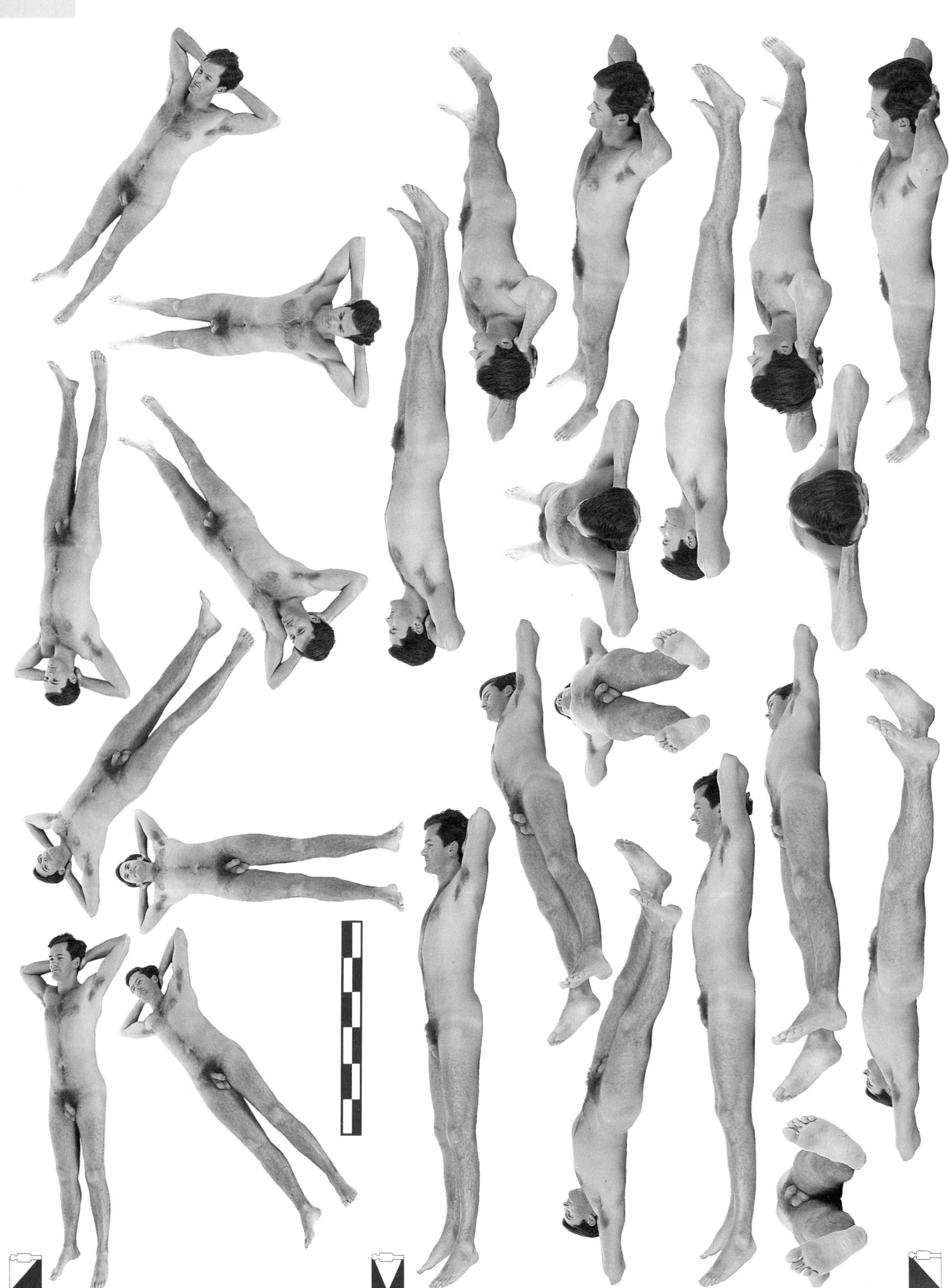

On back, limbs by the side

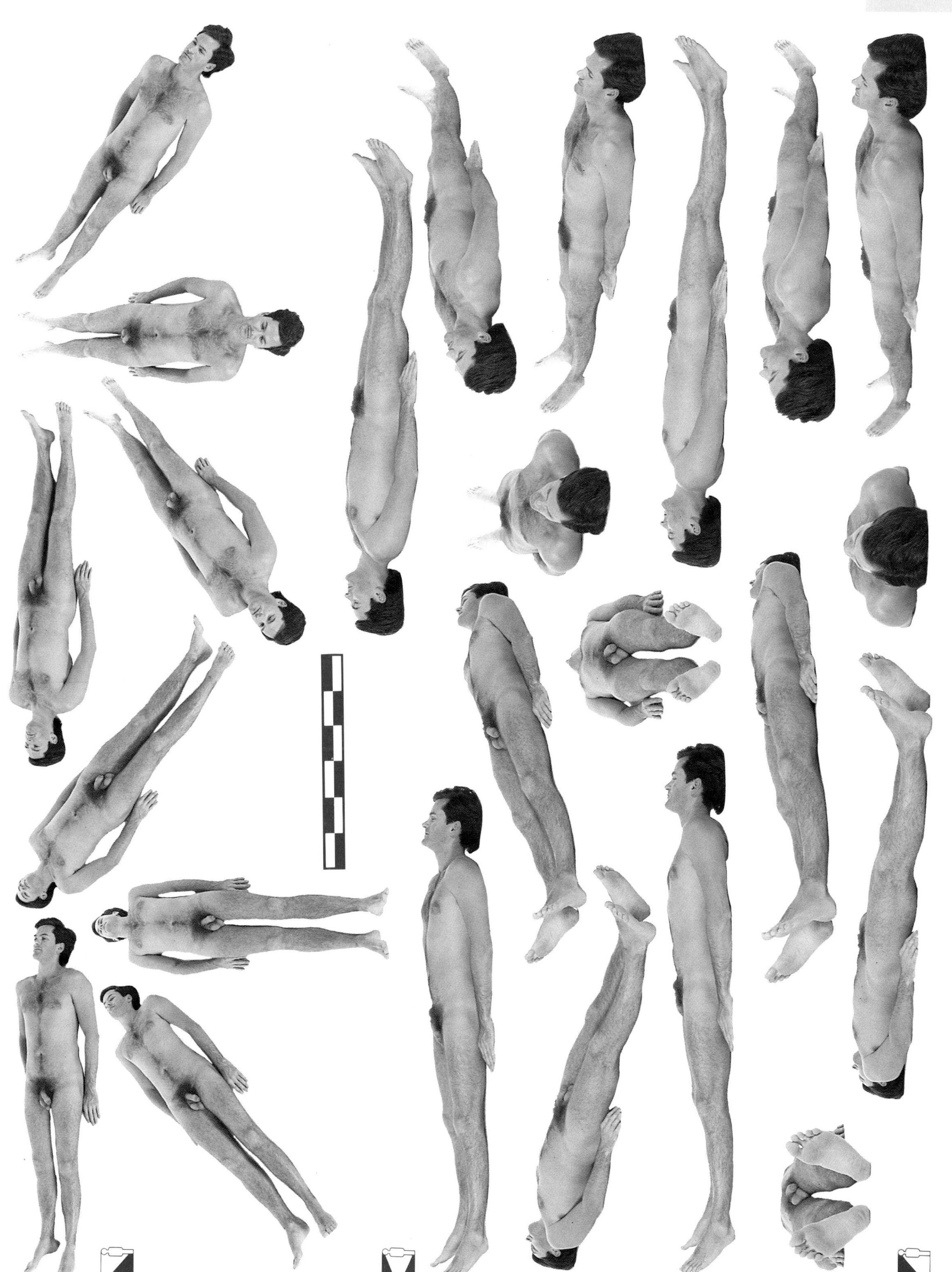

On back, limbs outstretched

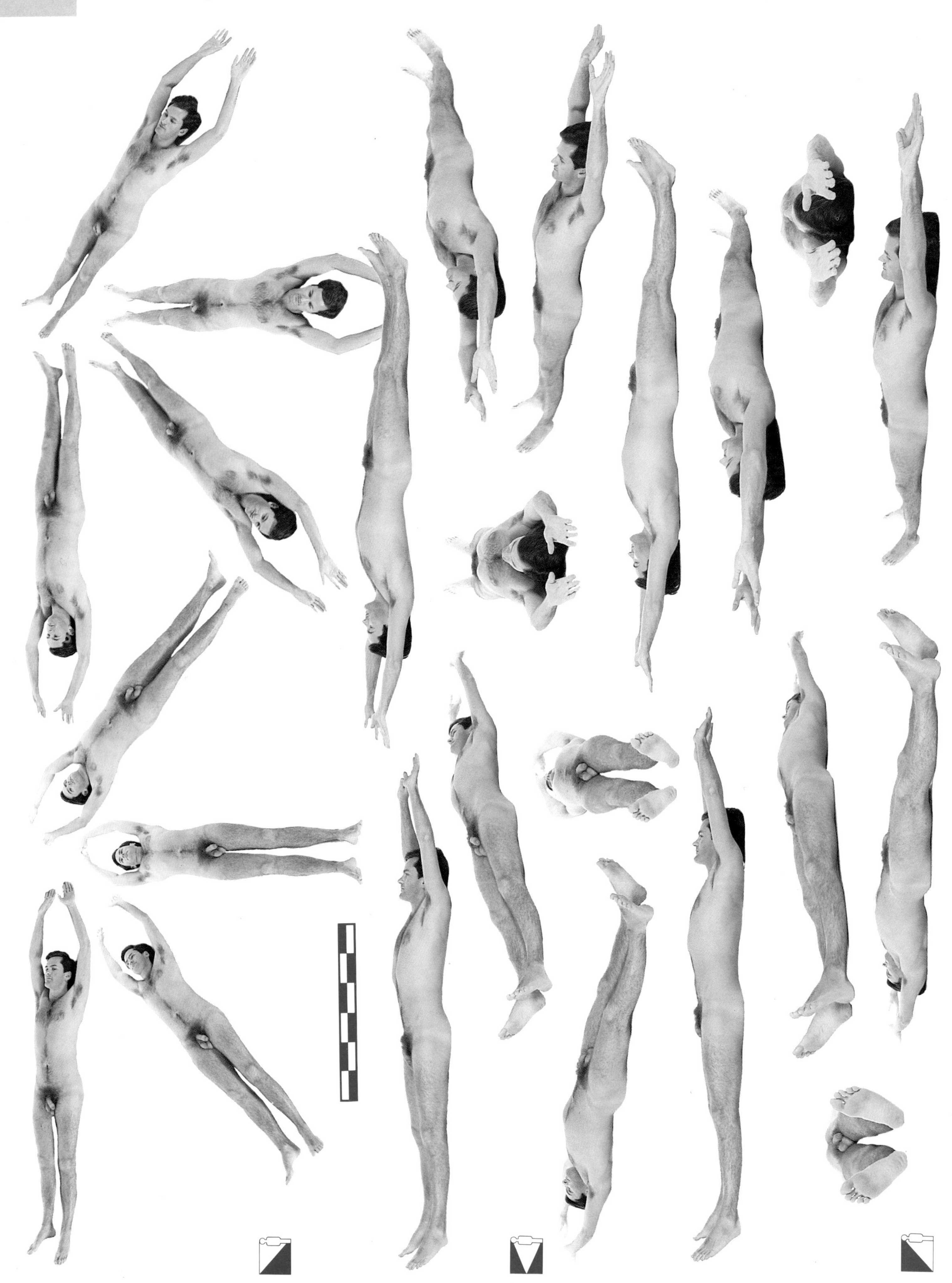

On side, limbs by the side

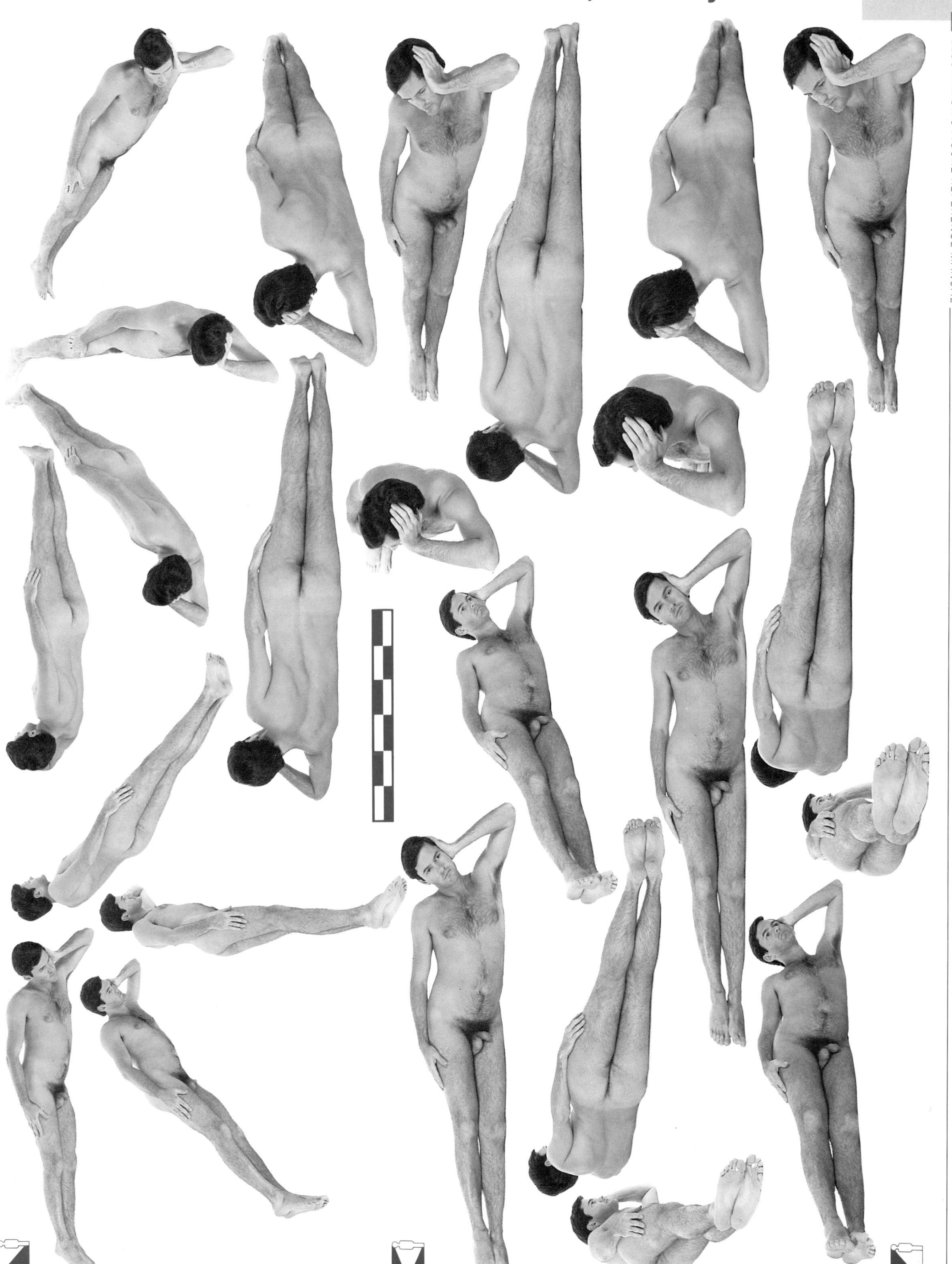

On side, one knee raised

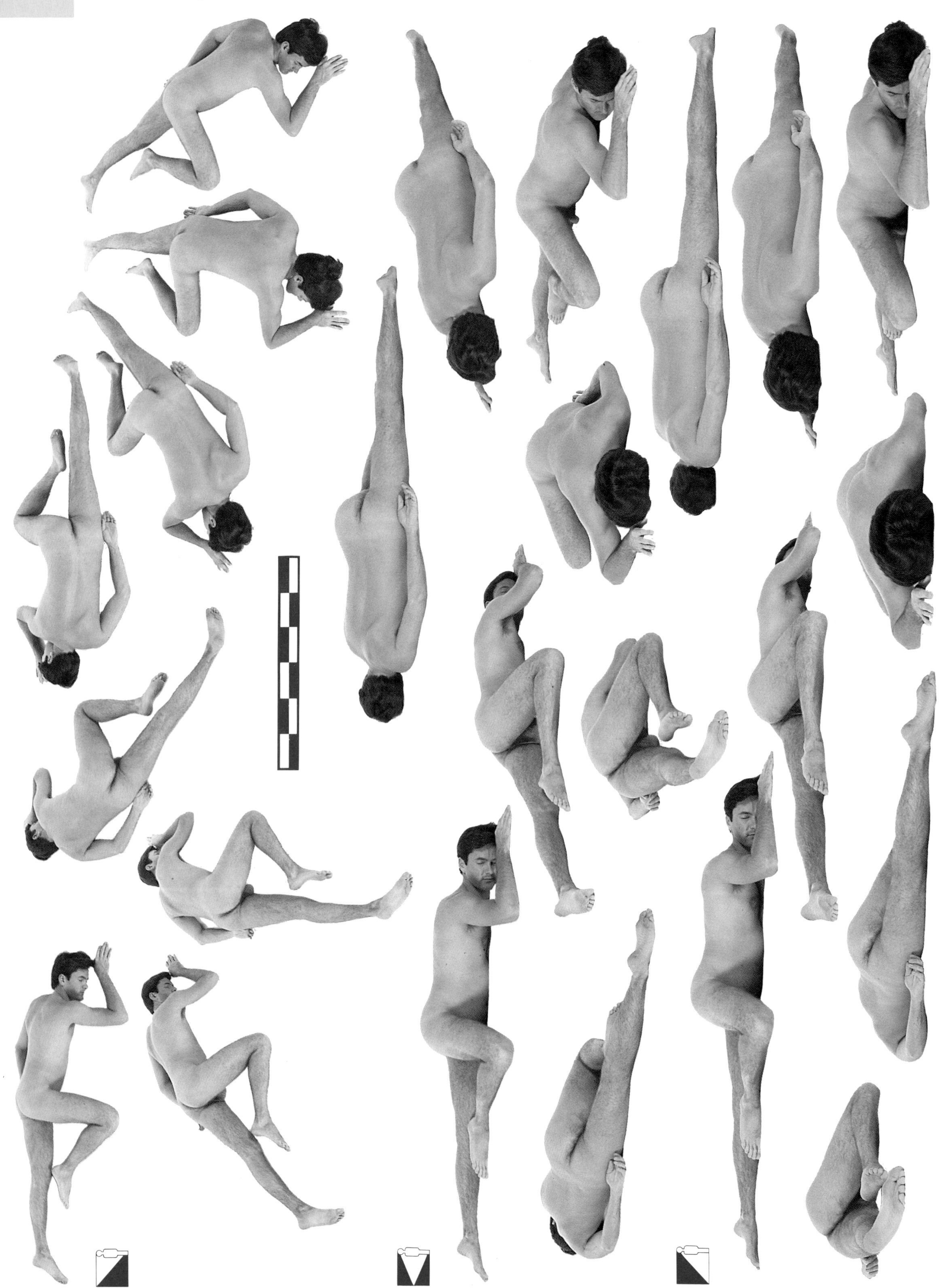

Face down, limbs by the side

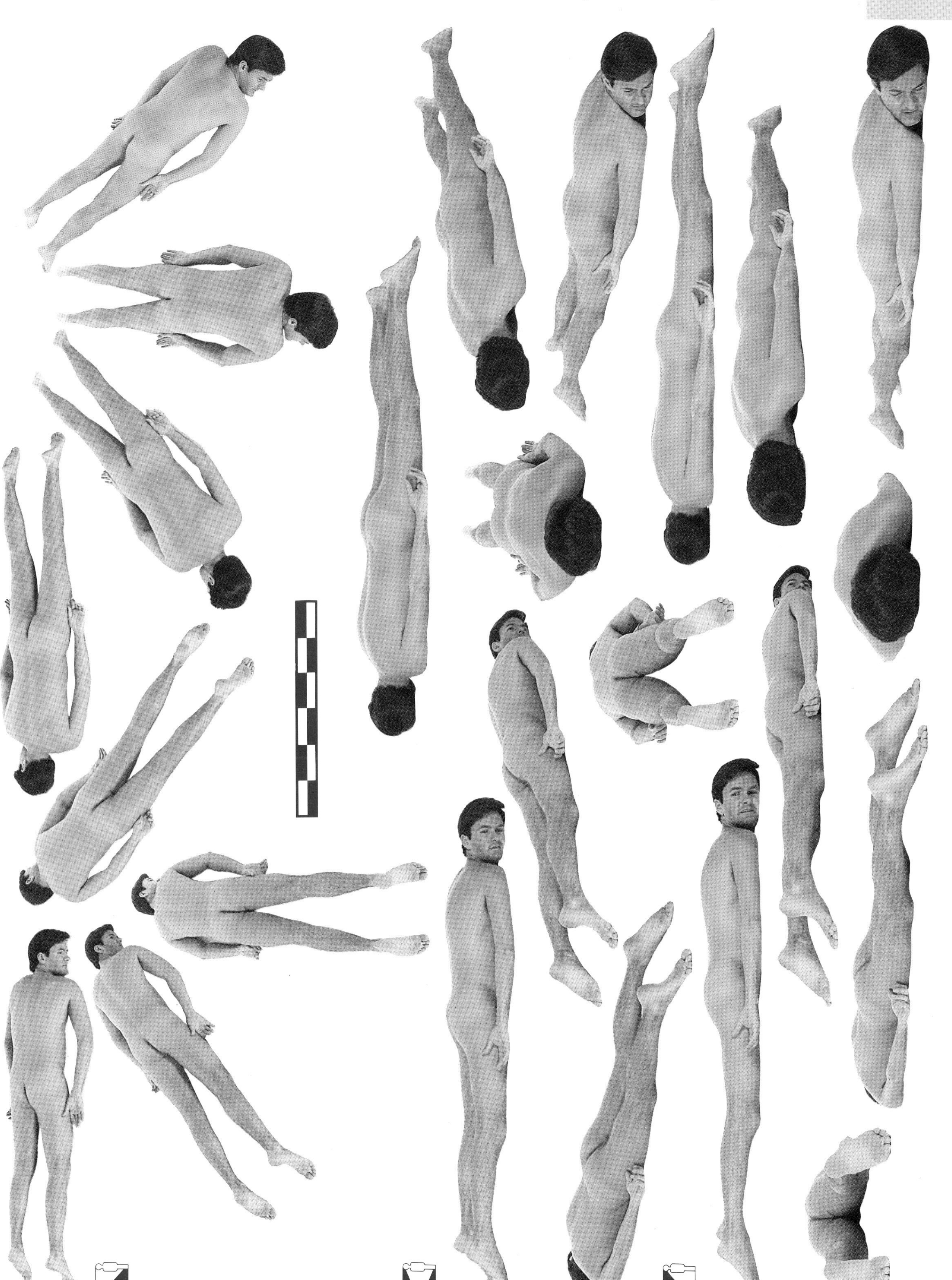

Skiing – schuss

FISCHER
VACUUM

Skiing – admiring the view

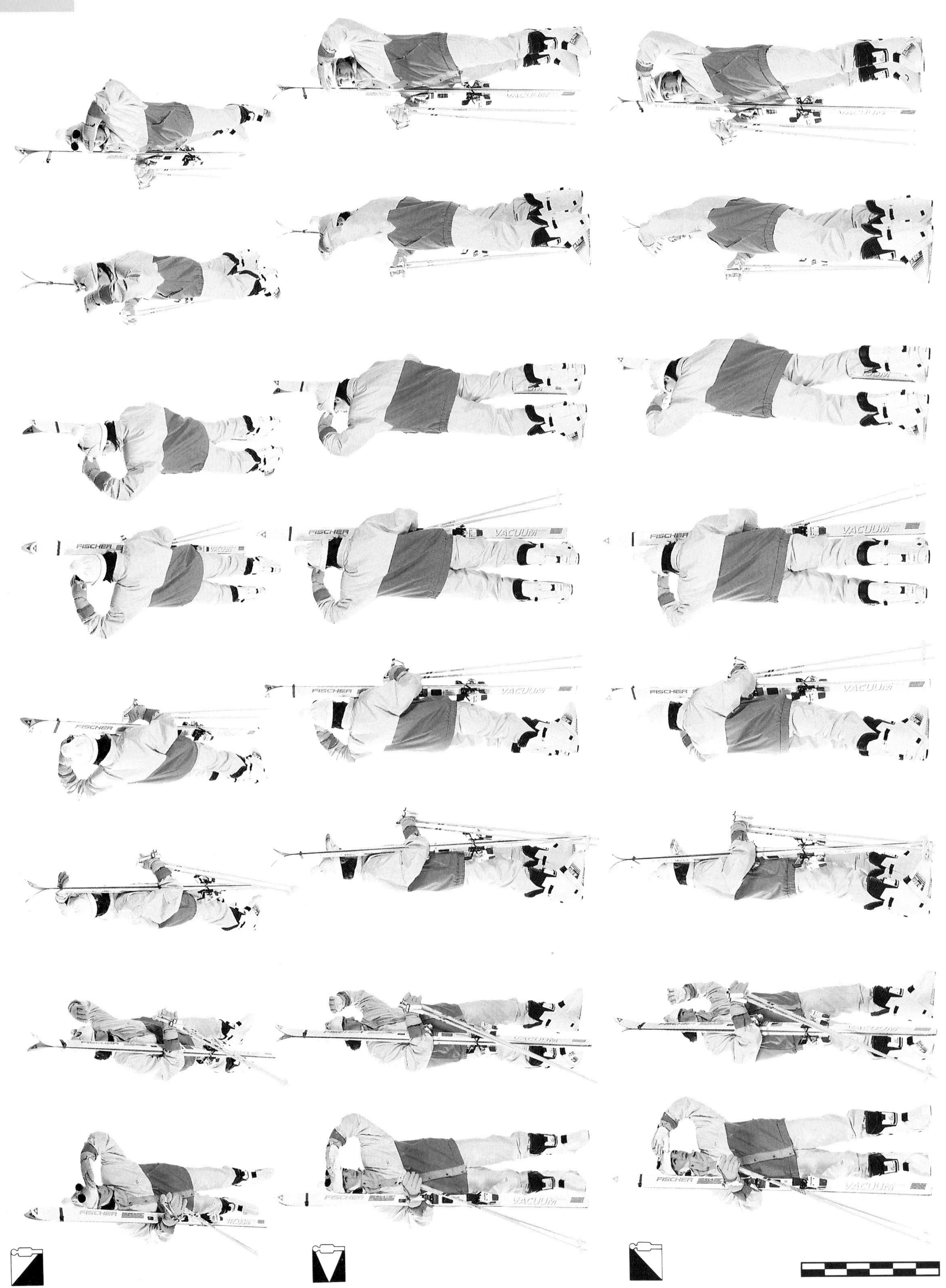

Skier – carrying skis

Golf – admiring the shot

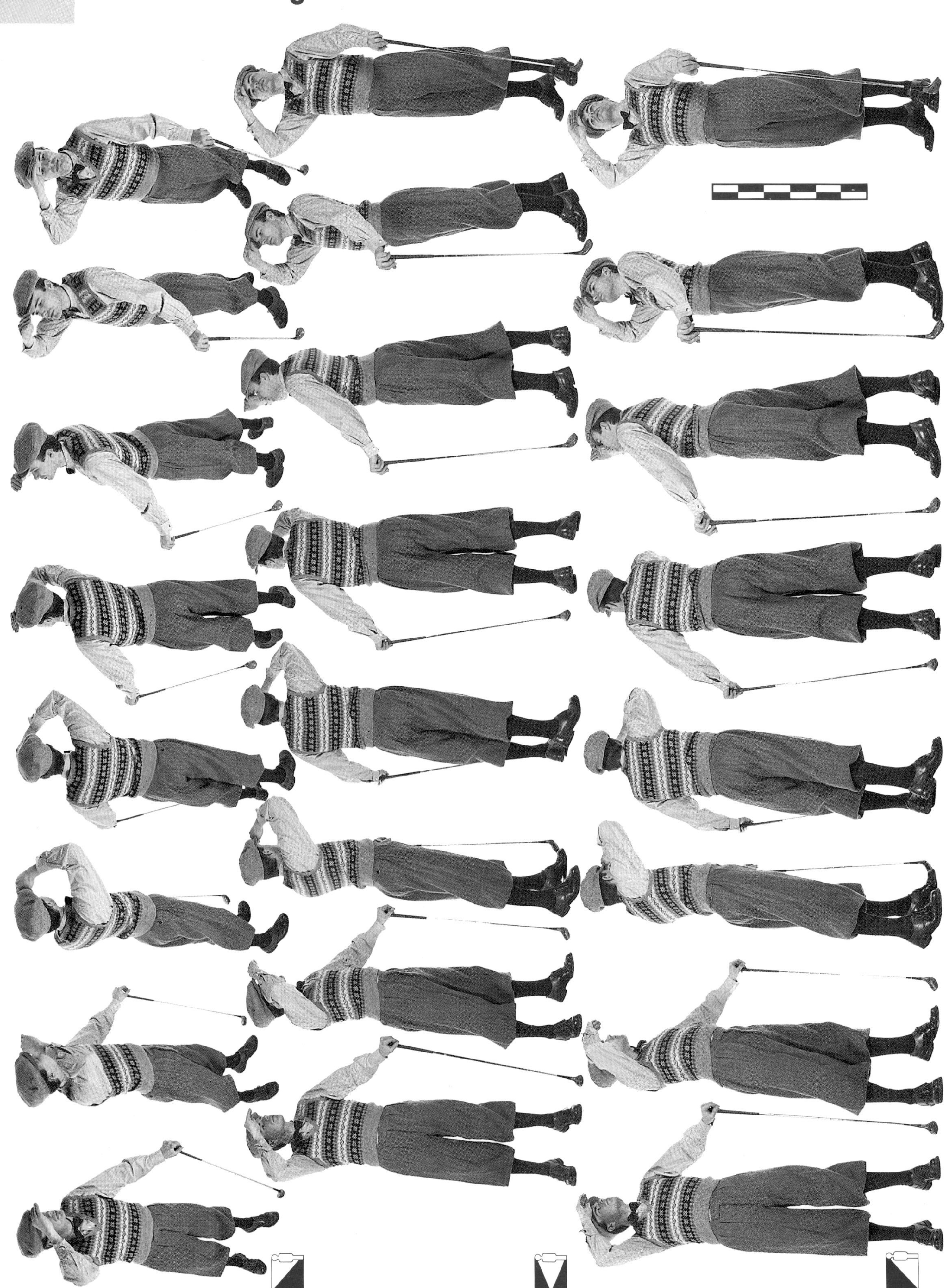

Golf – addressing the ball

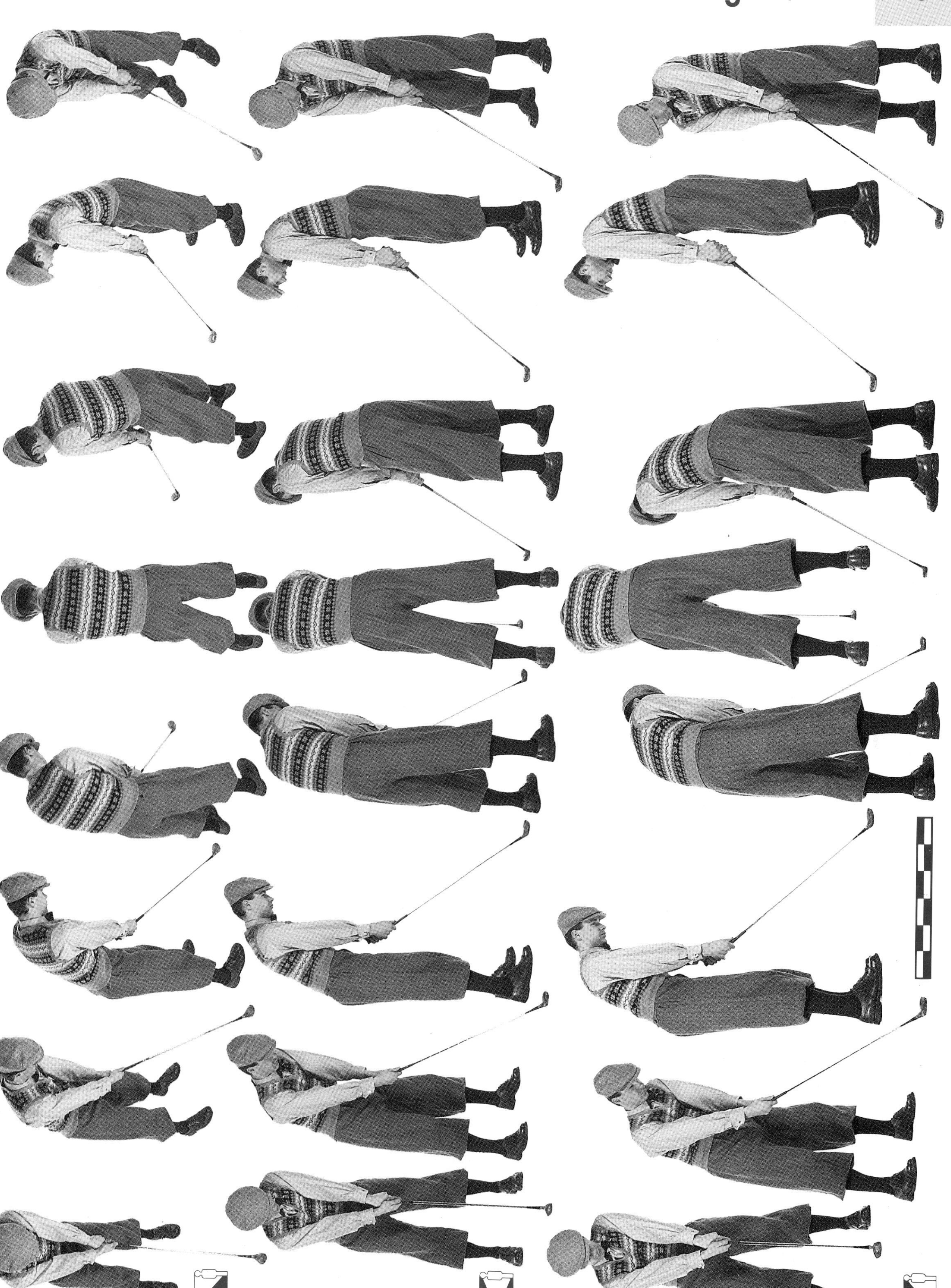

3·06 Golf – top of backswing

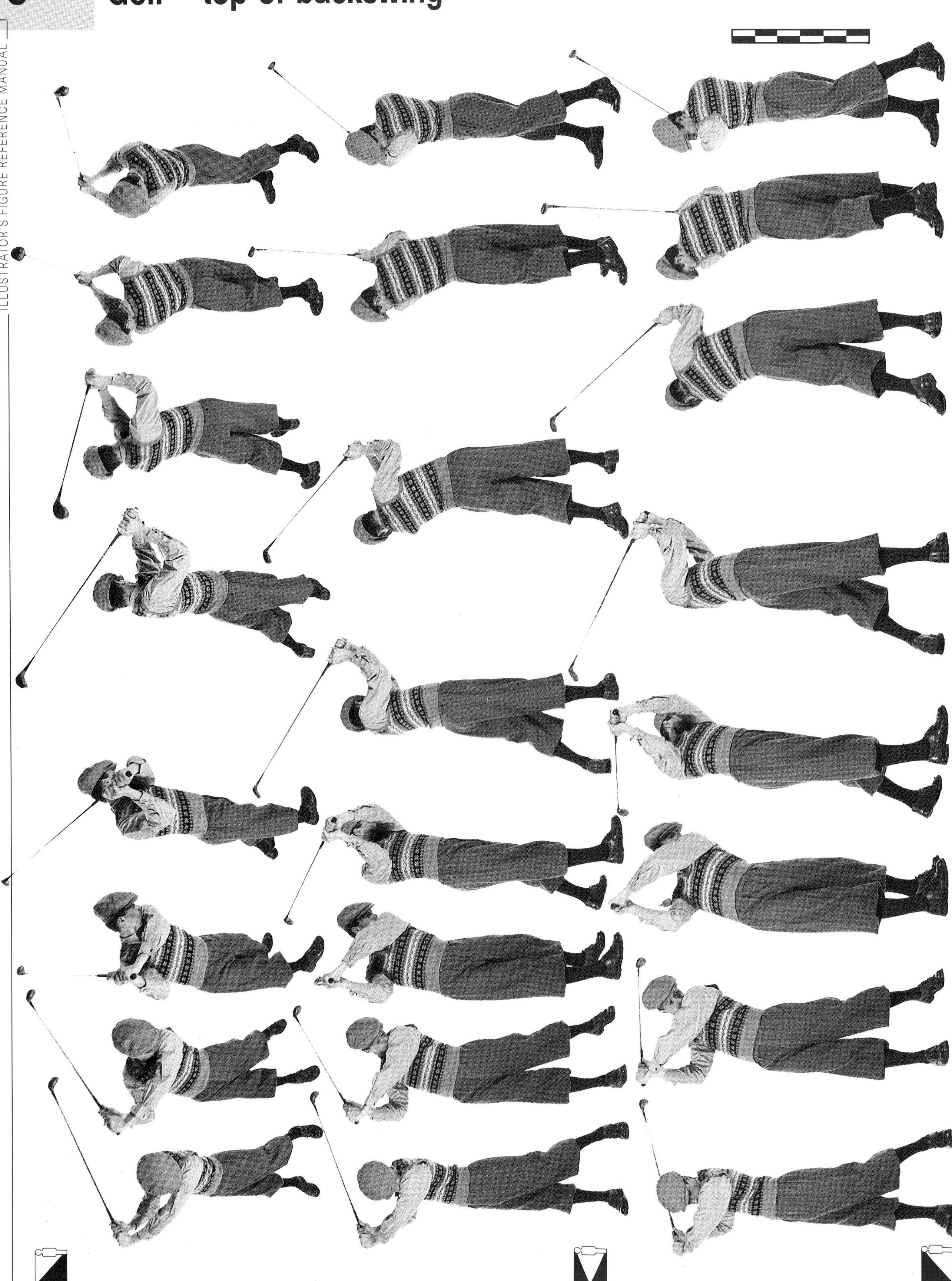

Tennis – ready to receive

Tennis – forehand drive

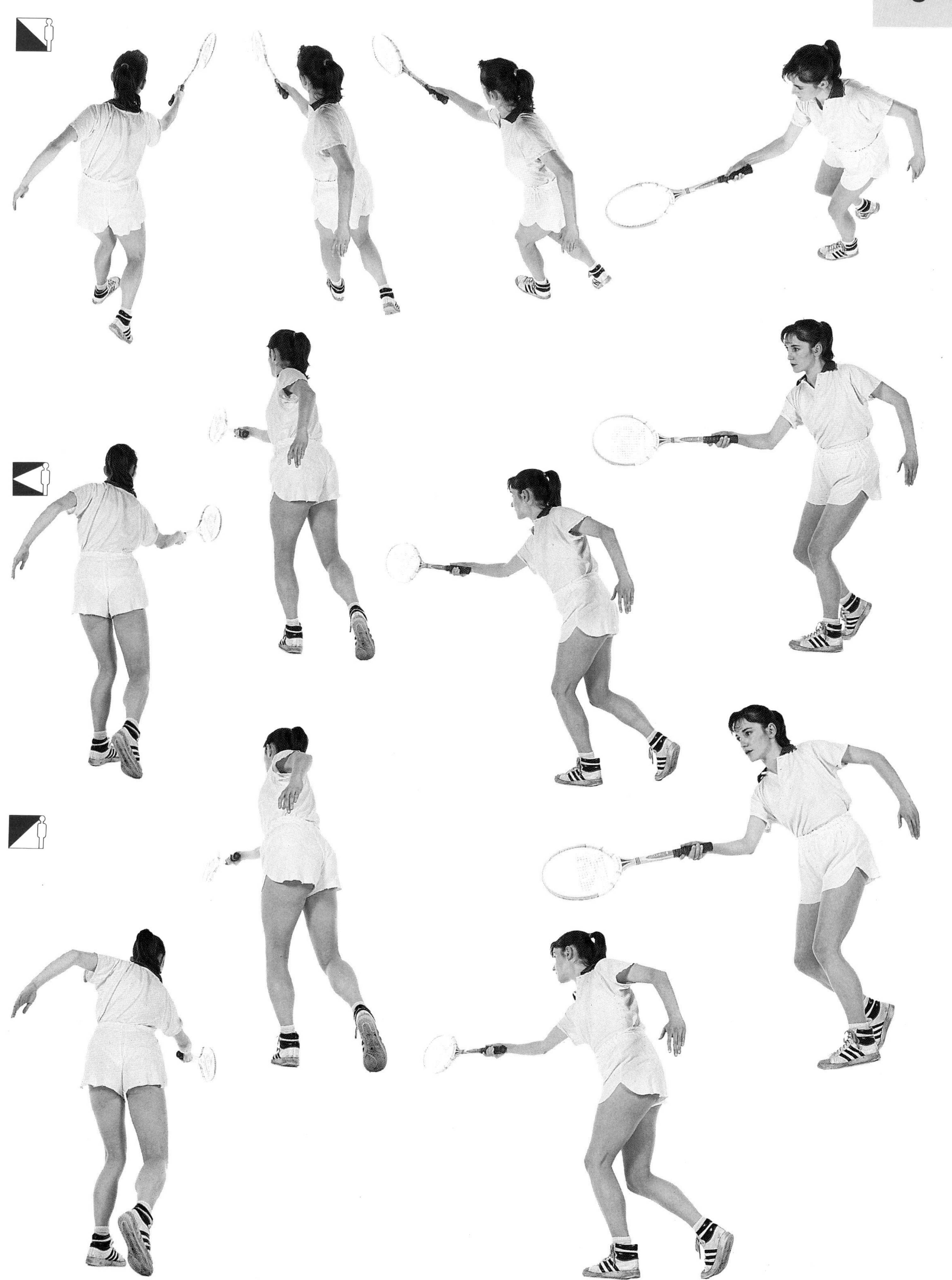

Badminton – smash

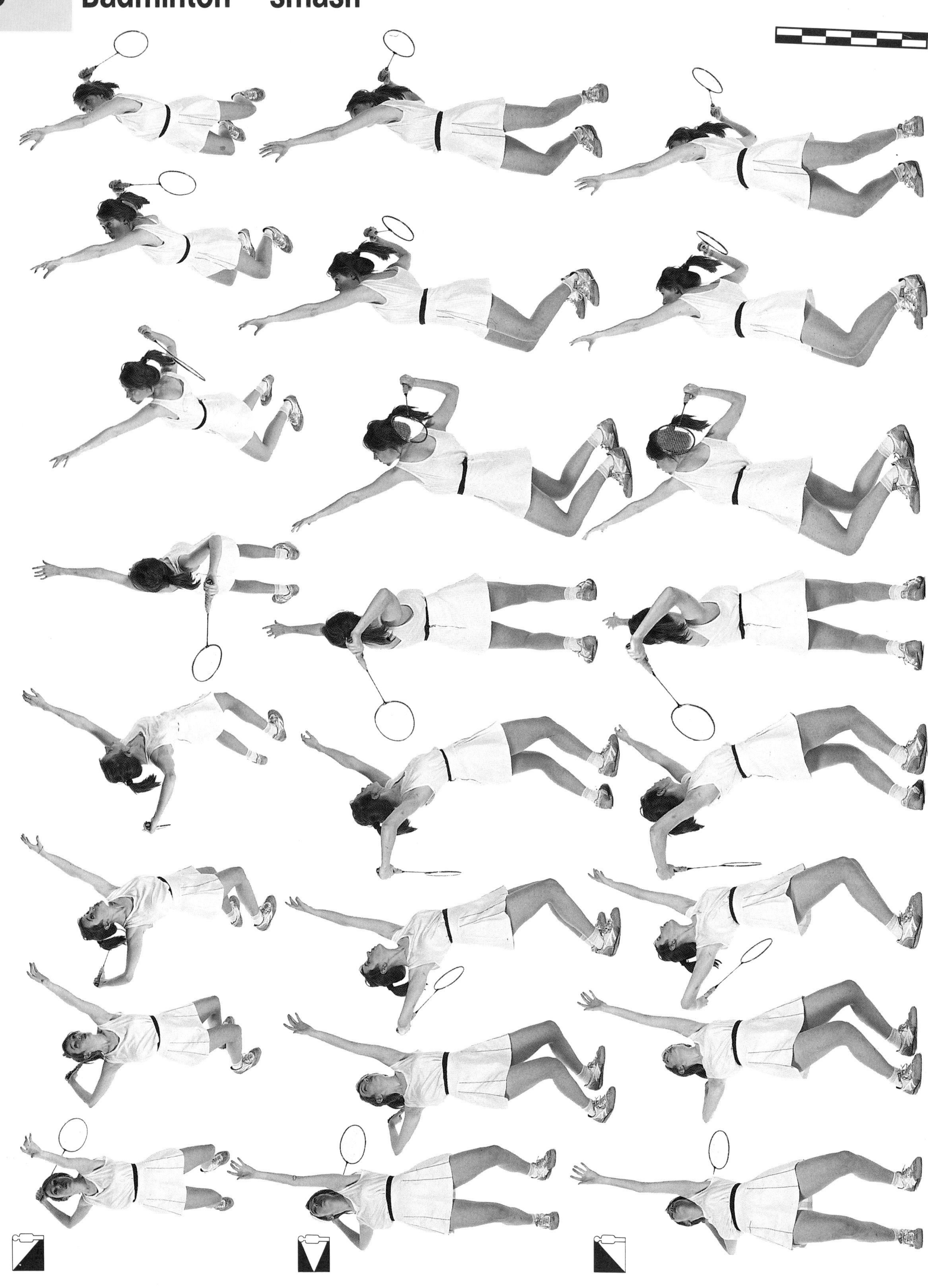

Squash – forehand

Squash – backhand

Cricket – defensive block

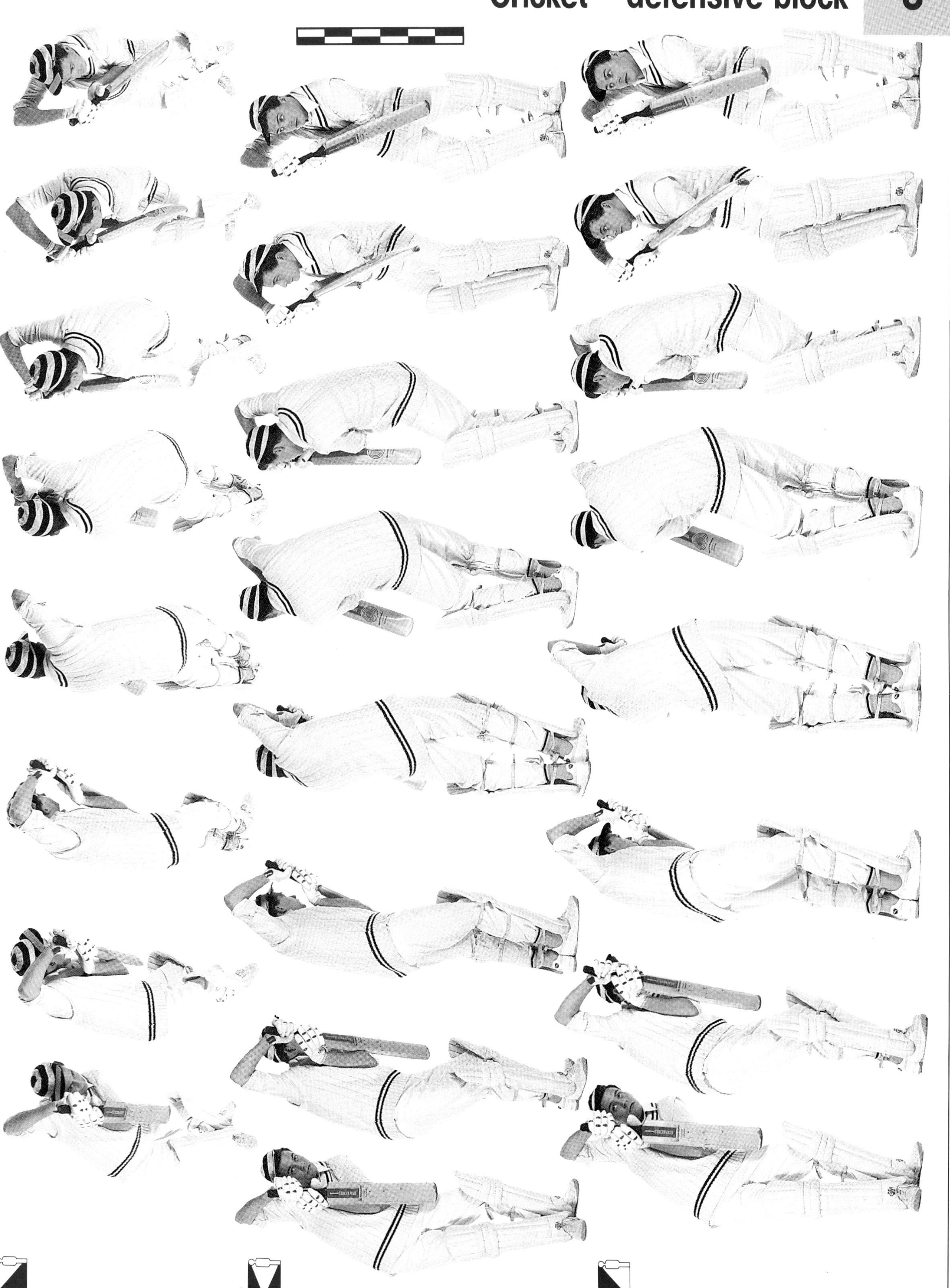

Cricket – waiting to bat

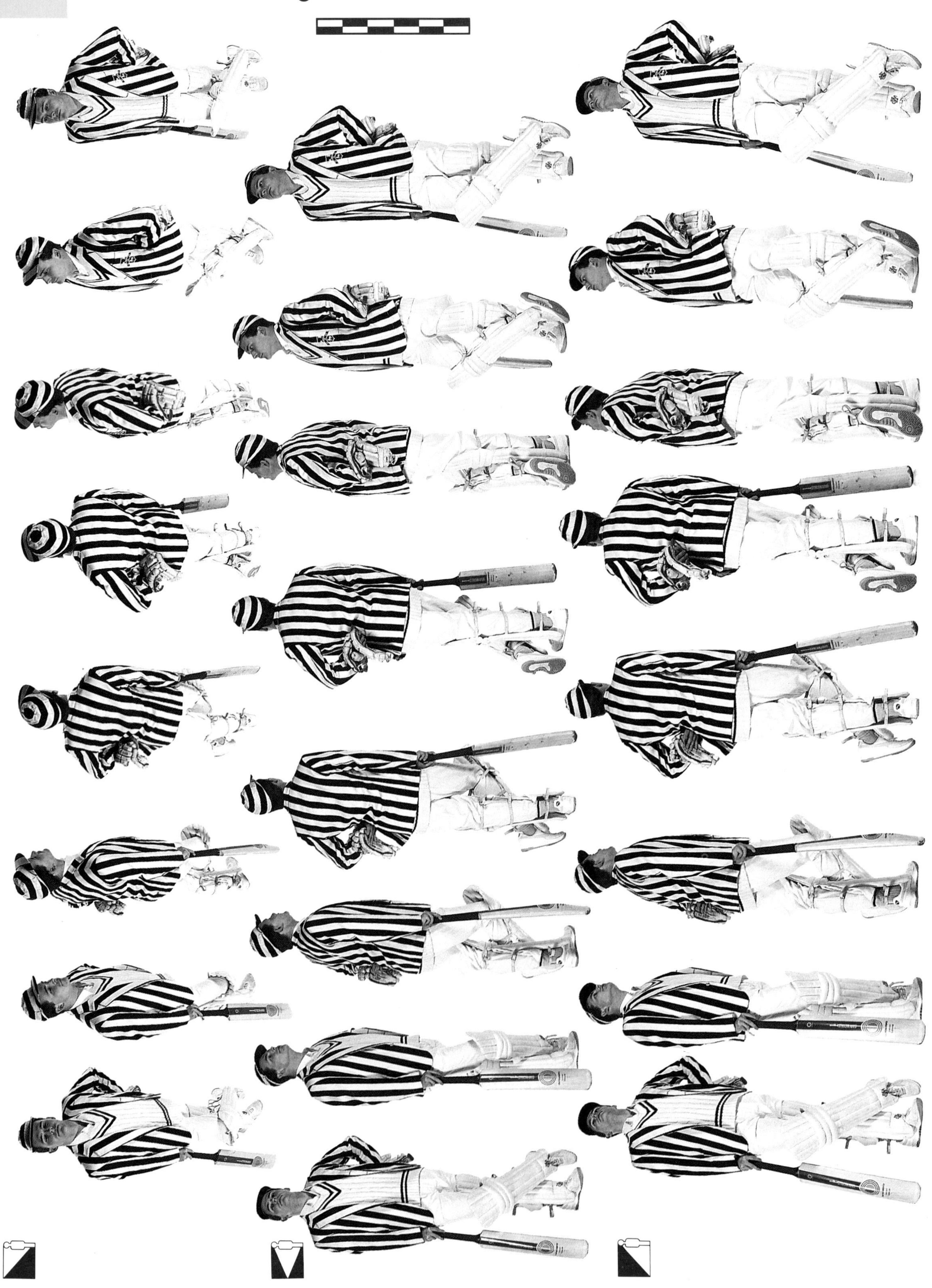

Throwing a ball

Tossing a ball up

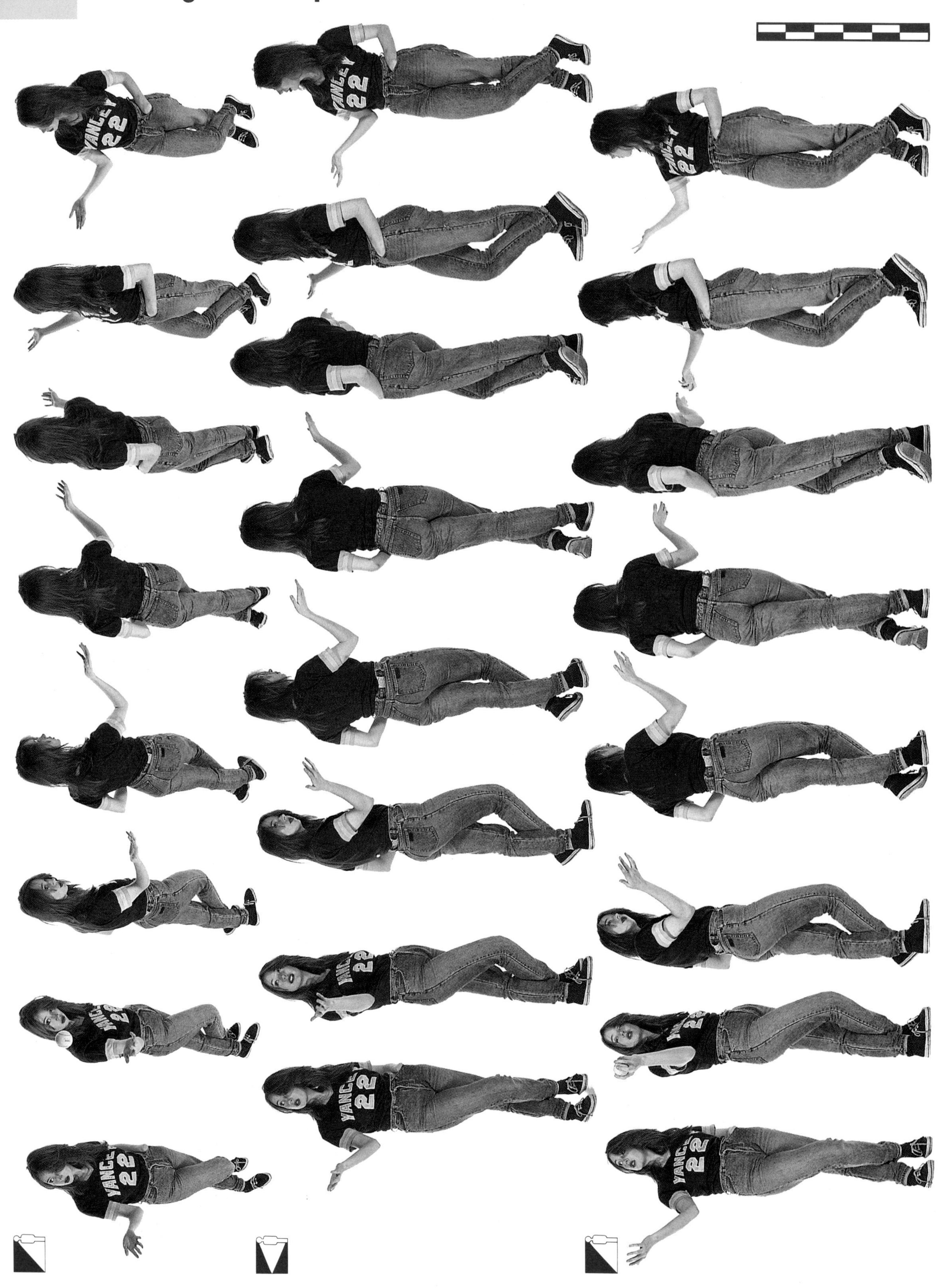

Snooker – long pot

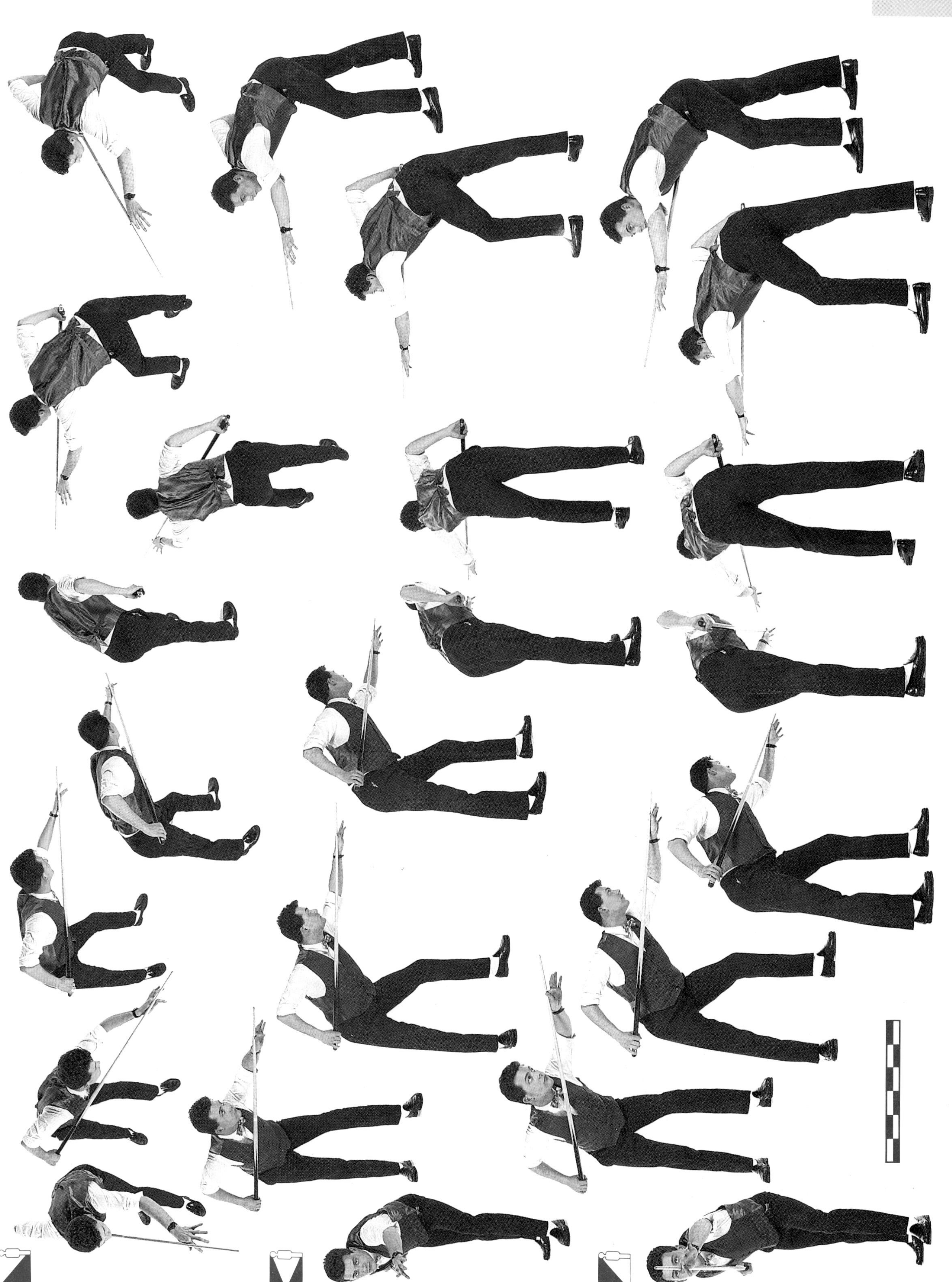

Tenpin bowling

Soccer – throw-in

Running – sprinter on the block

Rugby – passing

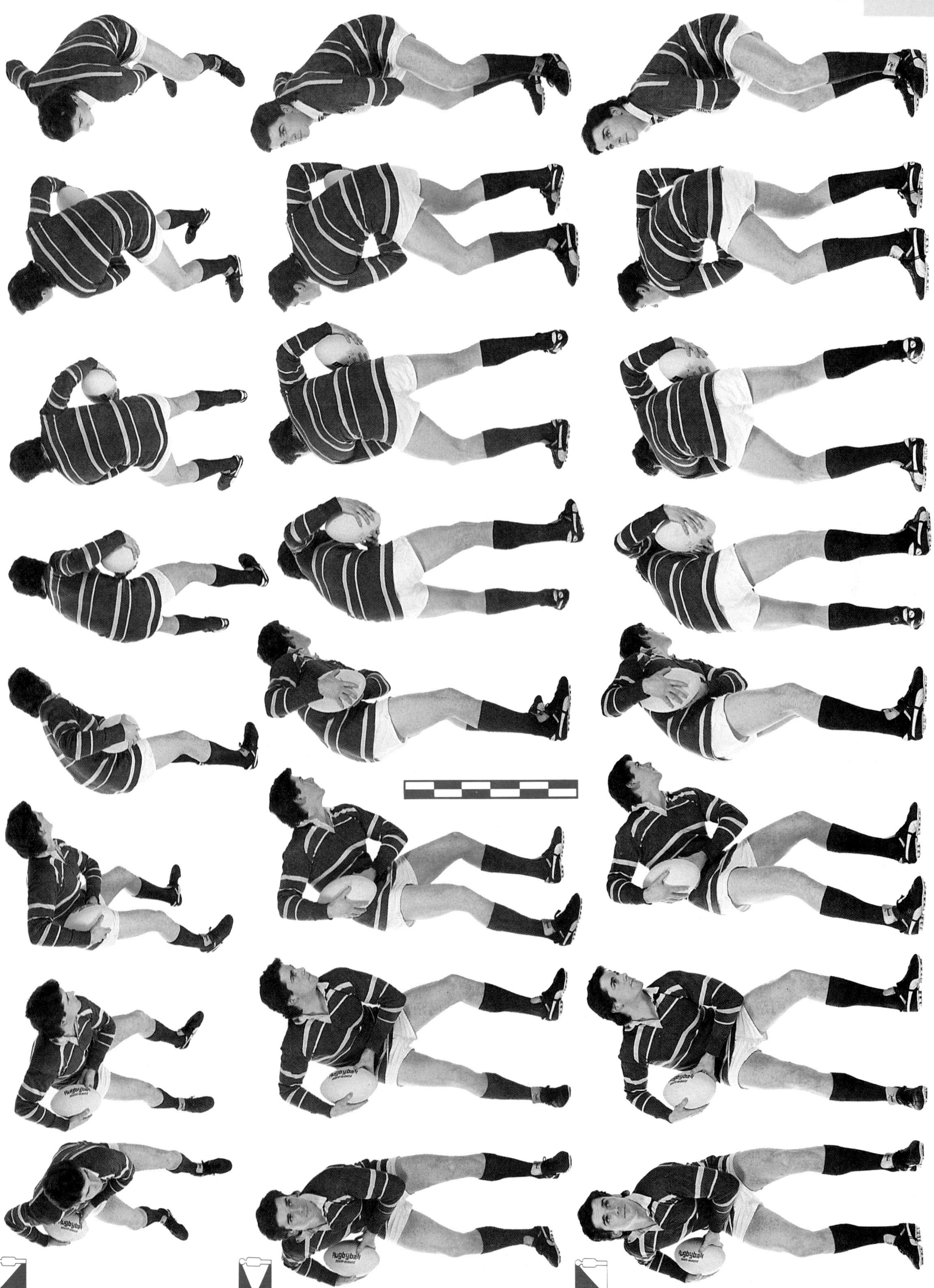

Rugby – drop kick

Basketball – dribbling

Basketball – shooting

Boxing – classic guard

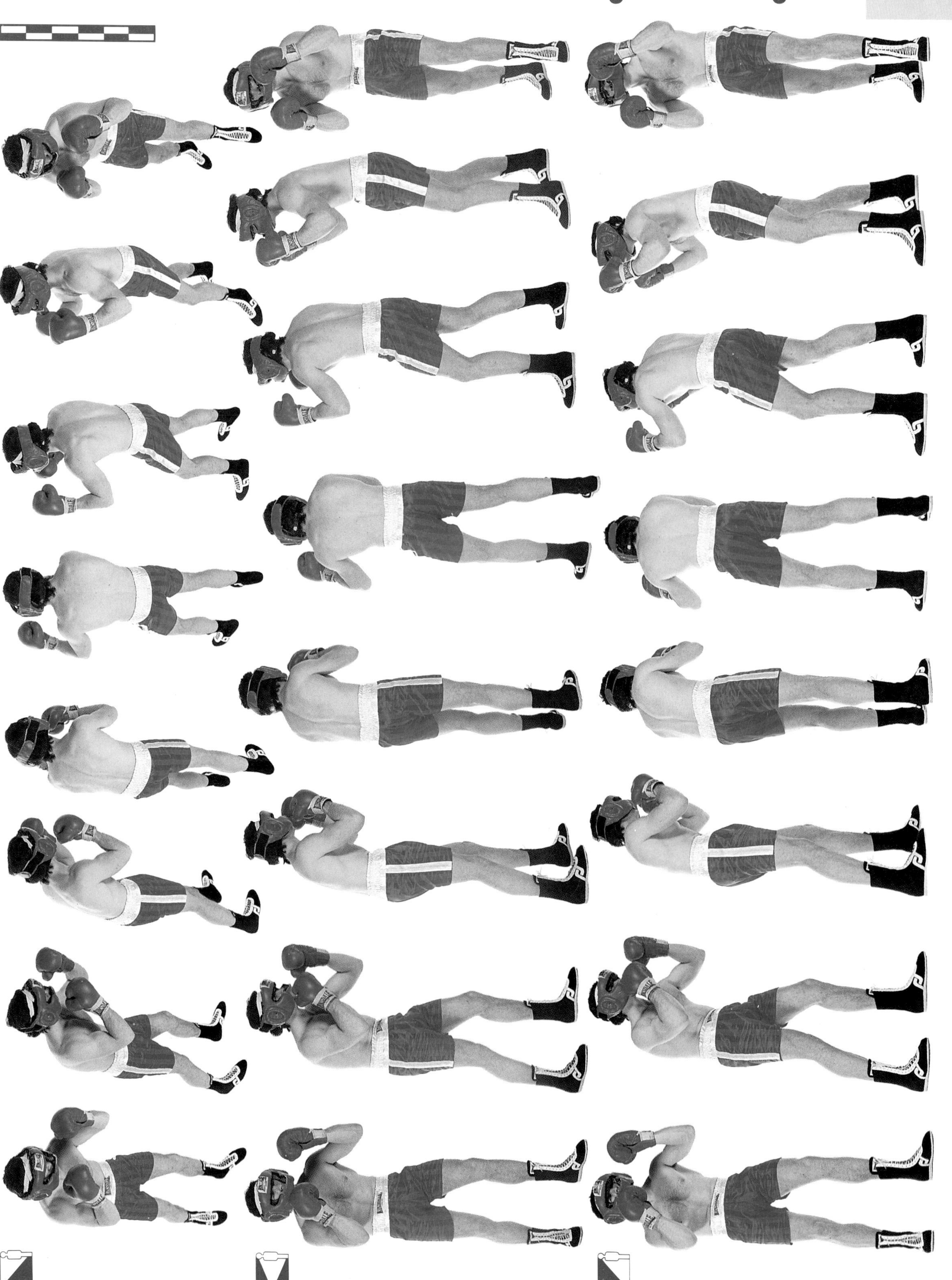

Boxing – jabbing

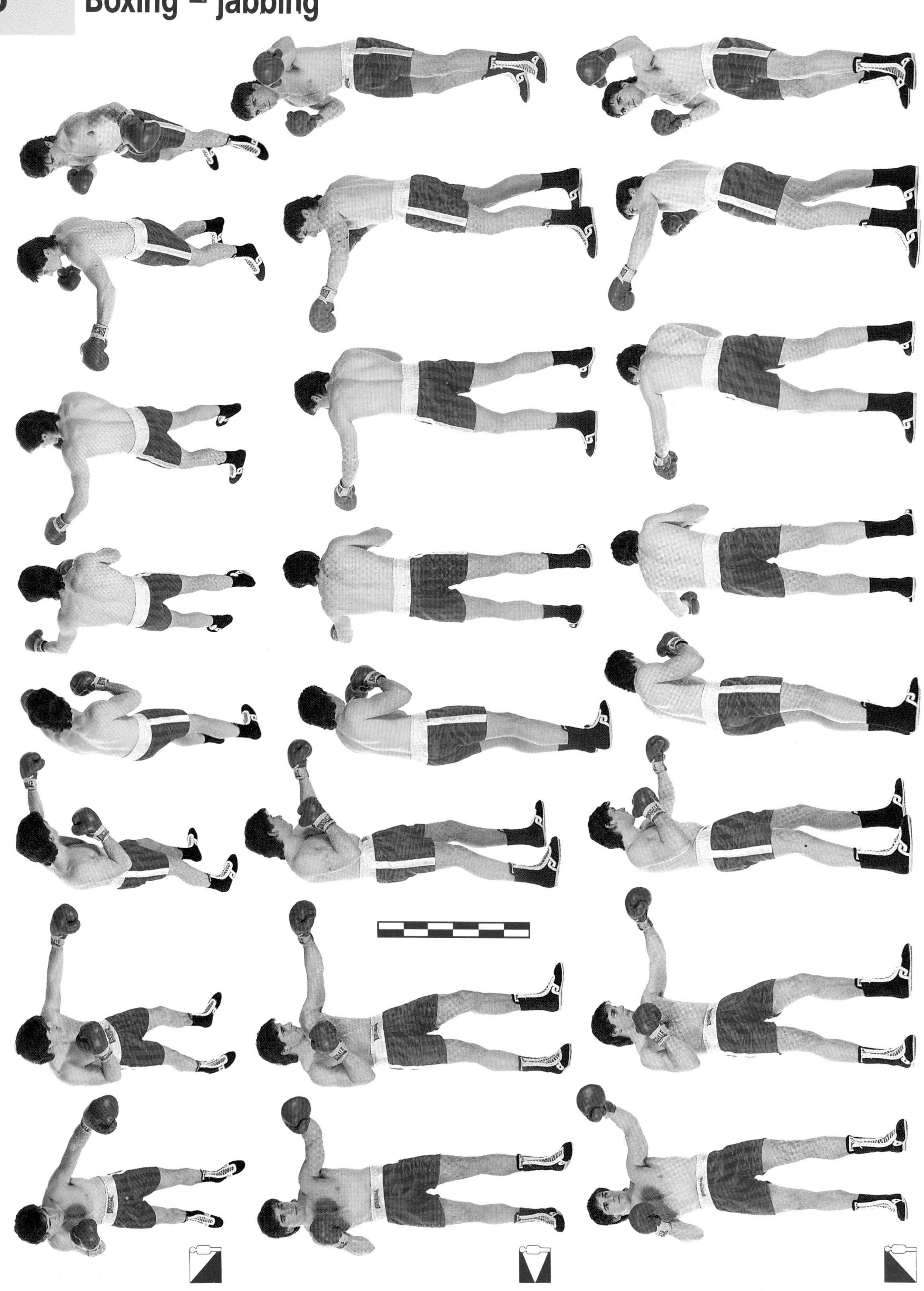

Boxing – the winner

Weightlifting – one arm dumb-bell

Weightlifting – bar under chin

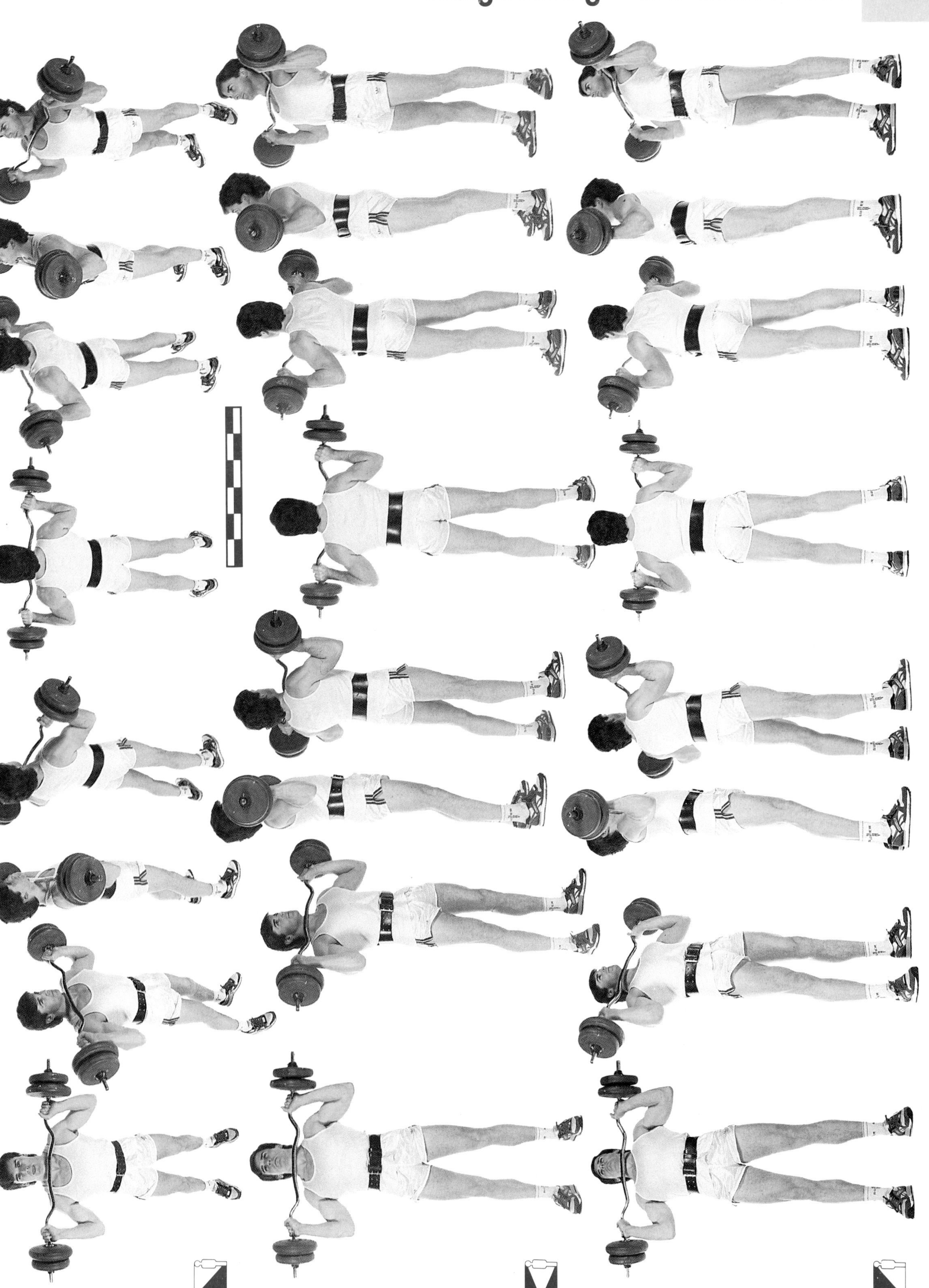

Skipping with rope

Gymnastics

Gymnastics – headstand

Gymnastics – crab

Keep fit

Keep fit

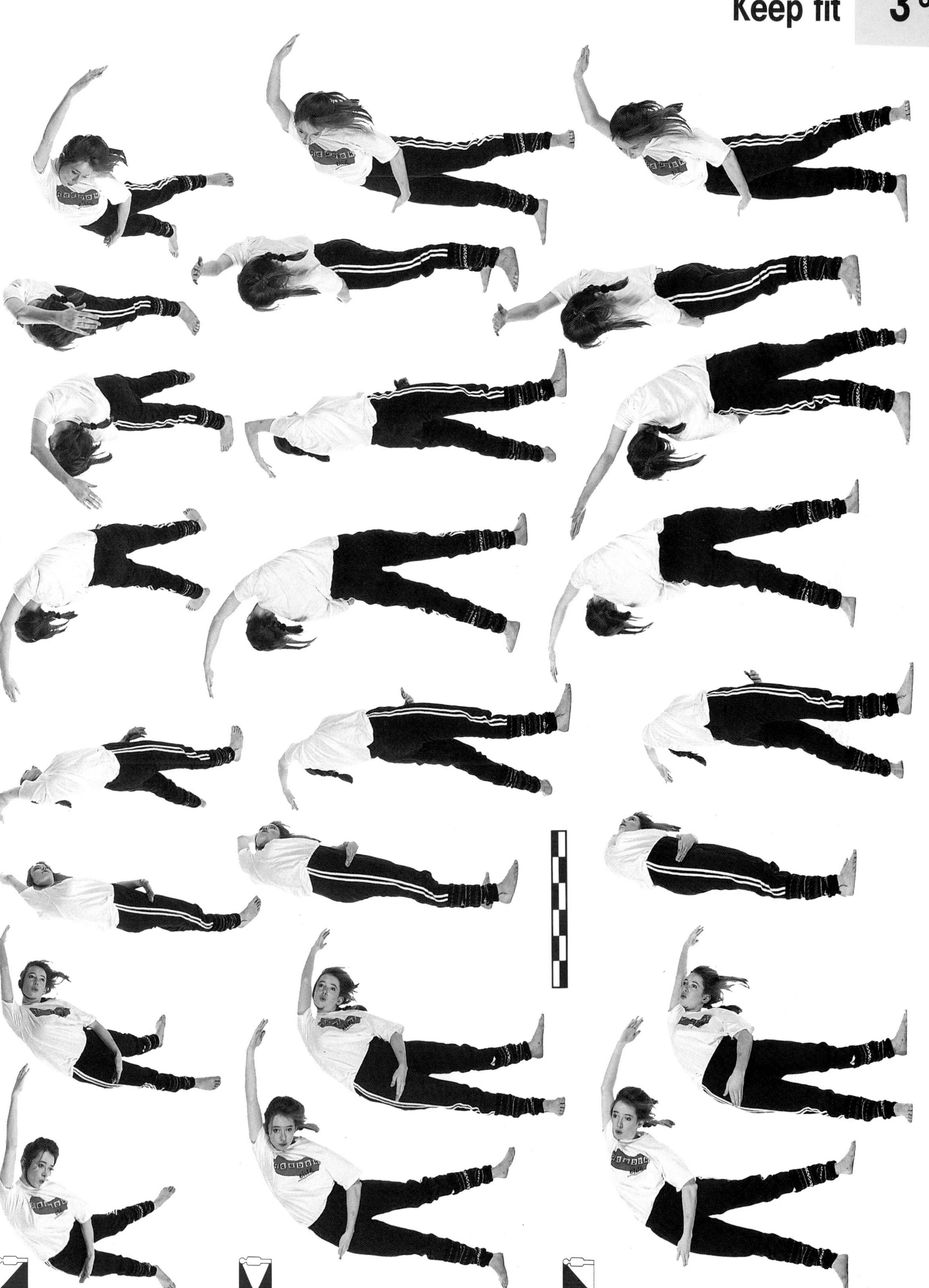

Yoga

Yoga

Walking the dog

Walking with walking stick

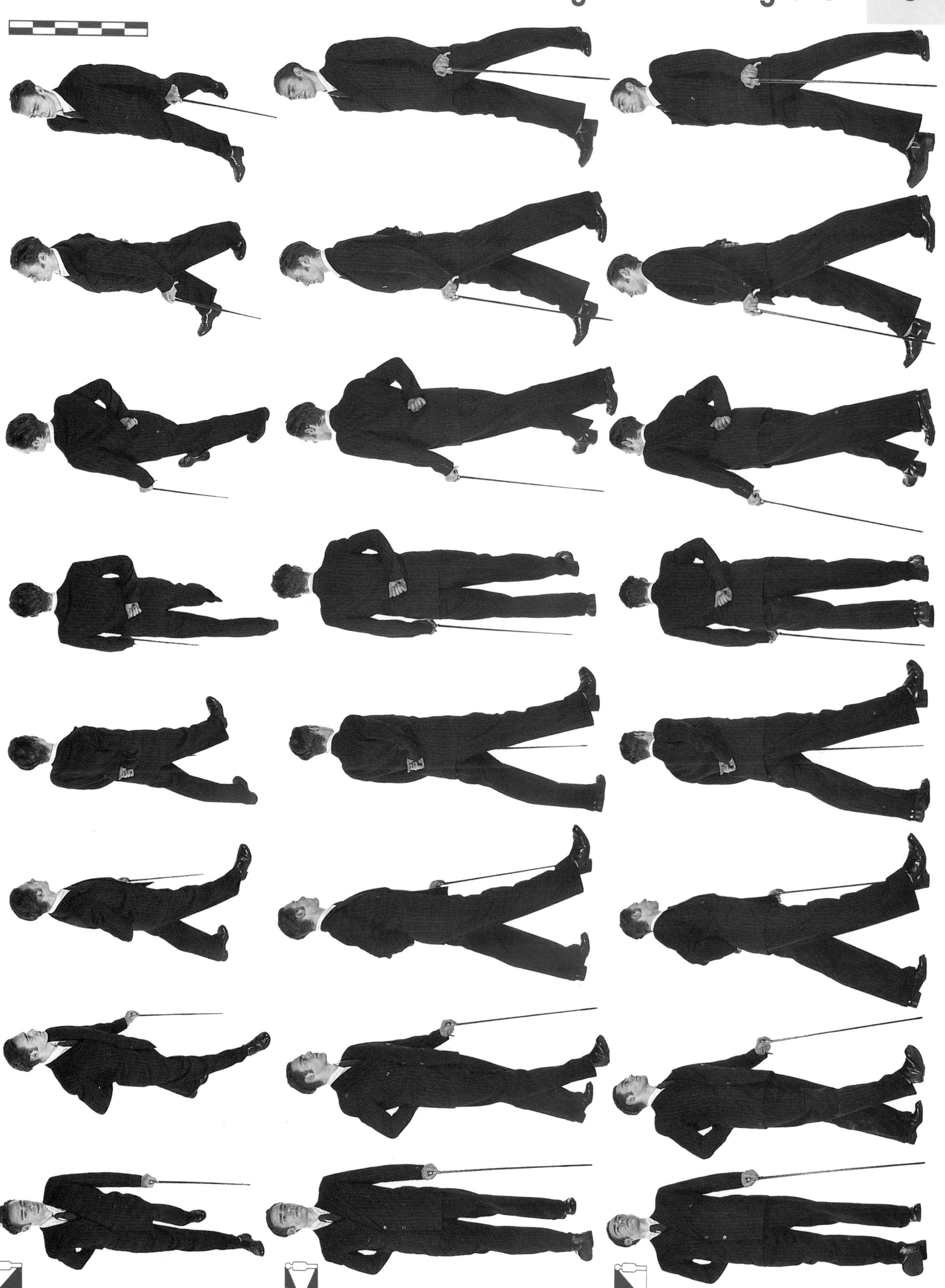

Couple playing chess

Playing cards

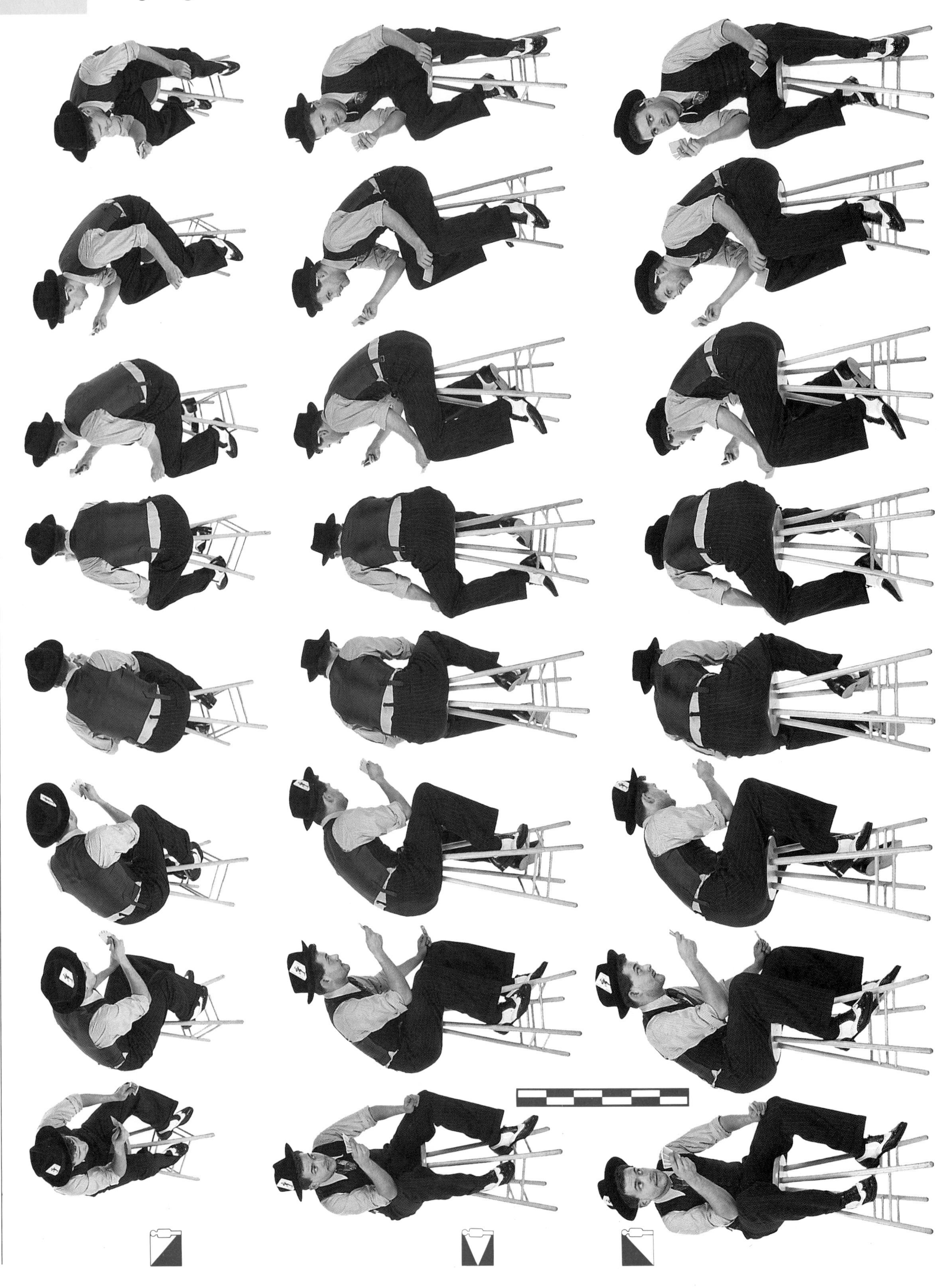

Artist painting

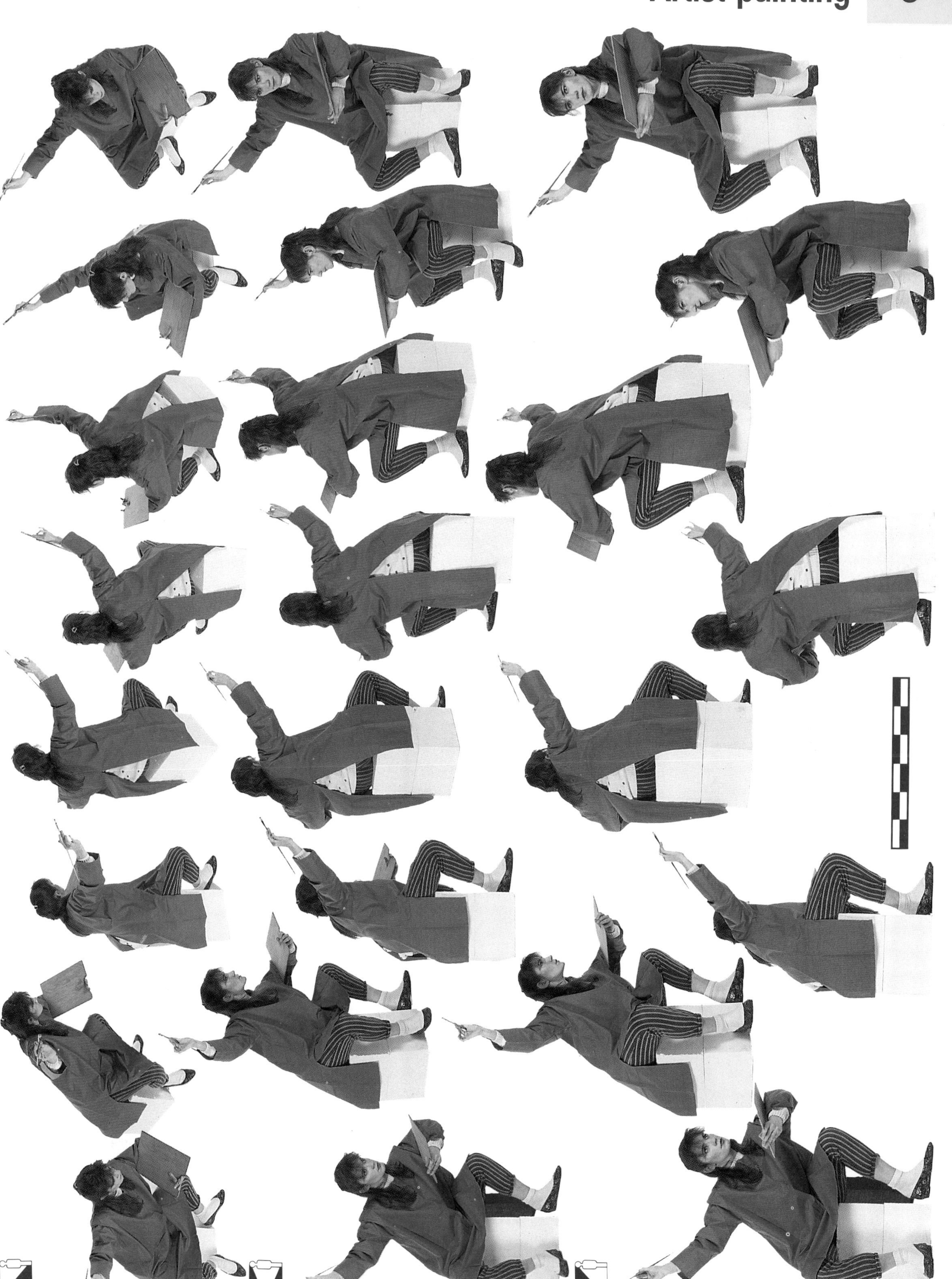

4·01 Backwards on a chair

In a chair doing the crossword

In a chair looking through filofax

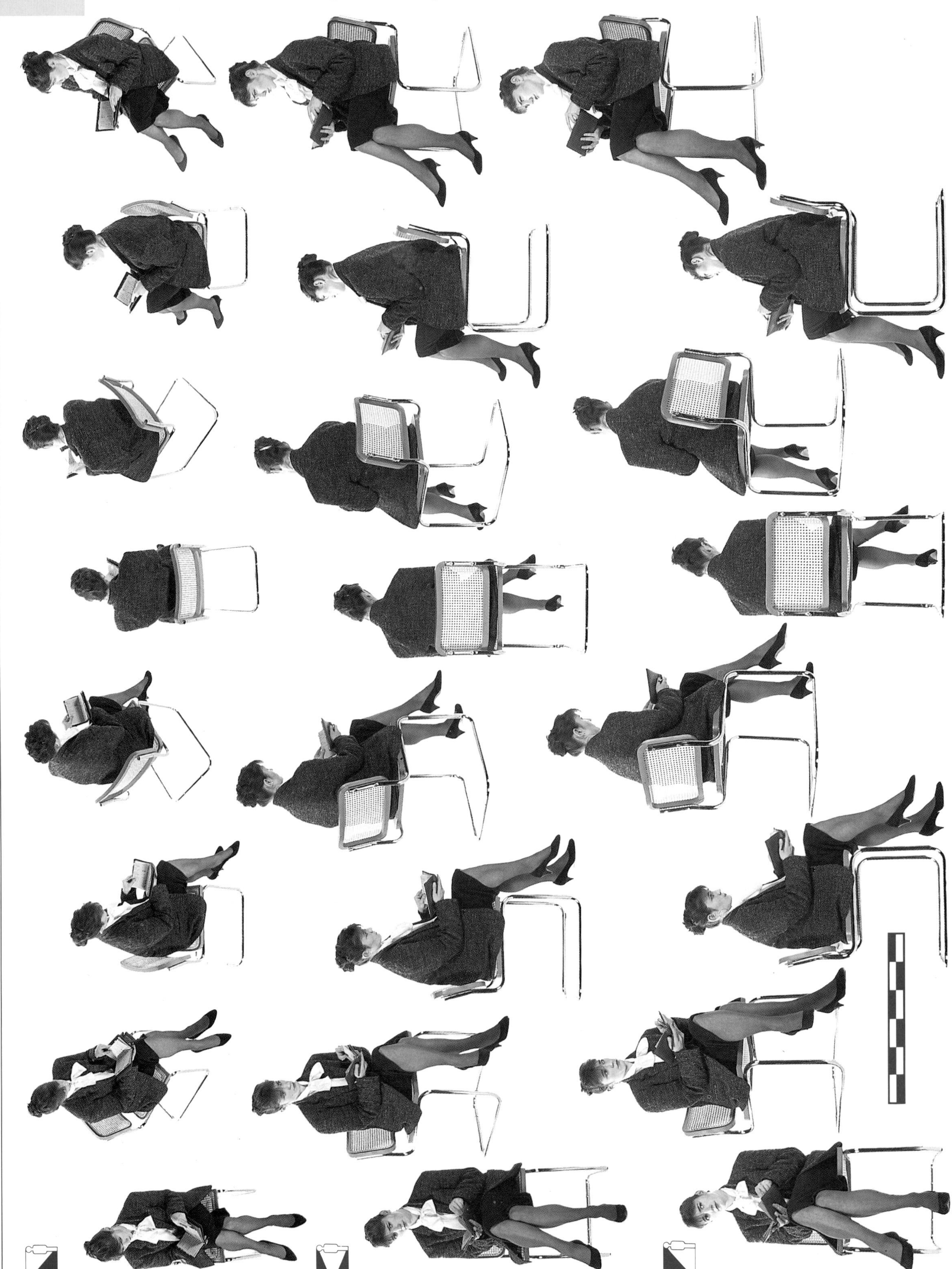

Sideways in a chair

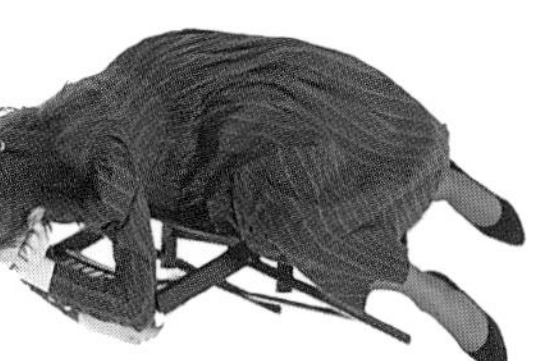

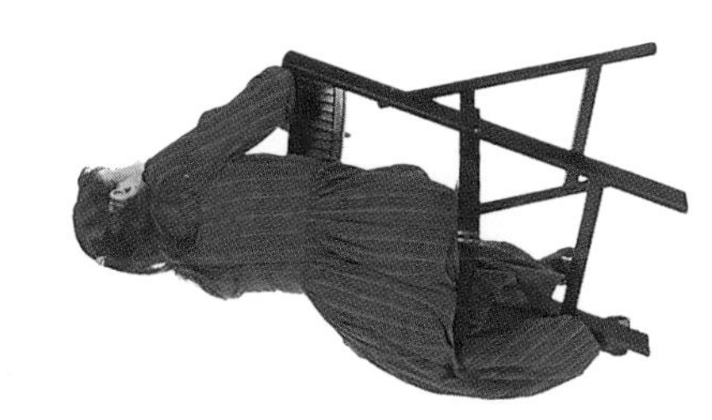

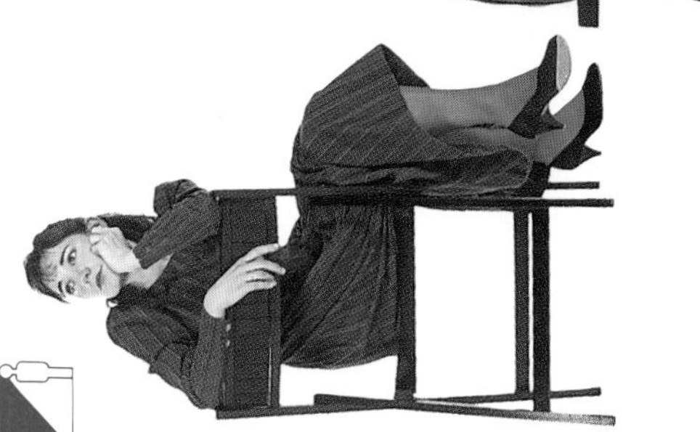

4·05

Kneeling on a chair talking on the phone

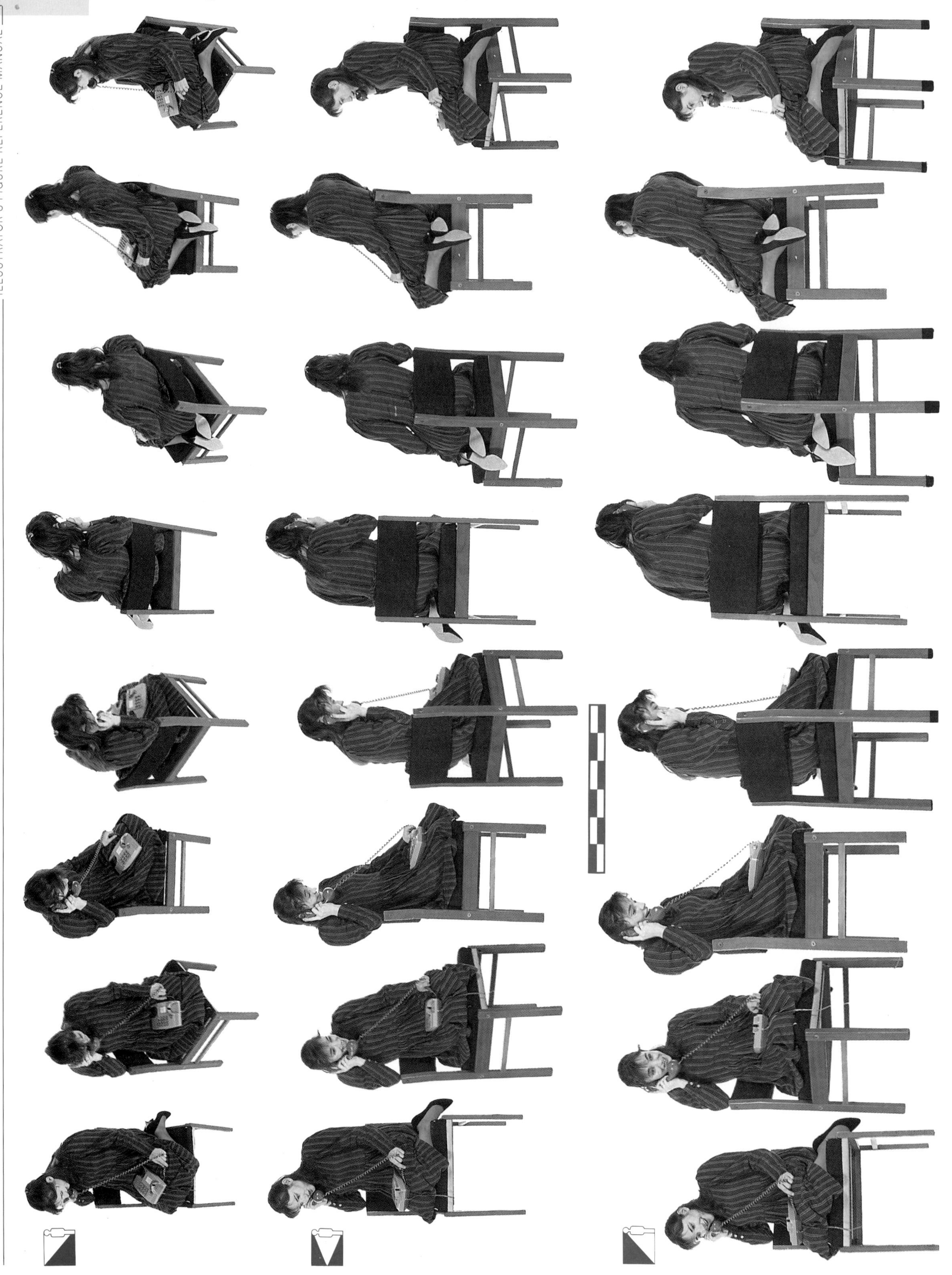

On a bar stool

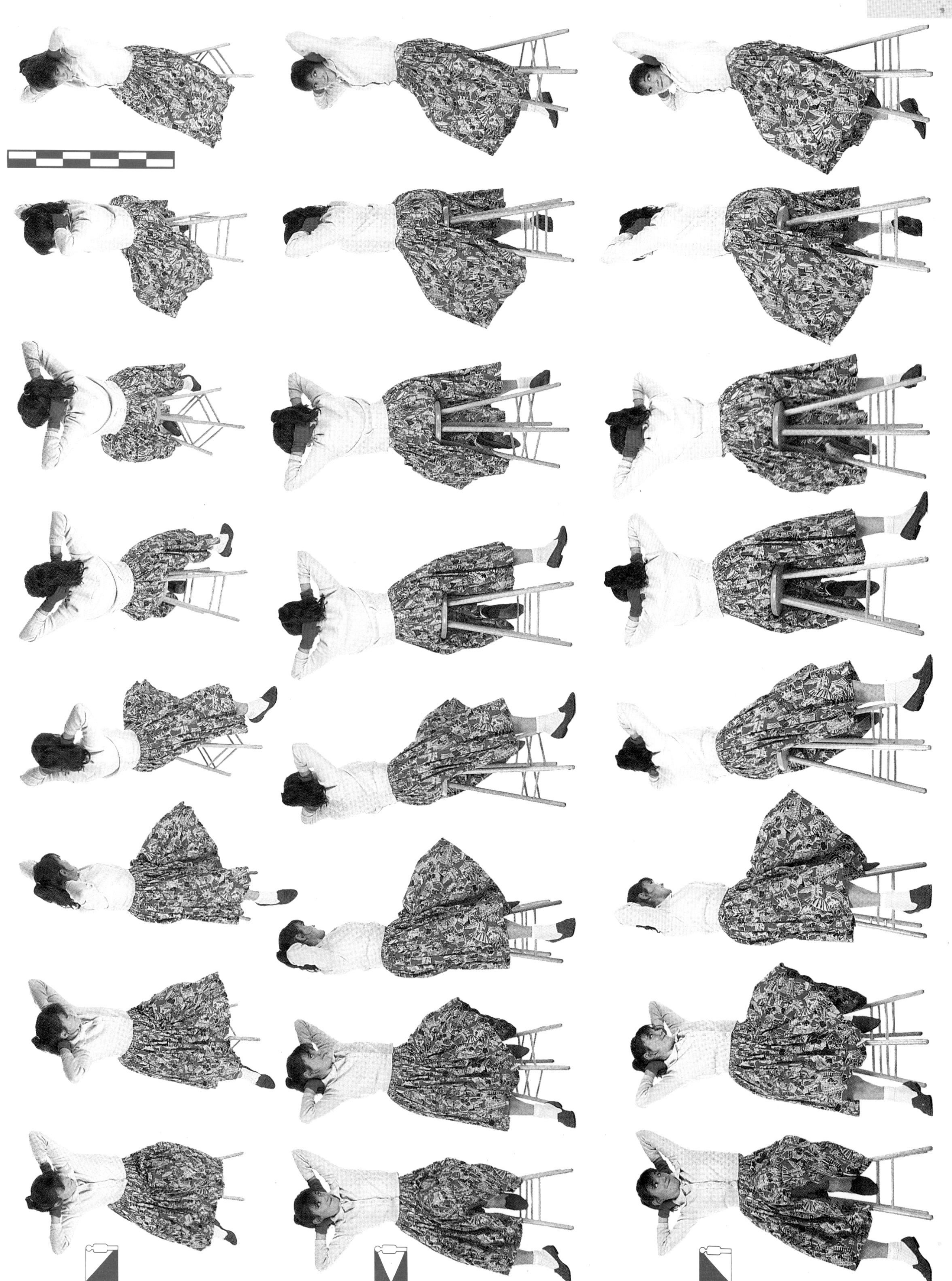

Vicar asleep in rocking chair

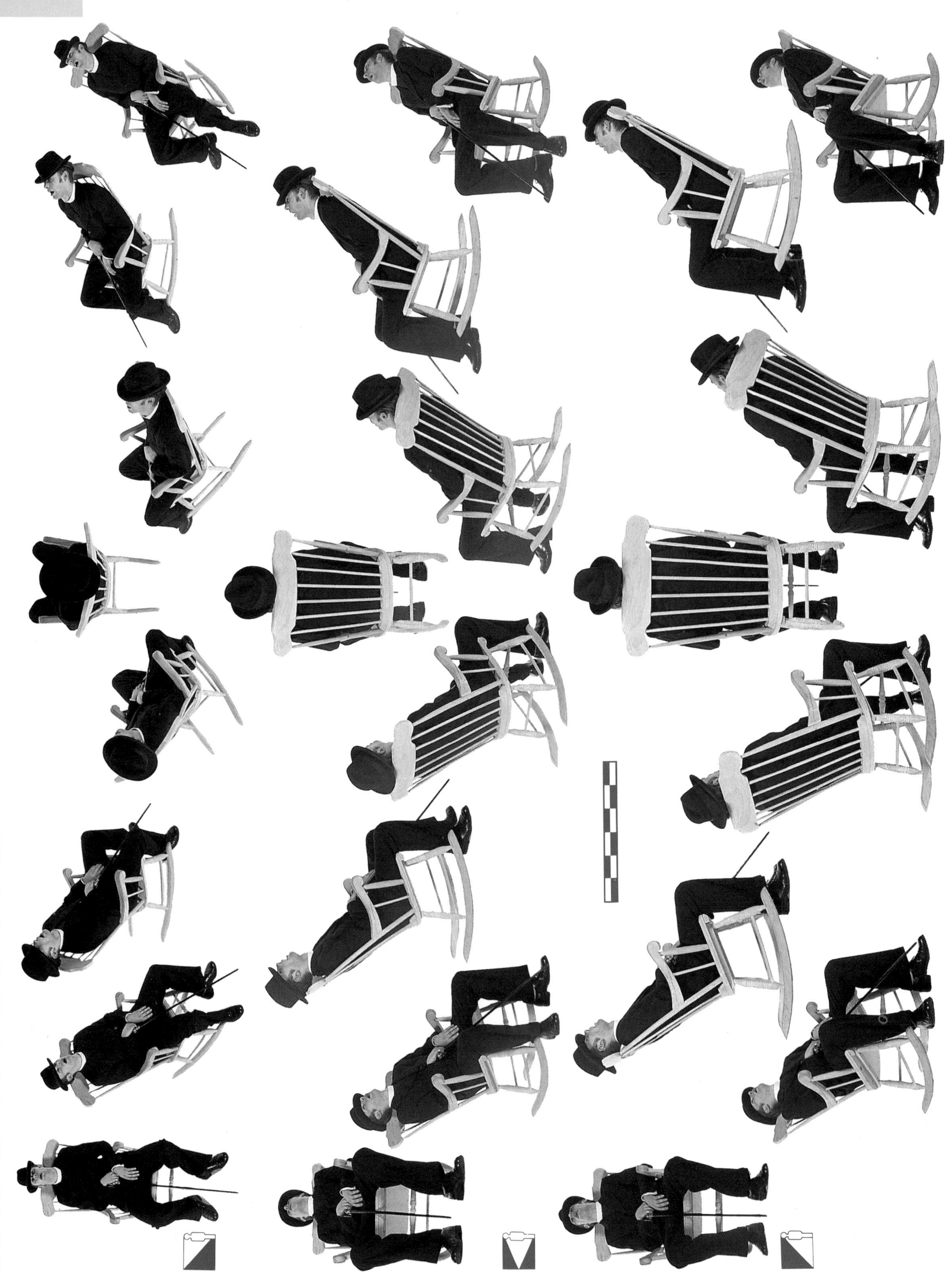

On the floor thinking

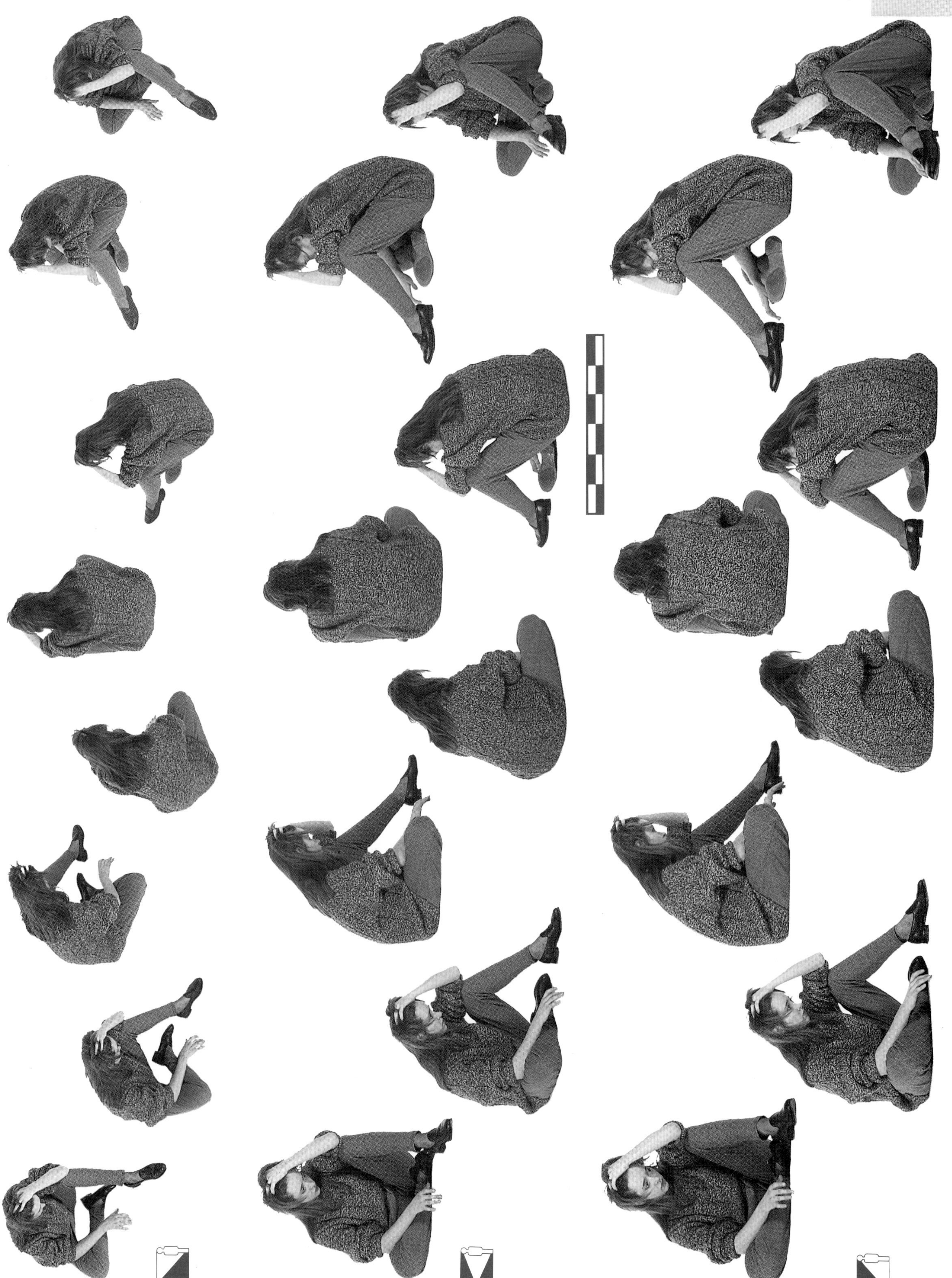

On a table talking on the phone

Relaxing in an armchair

Reclining on a sofa

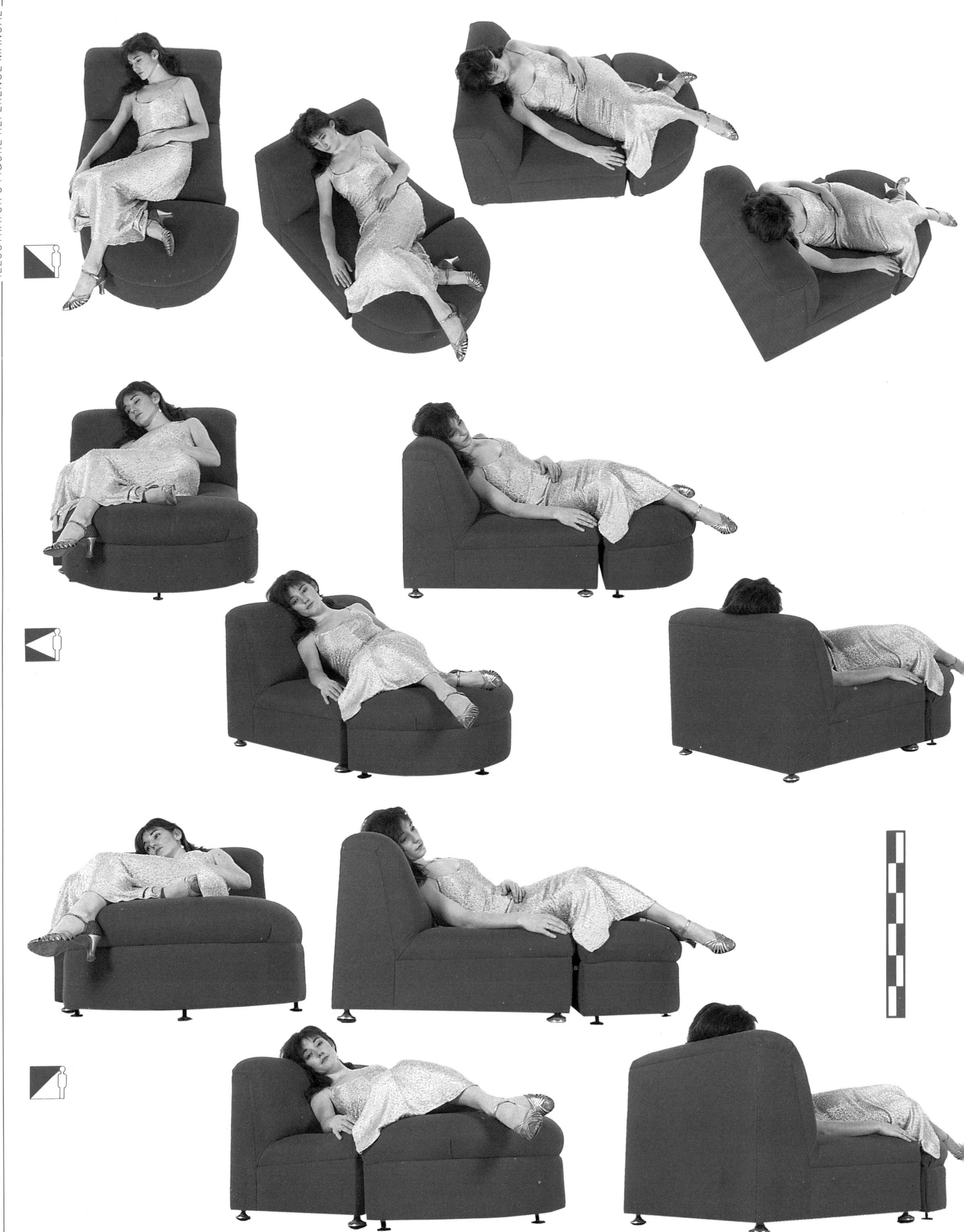

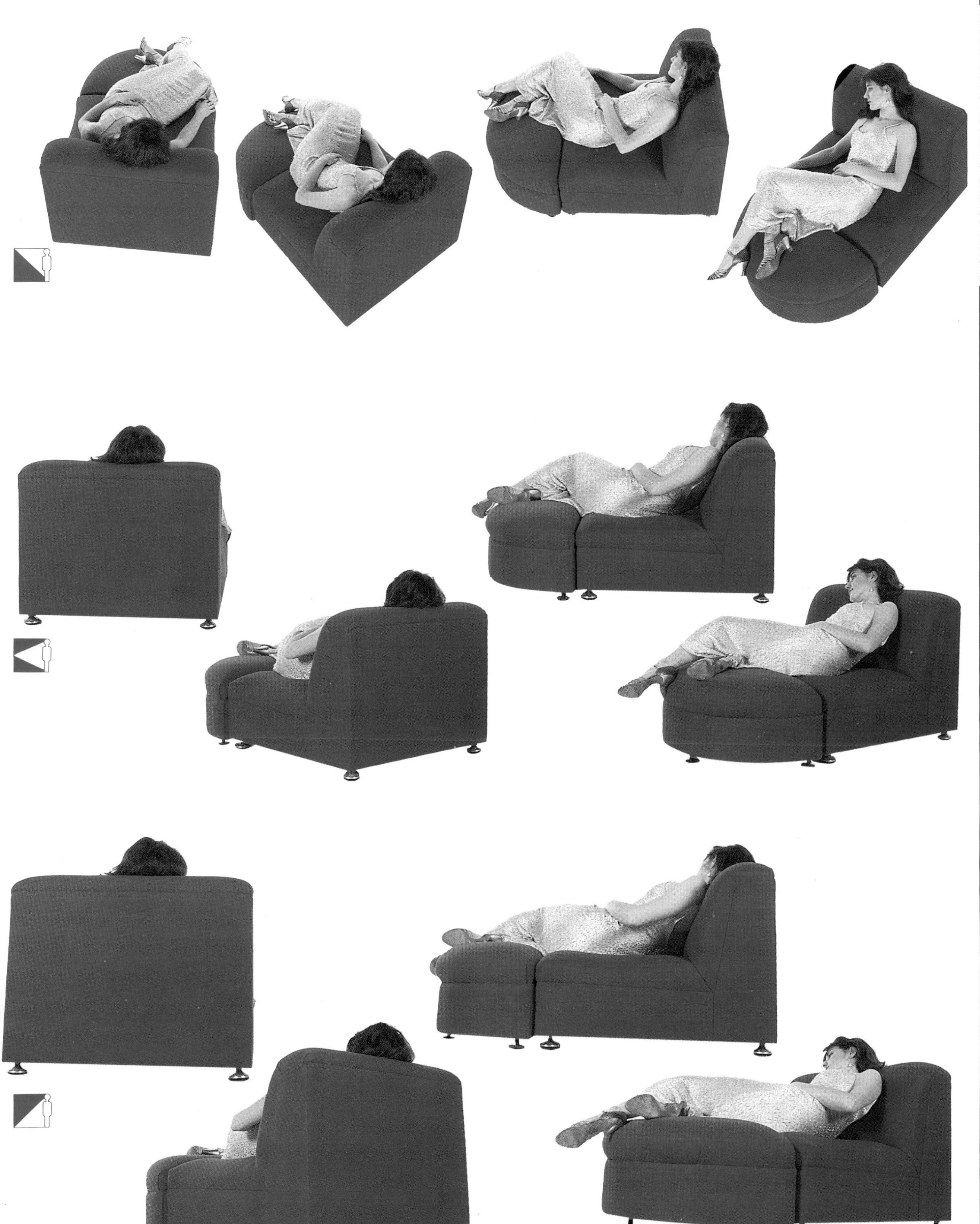

4·12 Couple sitting side by side

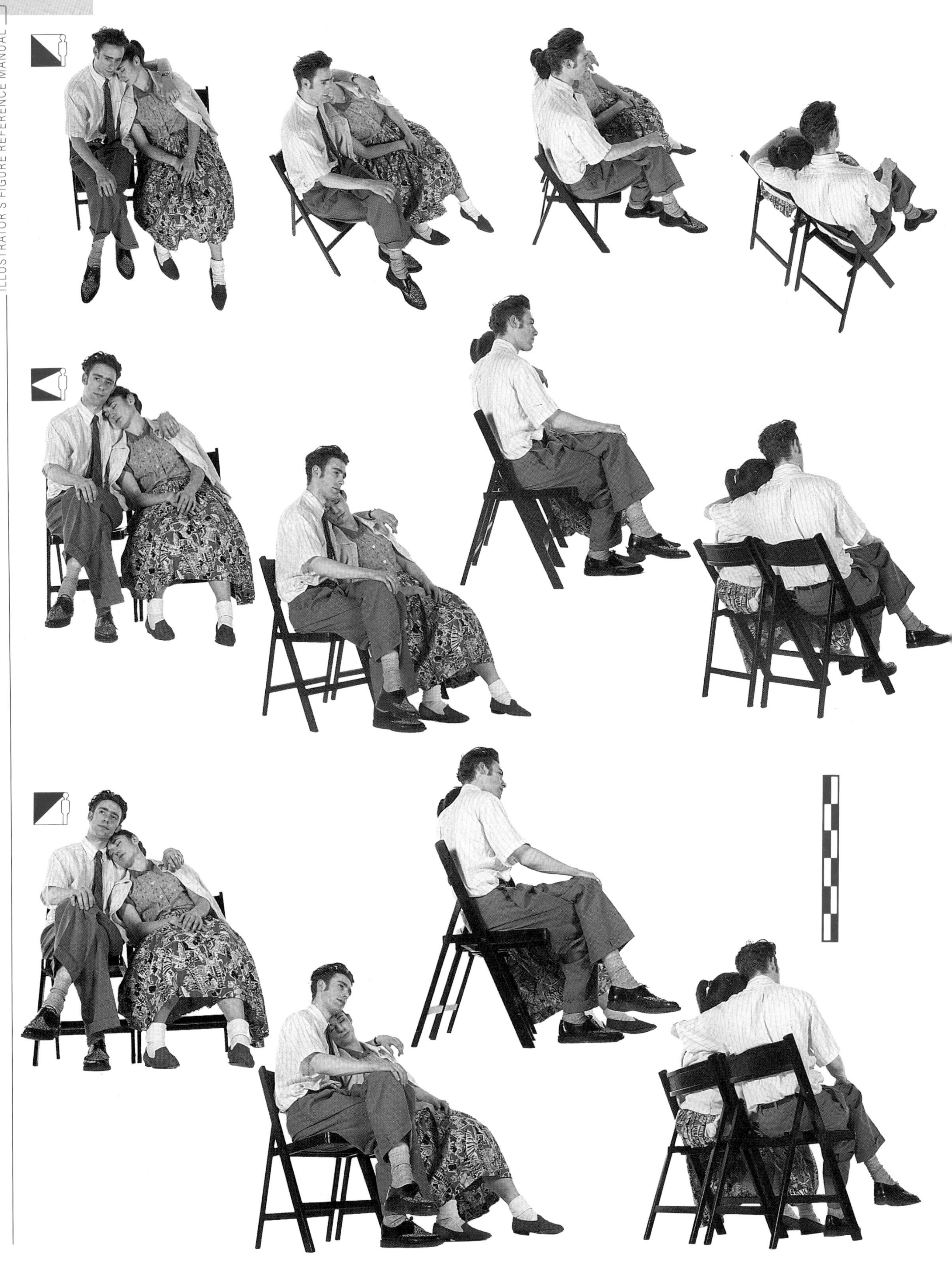

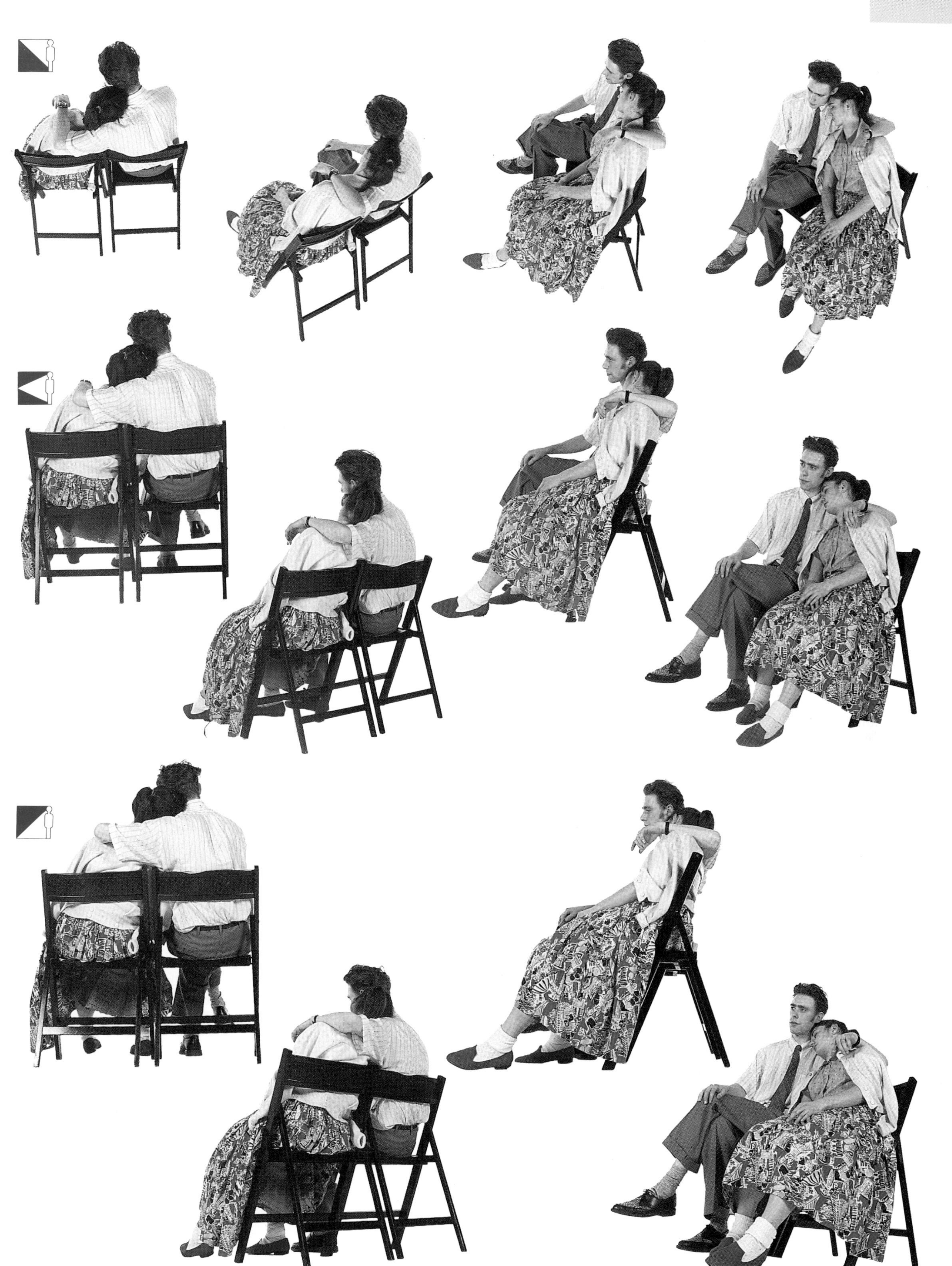

On the floor

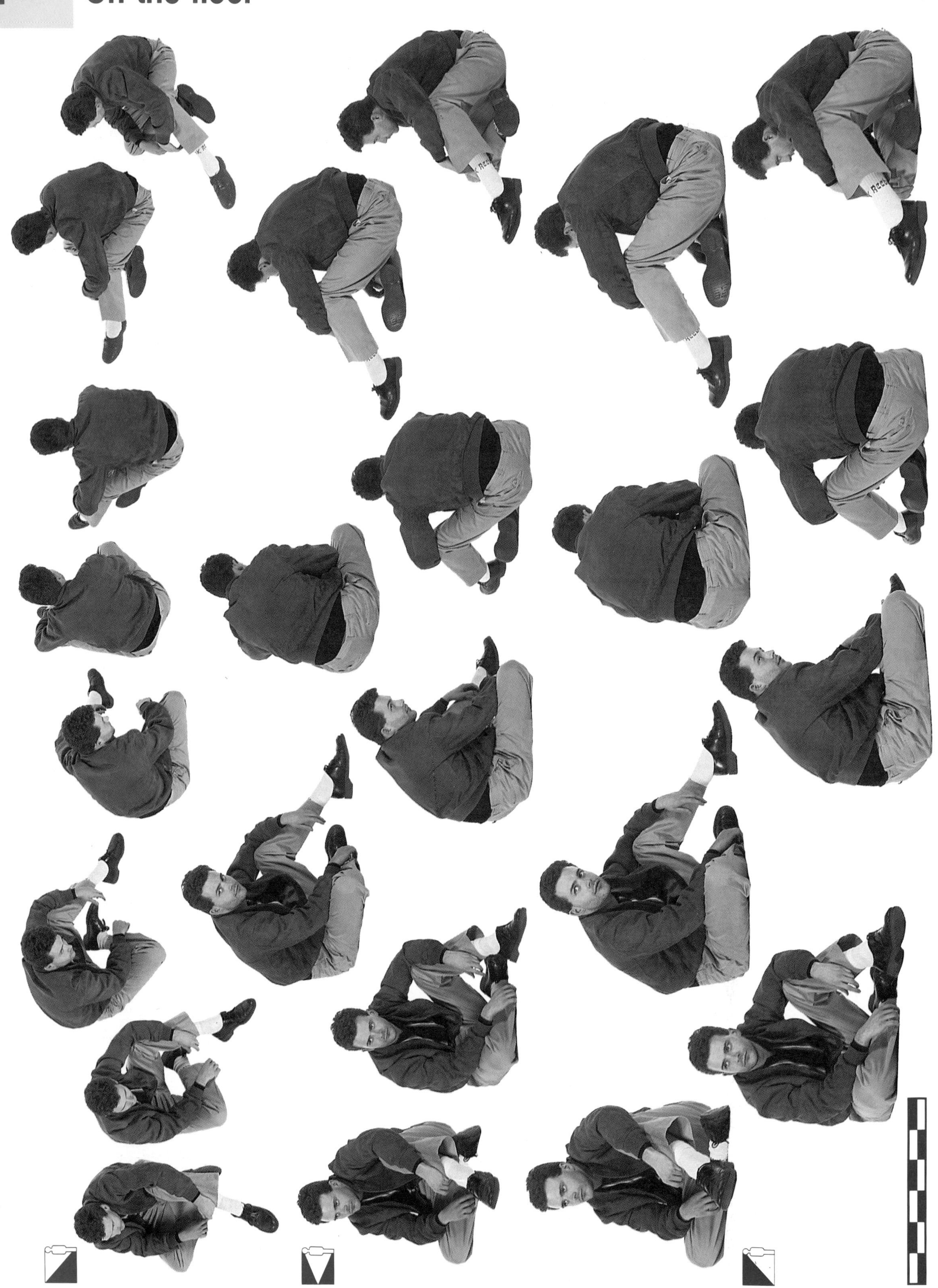

Couple kissing

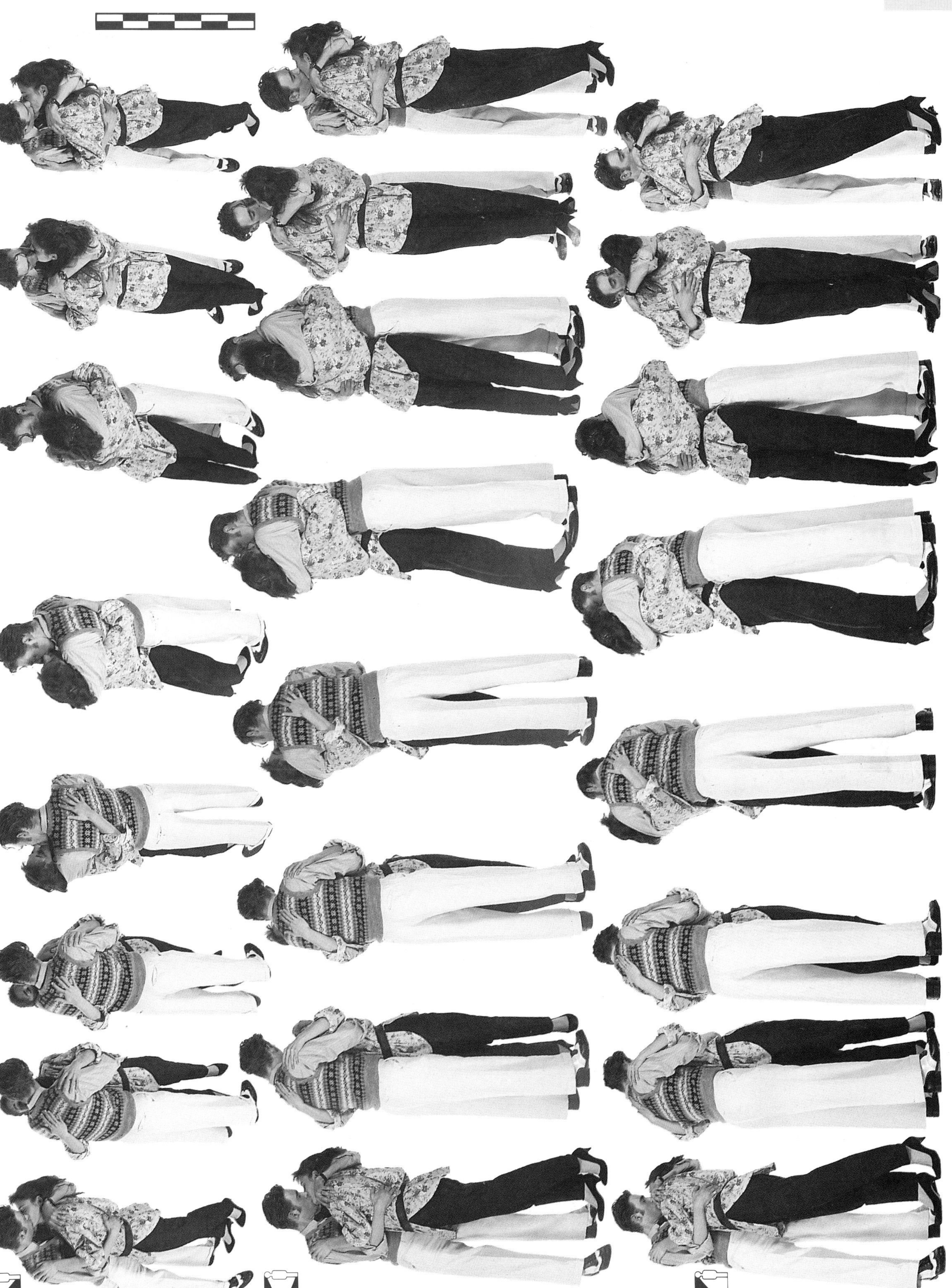

Kissing goodbye

Waving goodbye

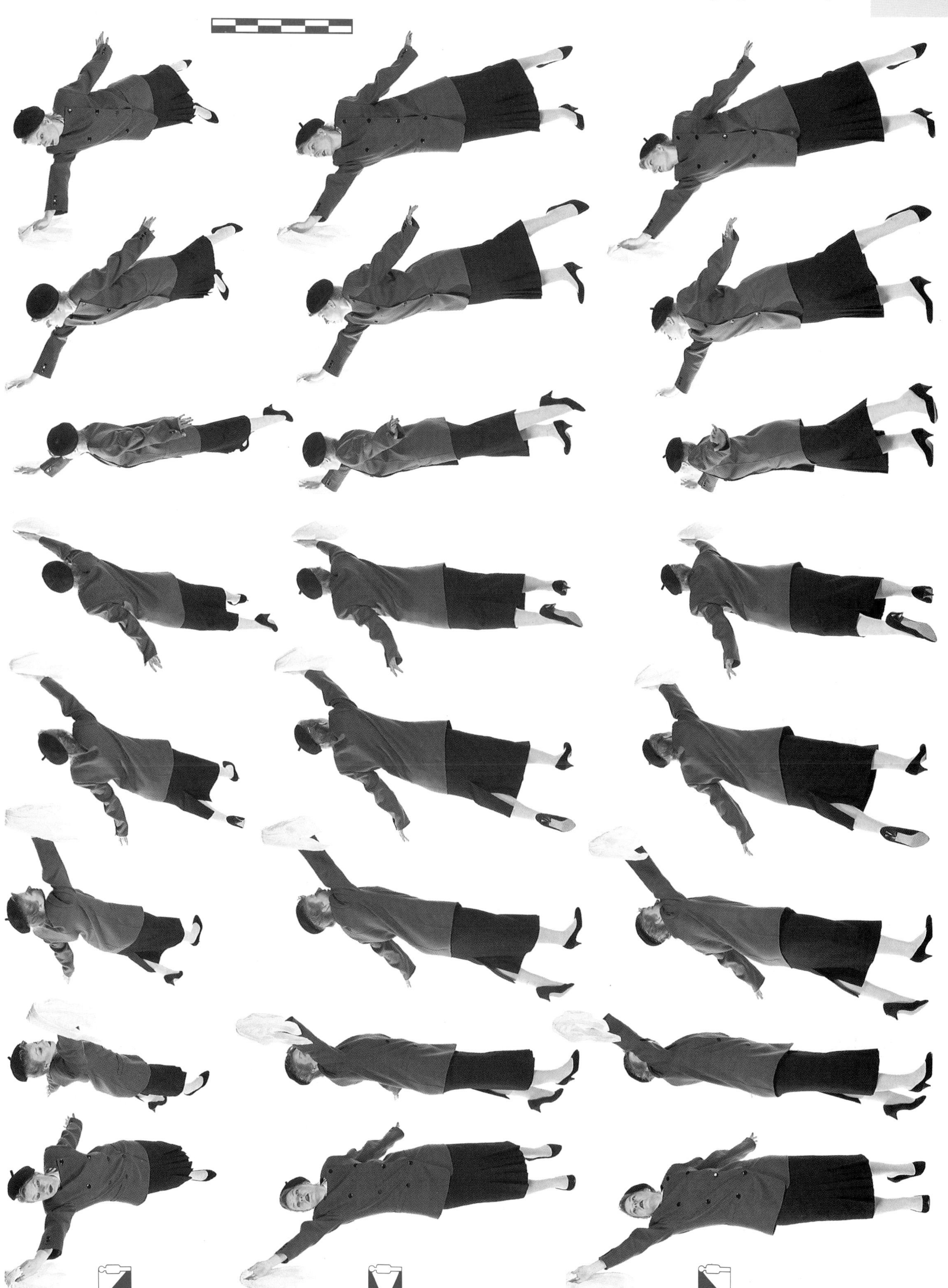

Crying into handkerchief

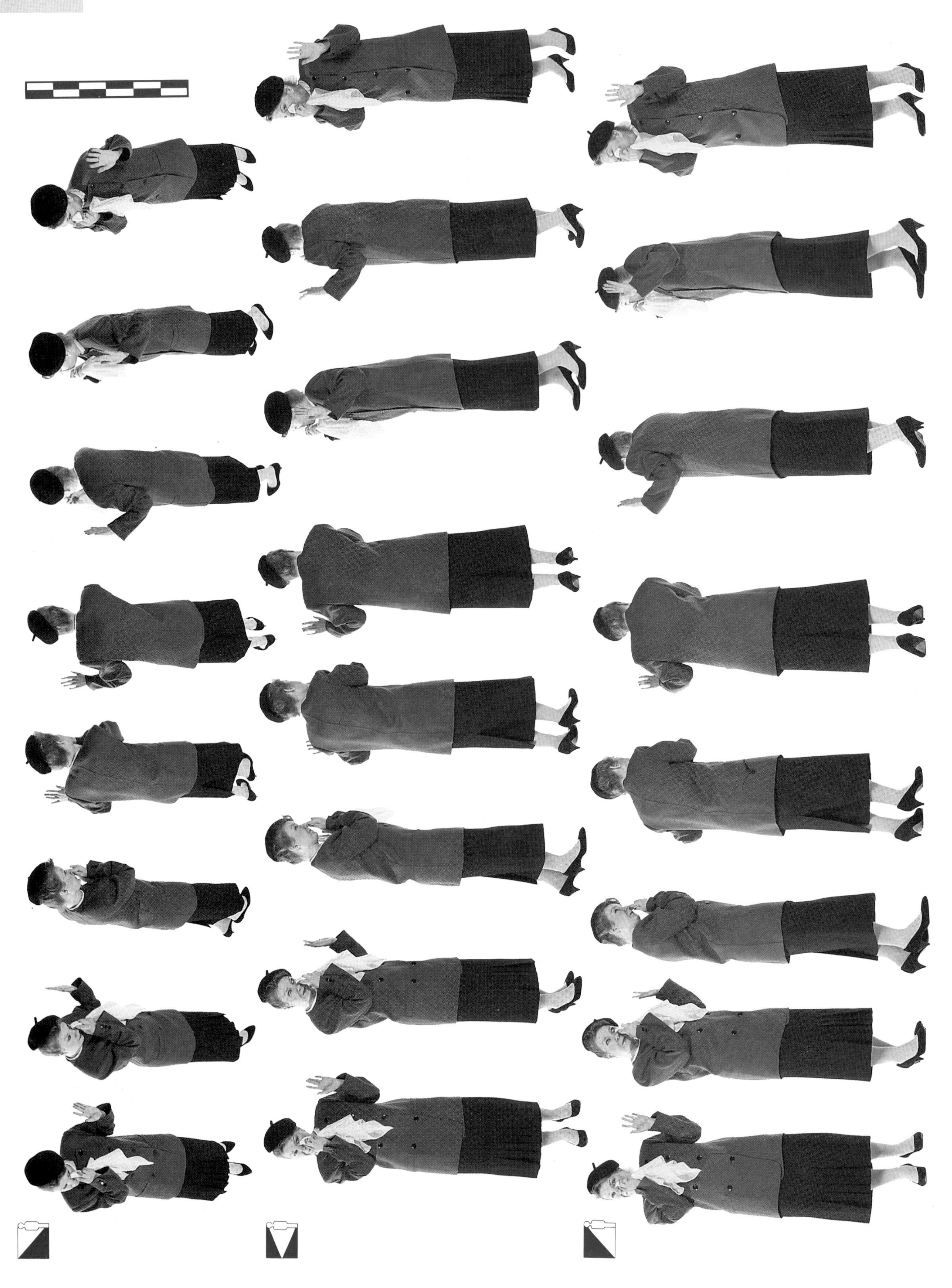

Macho man

Gent kissing lady's hand

5·07 Couple talking at dinner table

GI greeting his girl

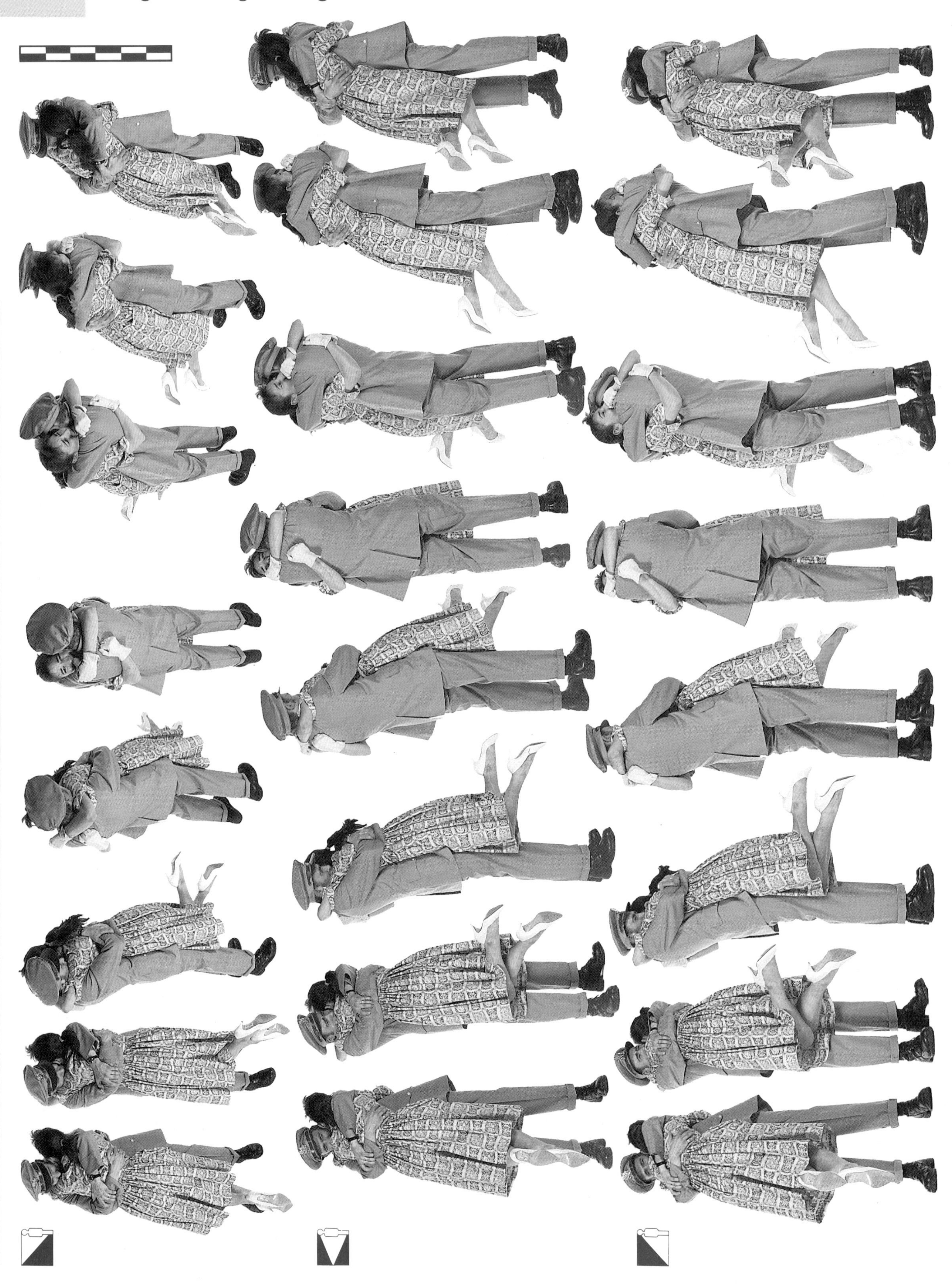

Couple at the races

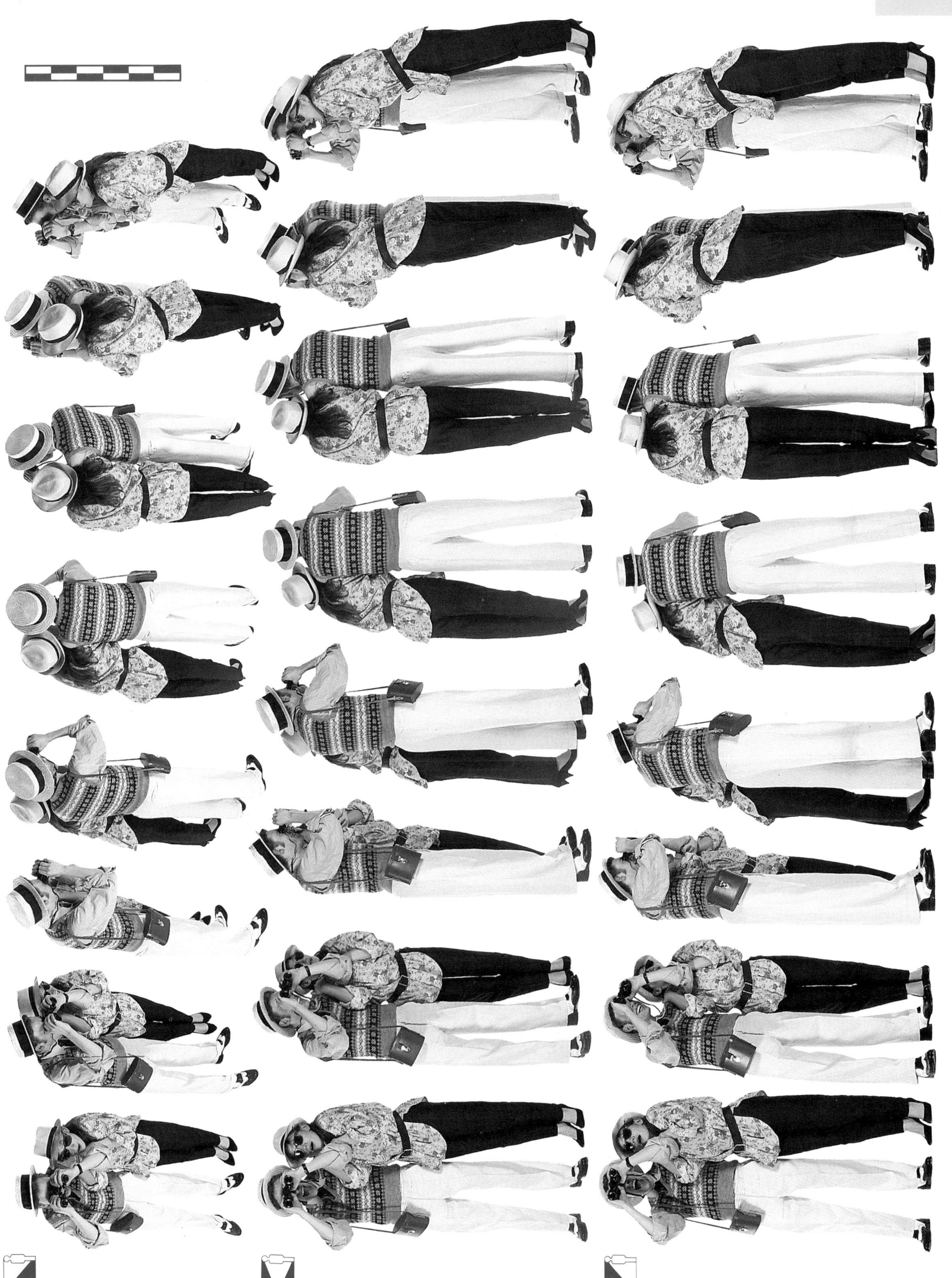

Bully threatening a small guy

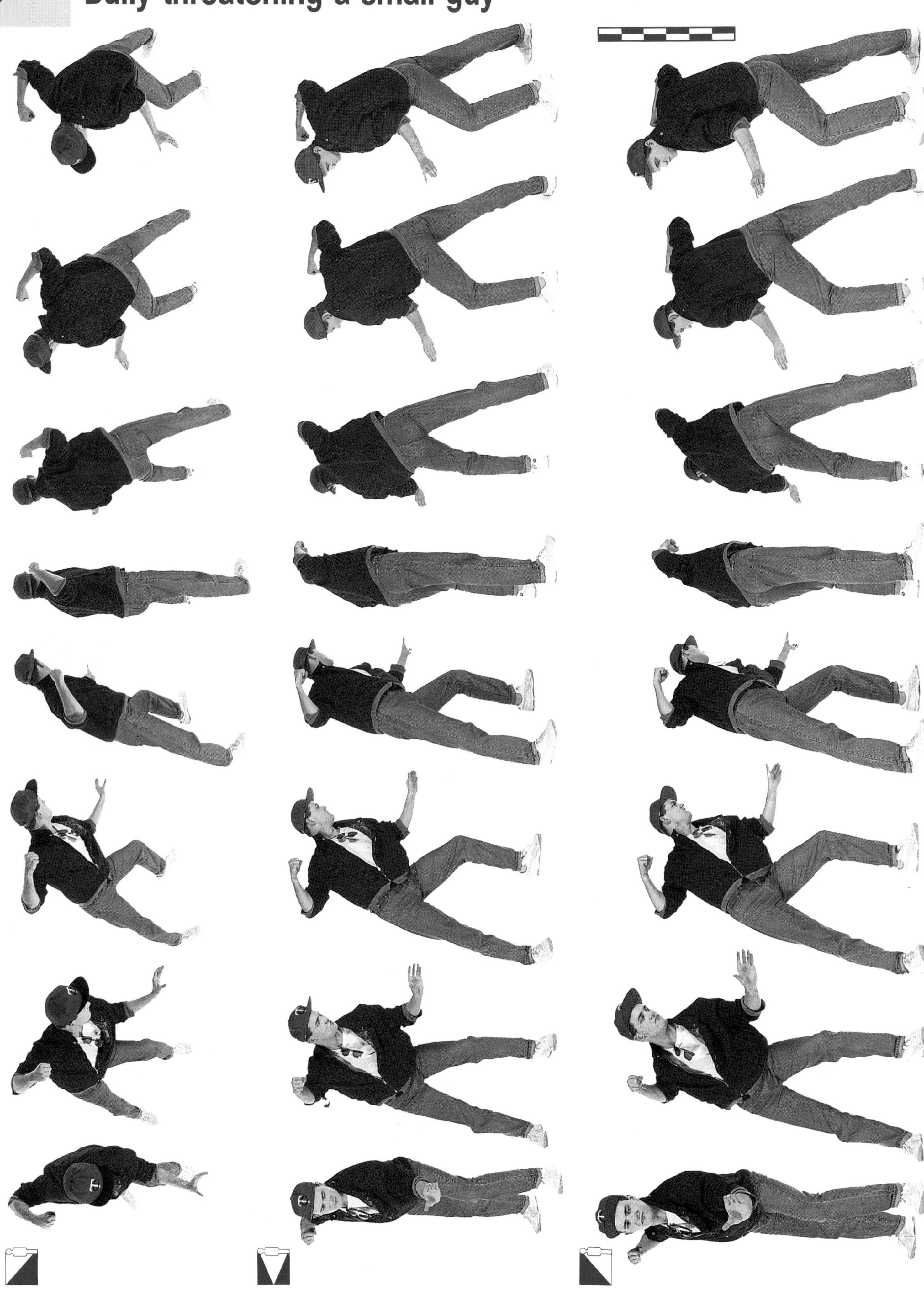

Cowering on the ground

Curtseying

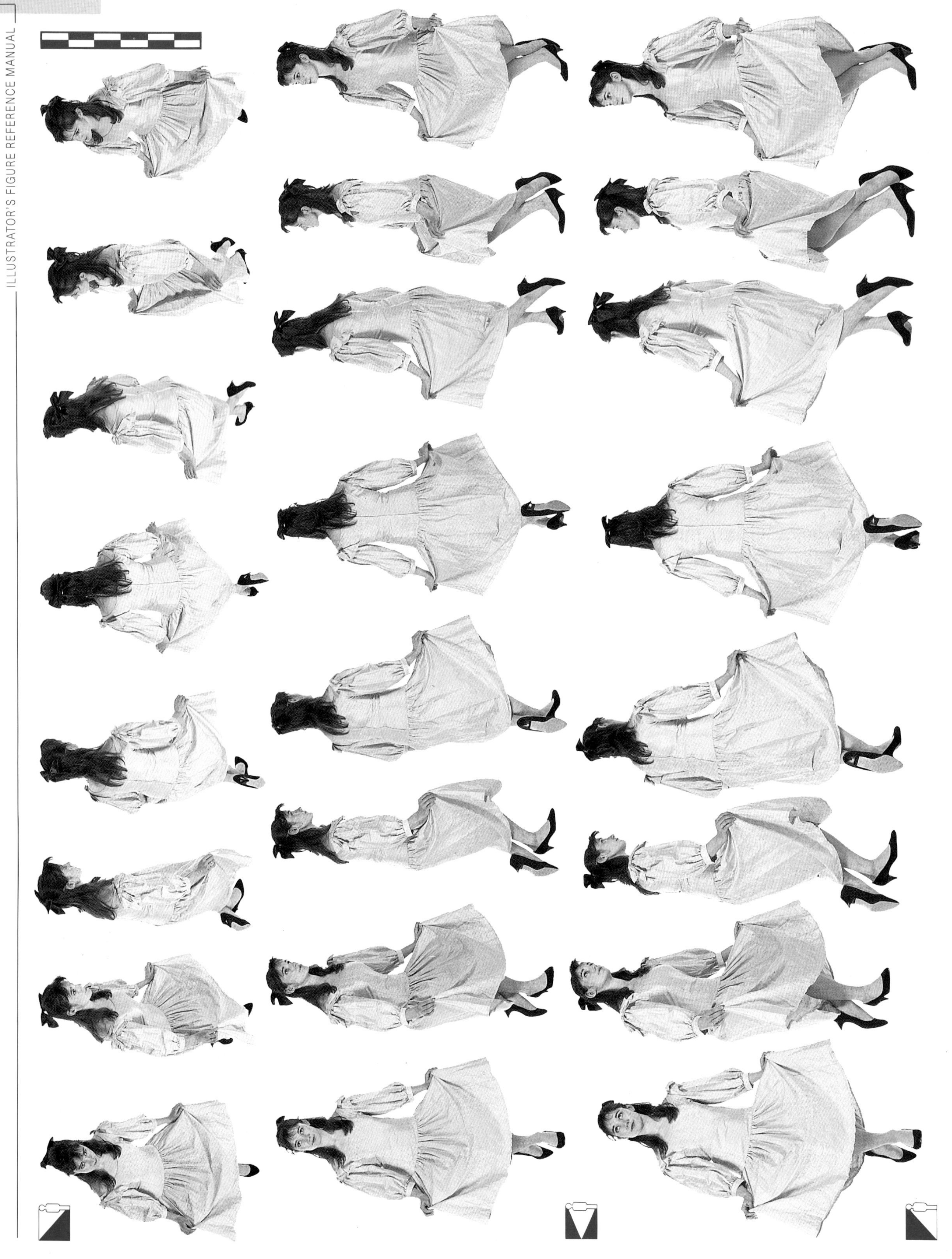

Greeting a friend

Taking the lady home

Couple at the beach

6·01 Genuflecting

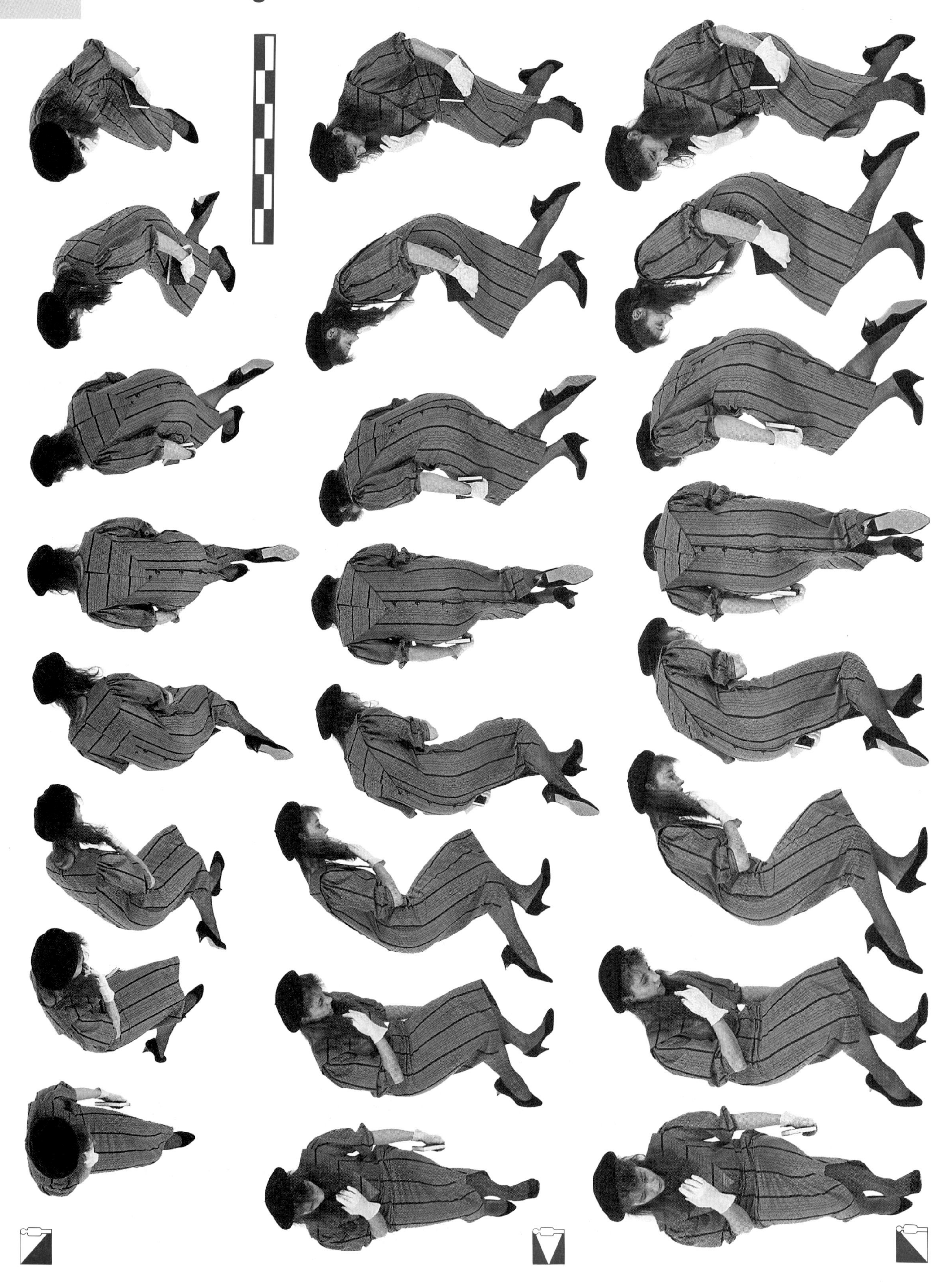

Vicar preaching

6·03 Vicar blessing girl

Girl praying

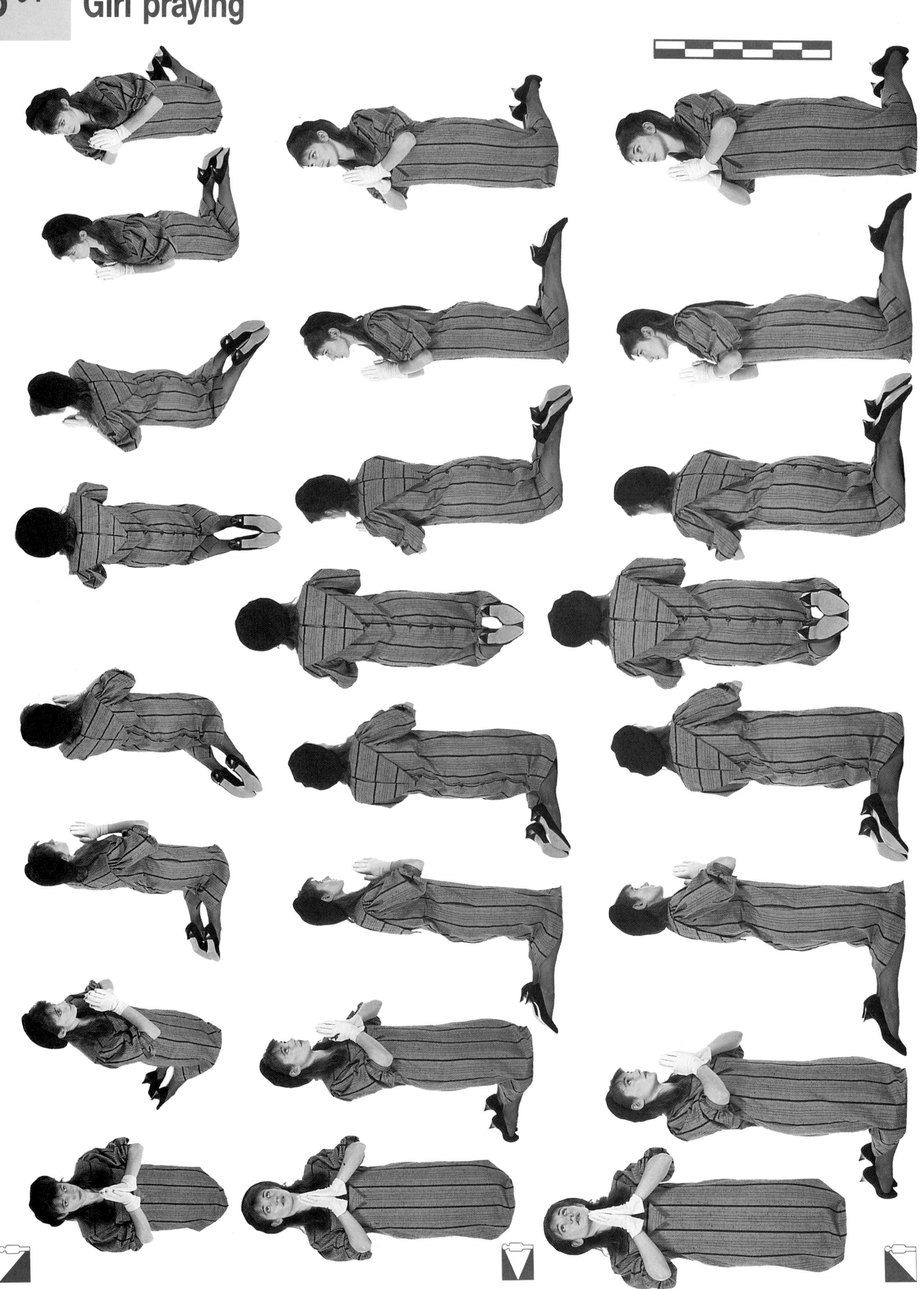

New York policeman – stop!

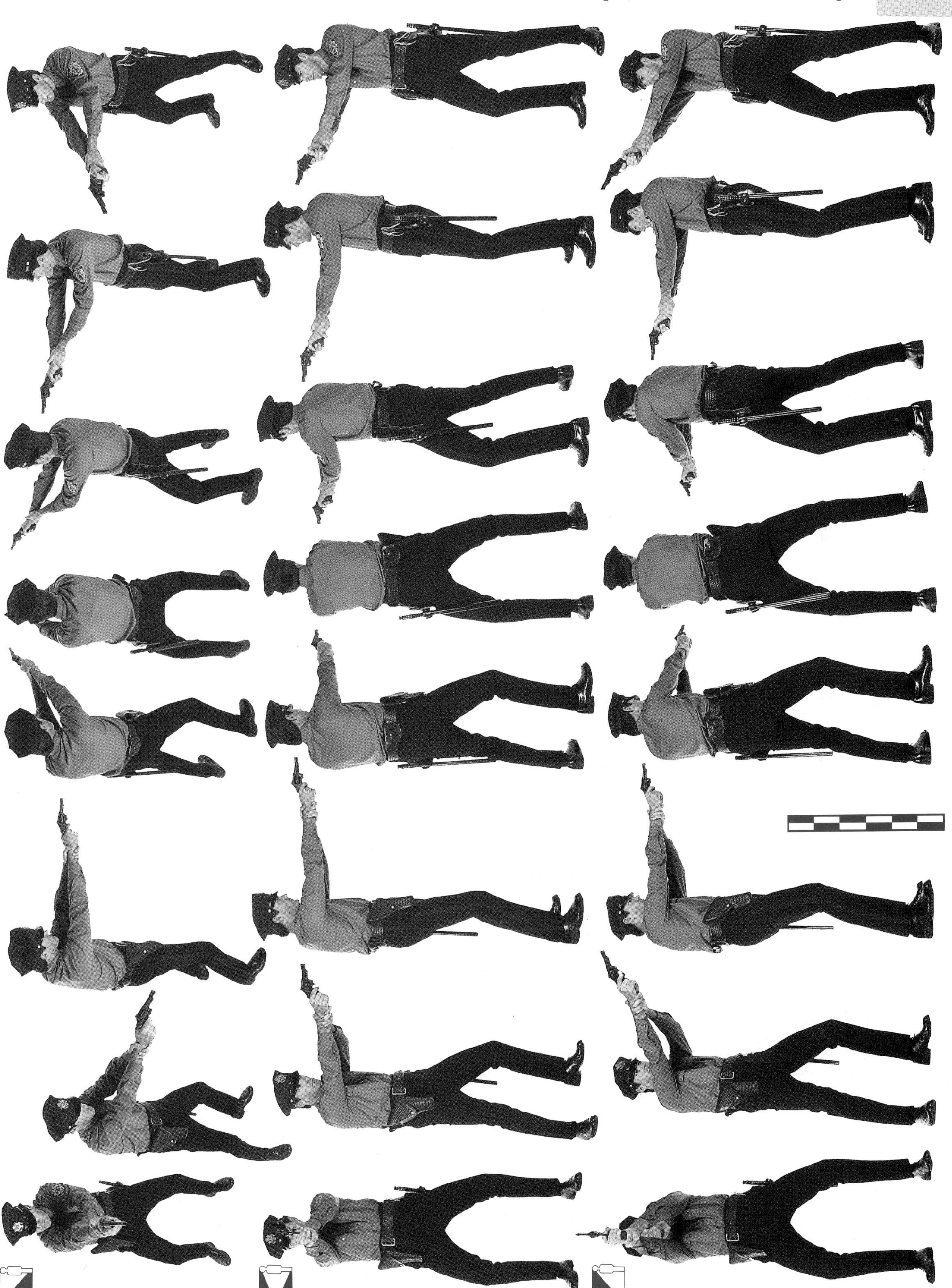

New York policeman directing traffic

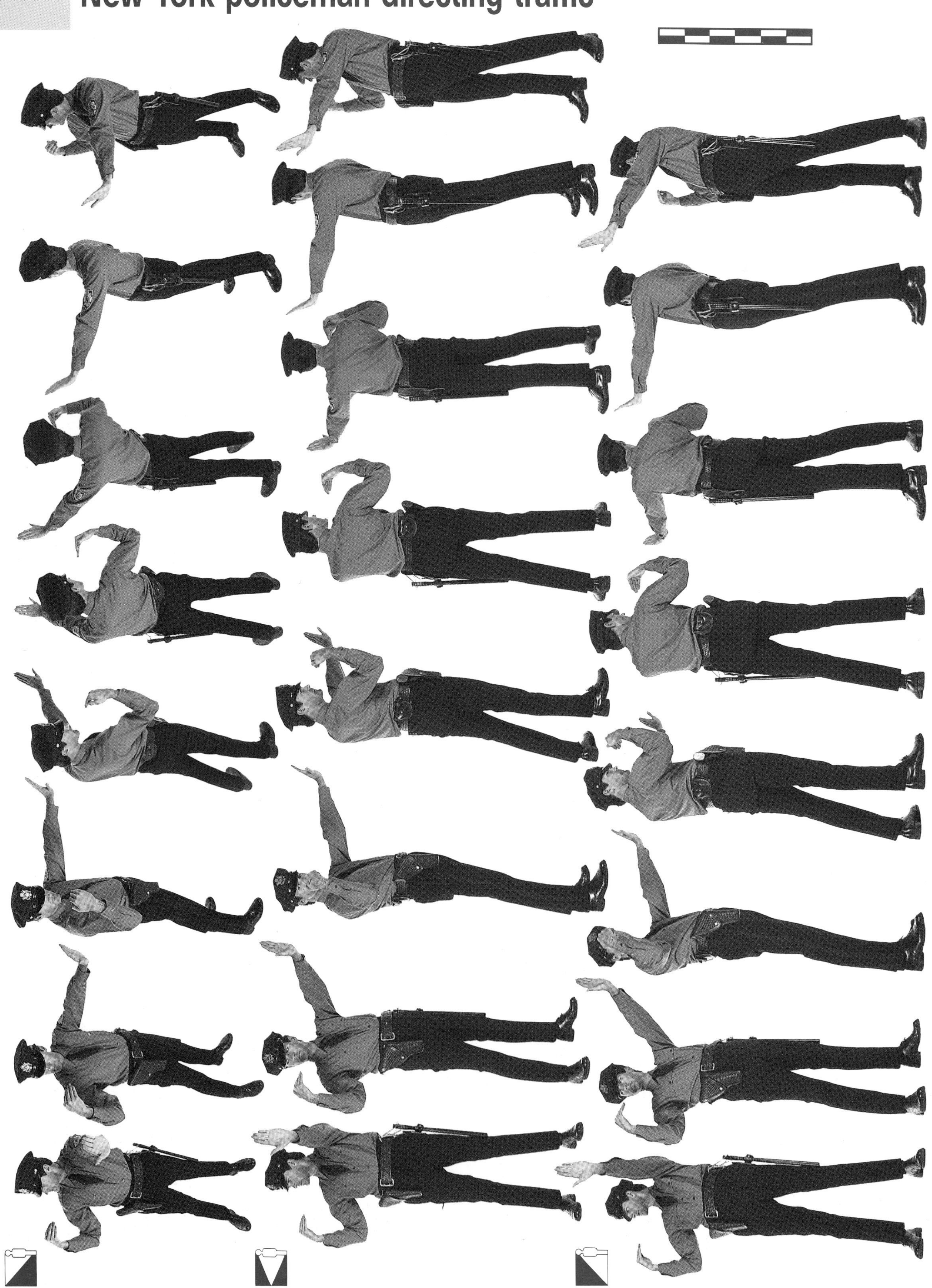

Cowgirl shooting

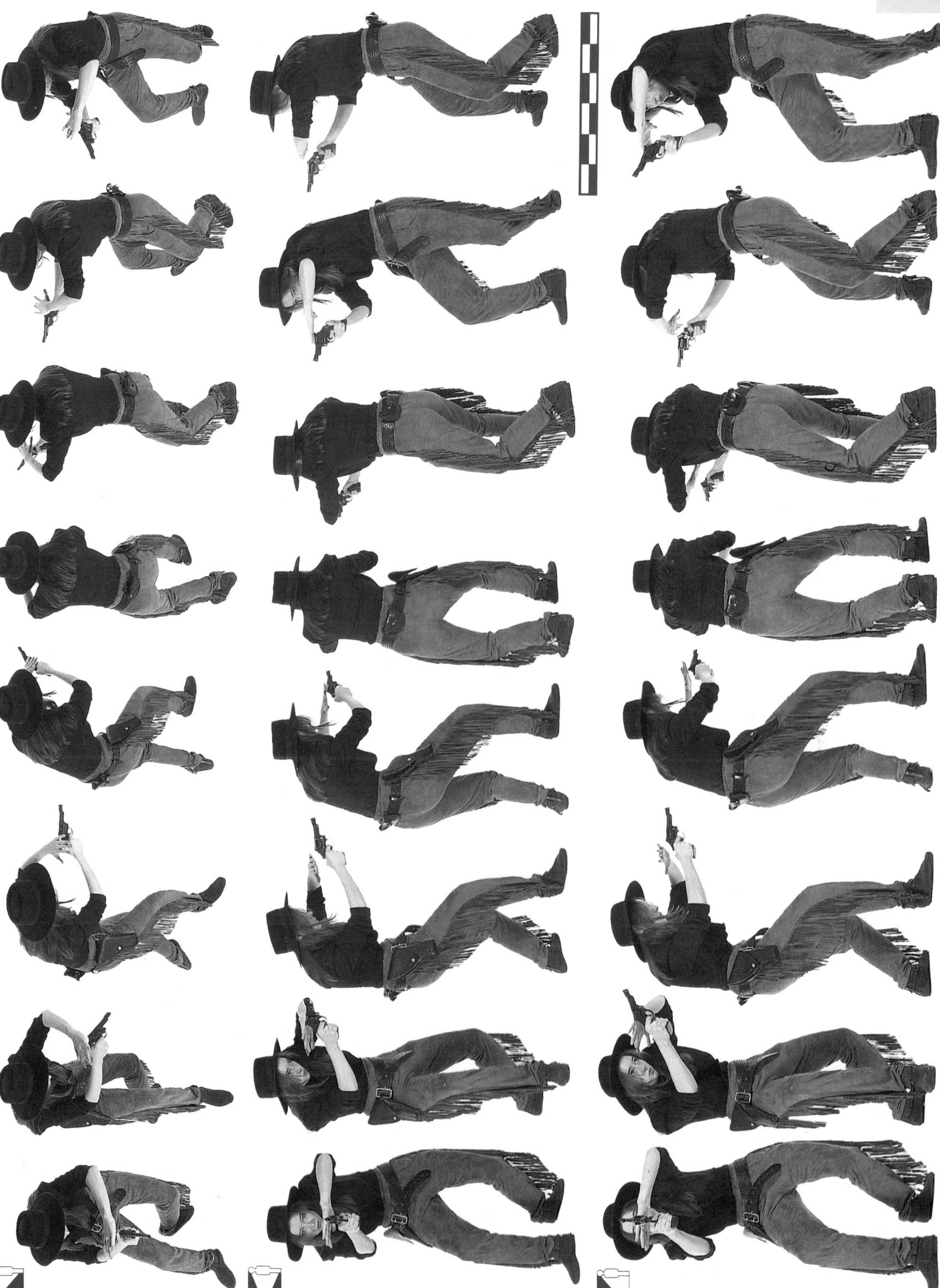

British policeman saluting

Gangster with violin case

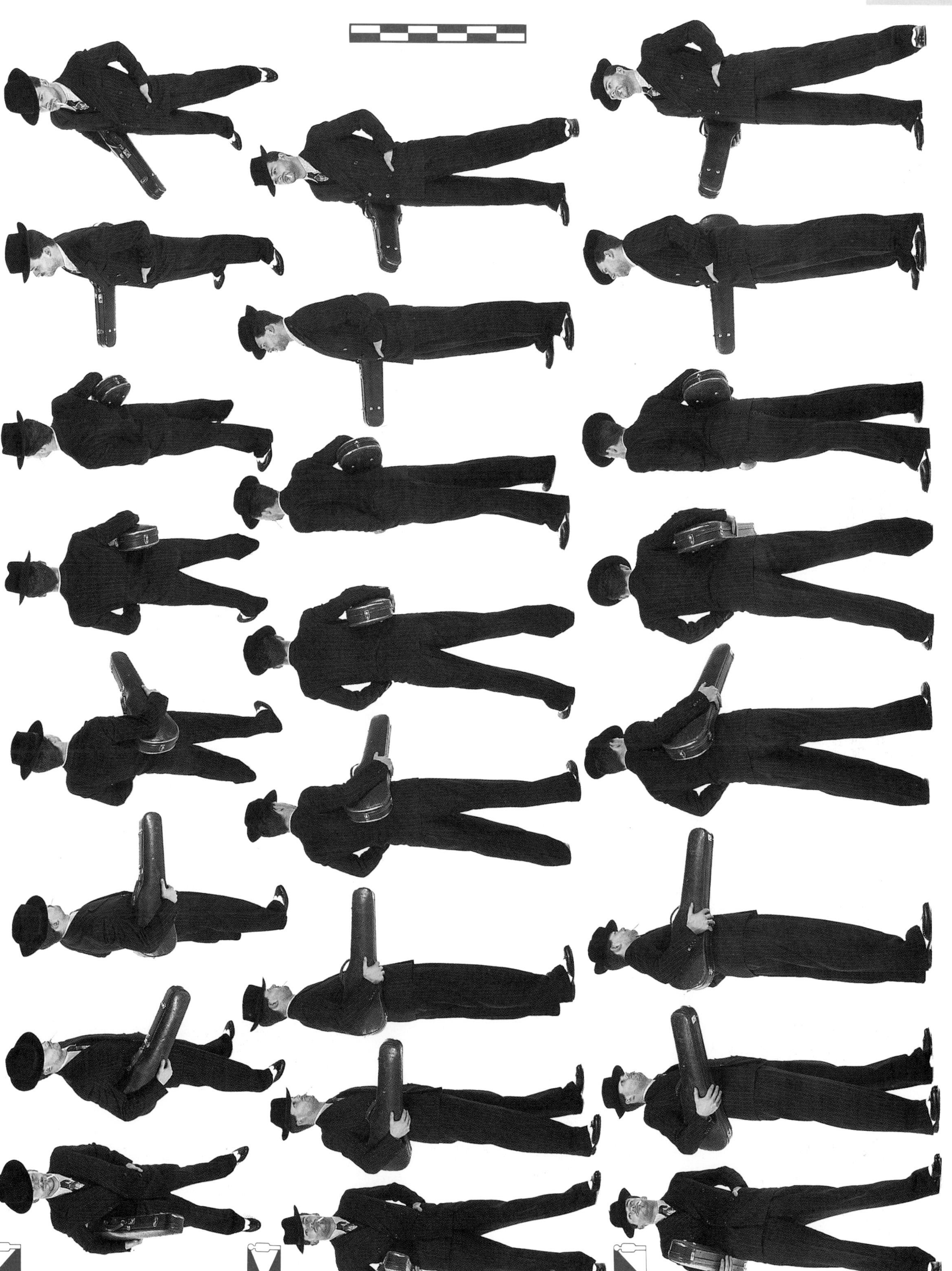

8·01 Businessman holding briefcase hailing taxi

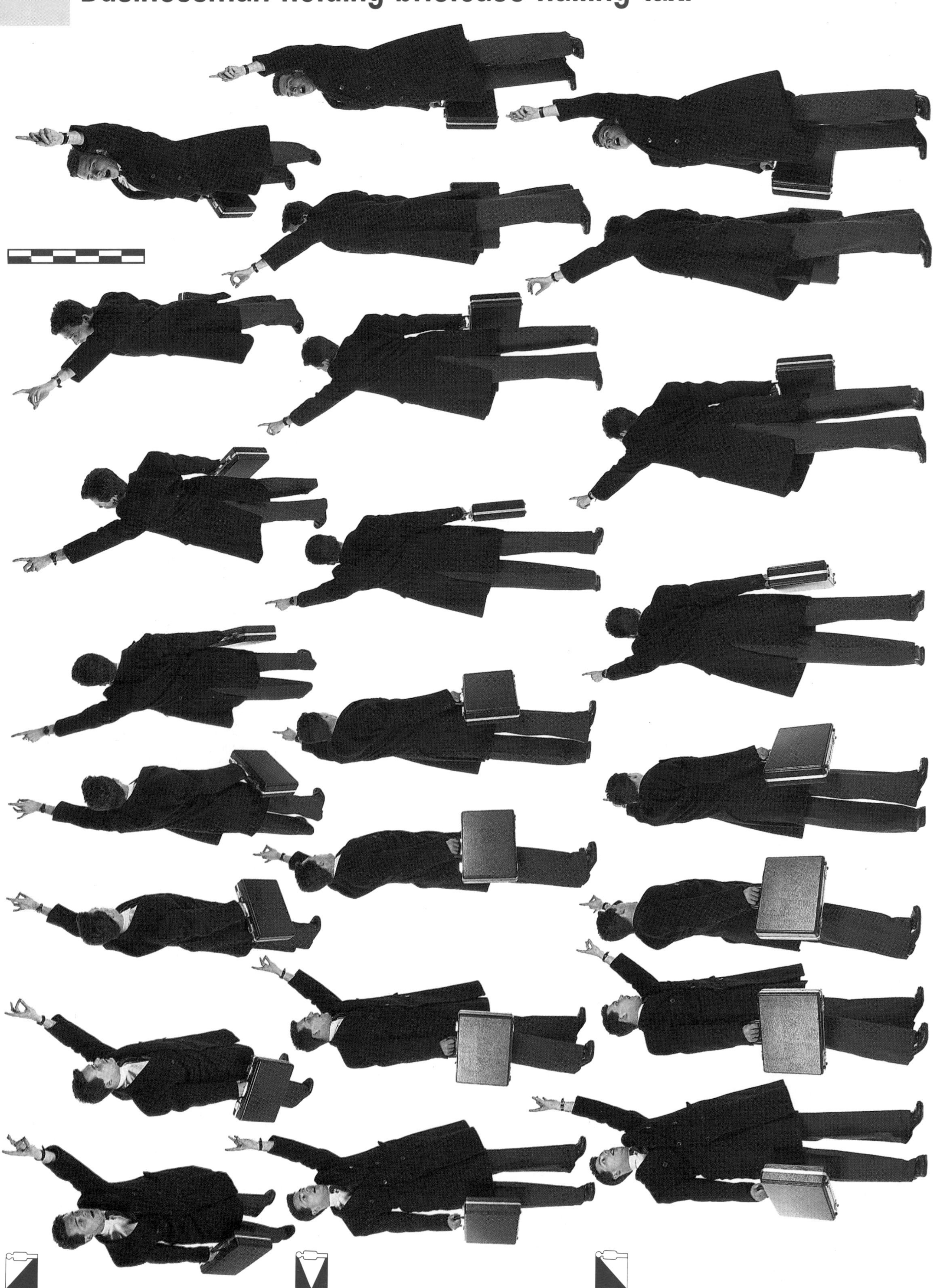

Secretary running looking at watch

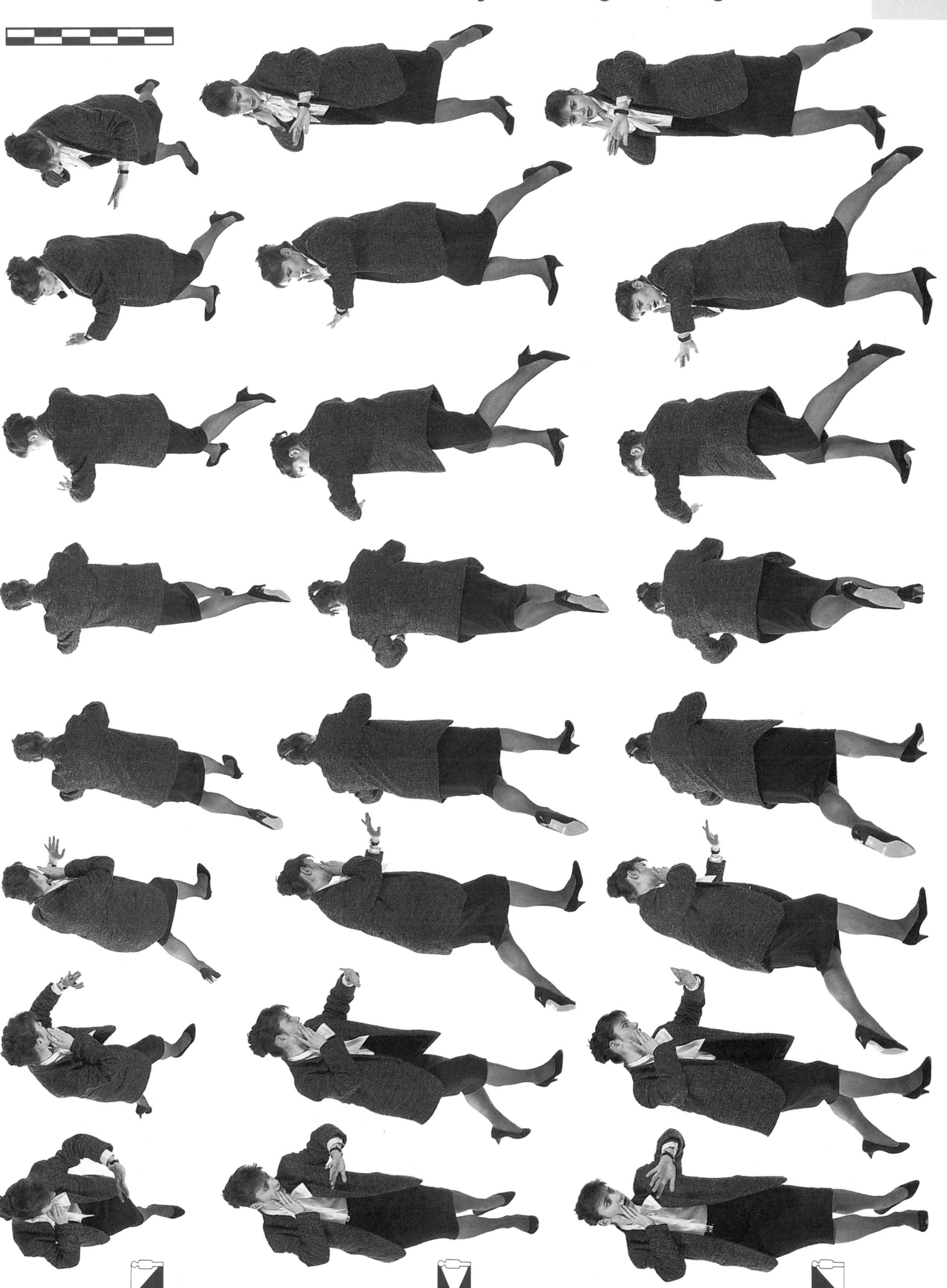

Businessman opening umbrella

8·04 Standing under an umbrella

8·05 Secretary taking dictation

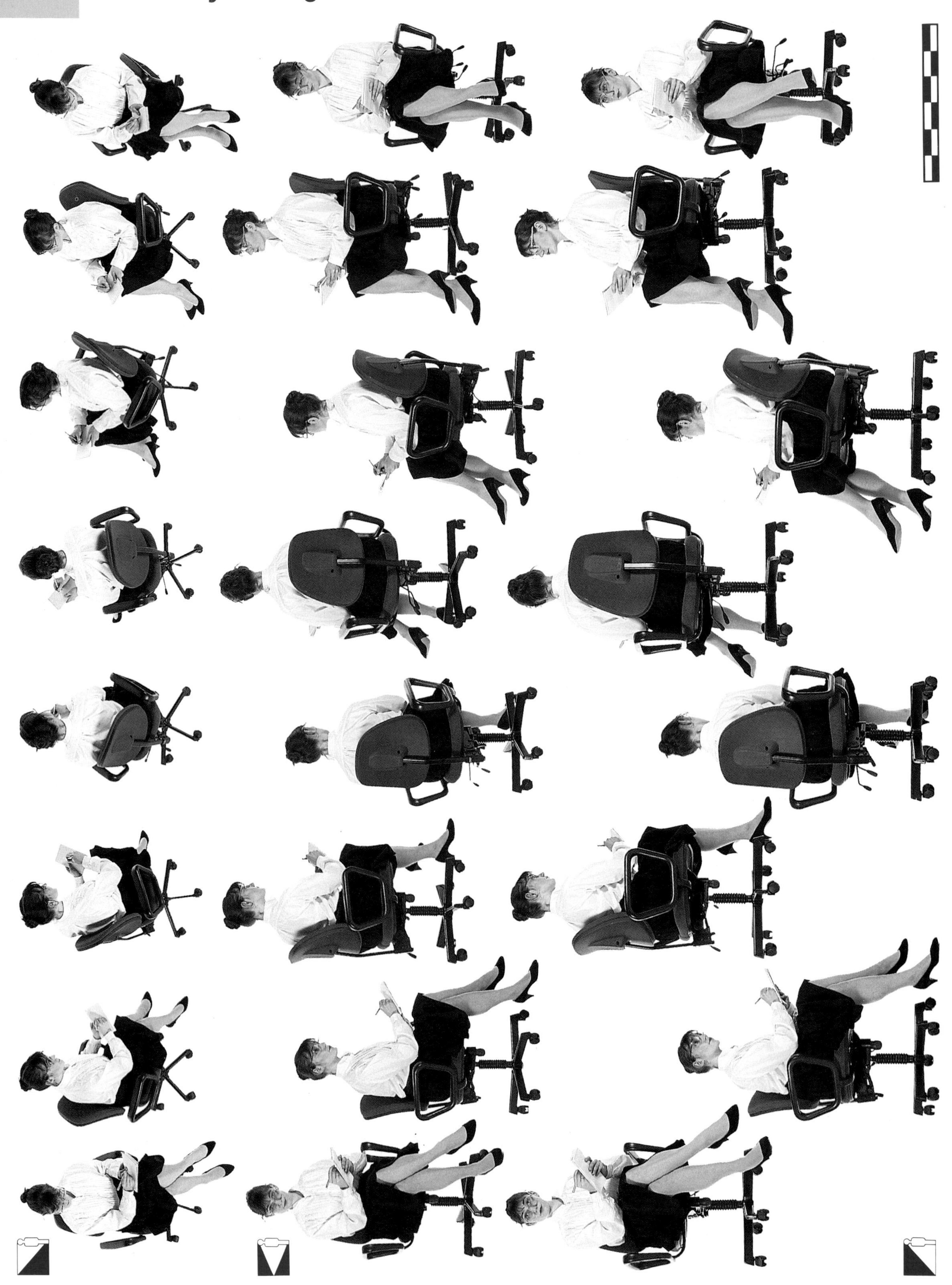

Businessman talking on phone looking at watch

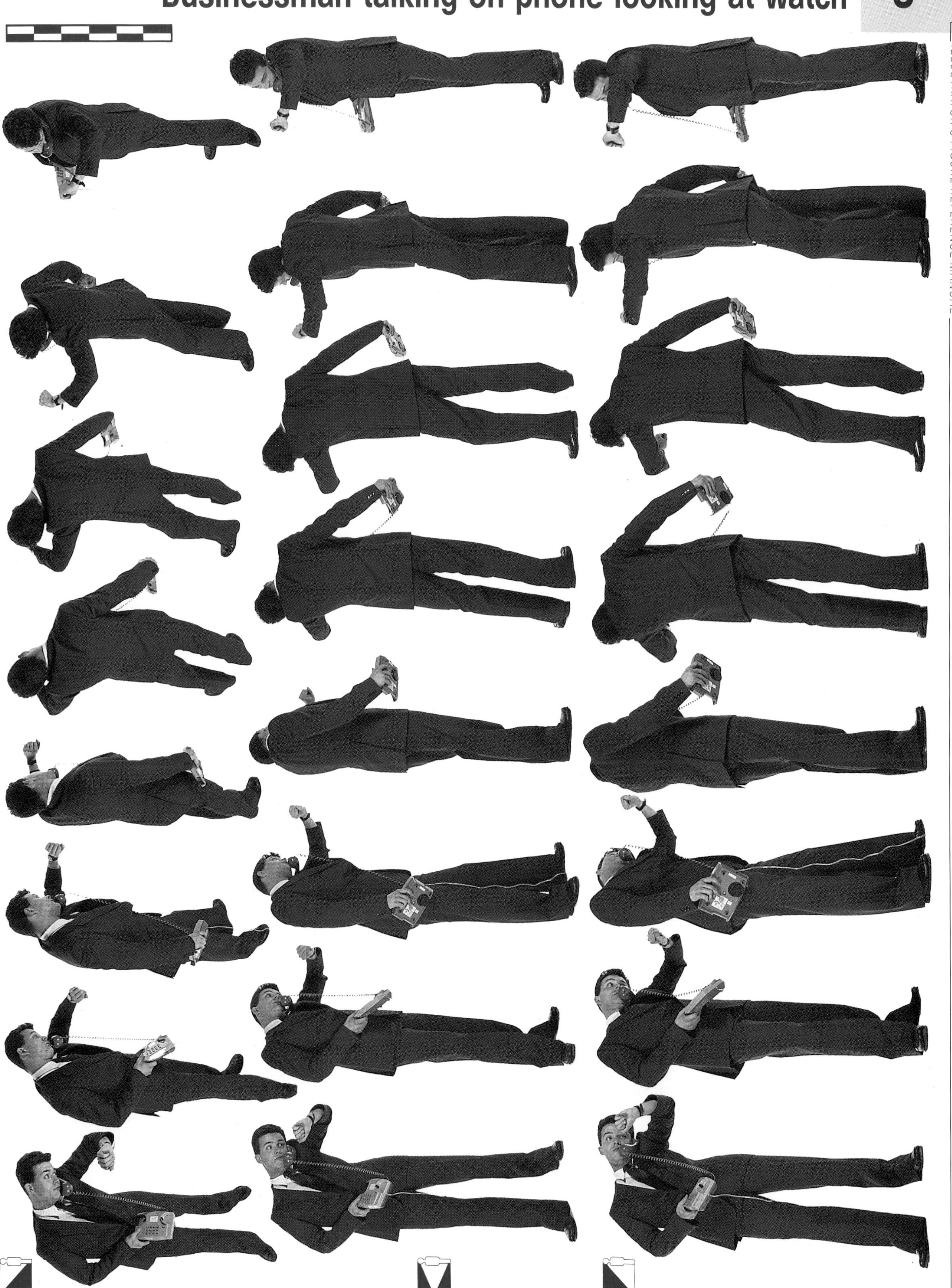

8·07 Secretary at typewriter

Secretary at desk talking on phone

8·09 Commuting

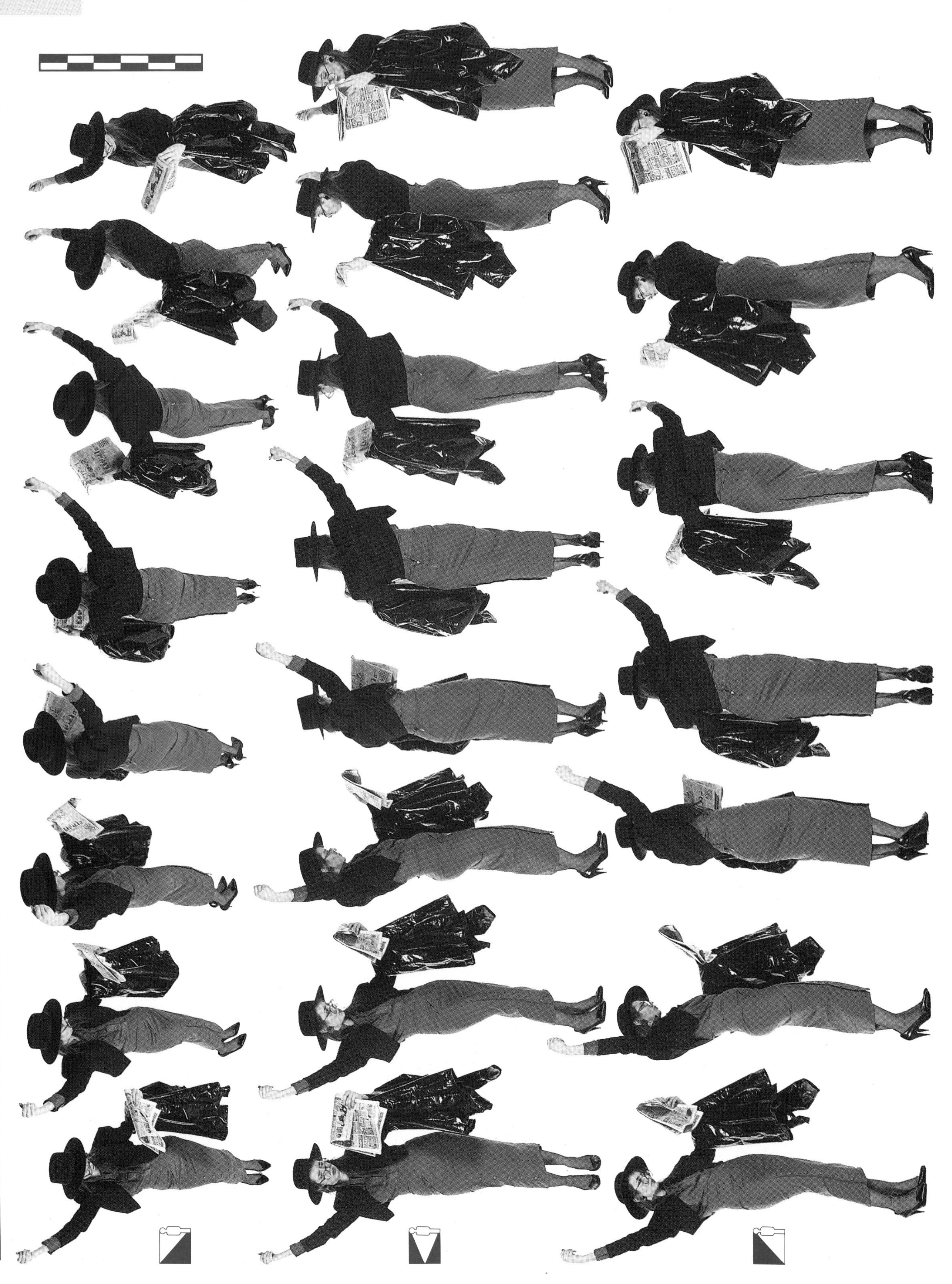

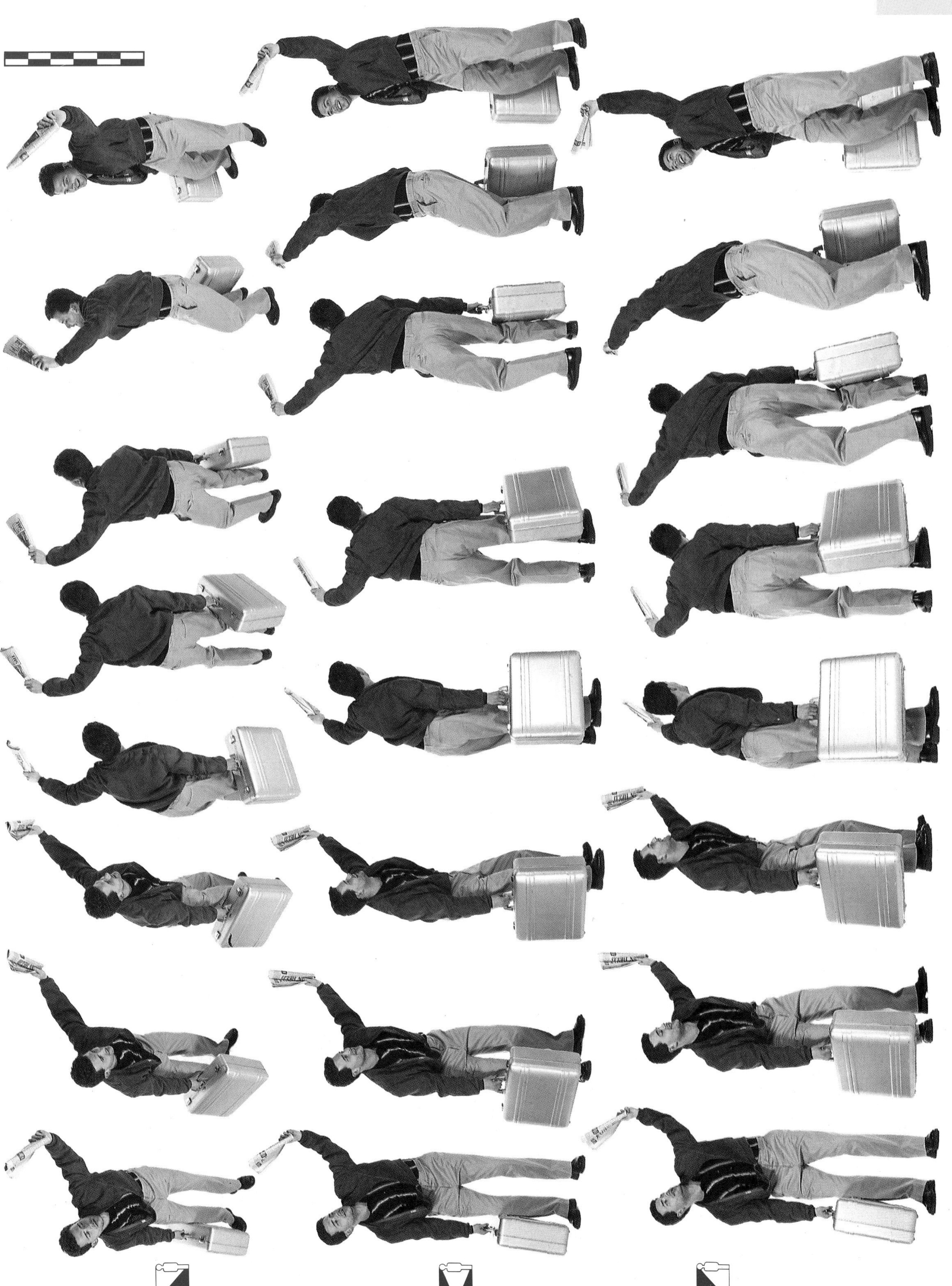

9·02 Stack of boxes

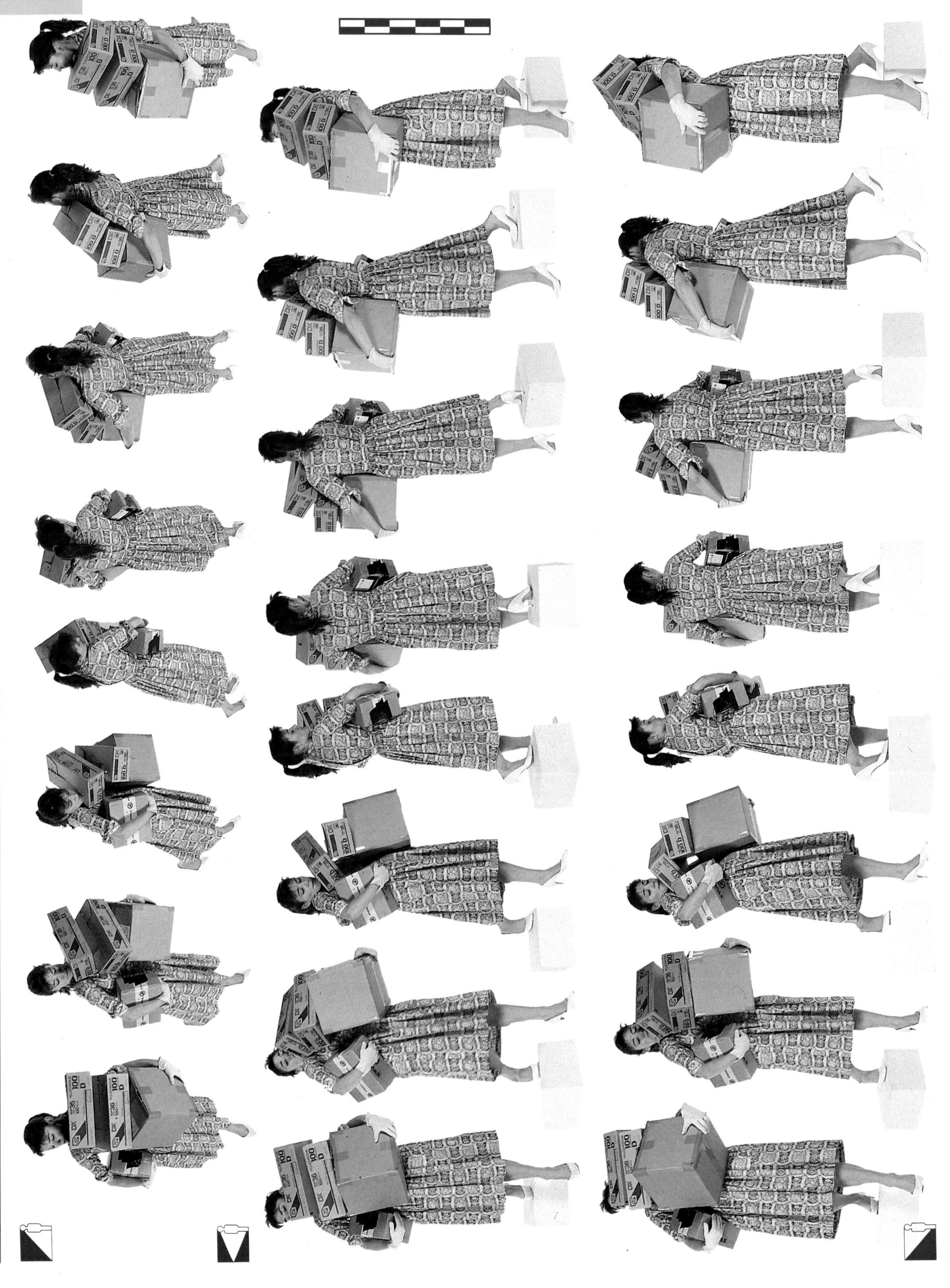

Large potted plant

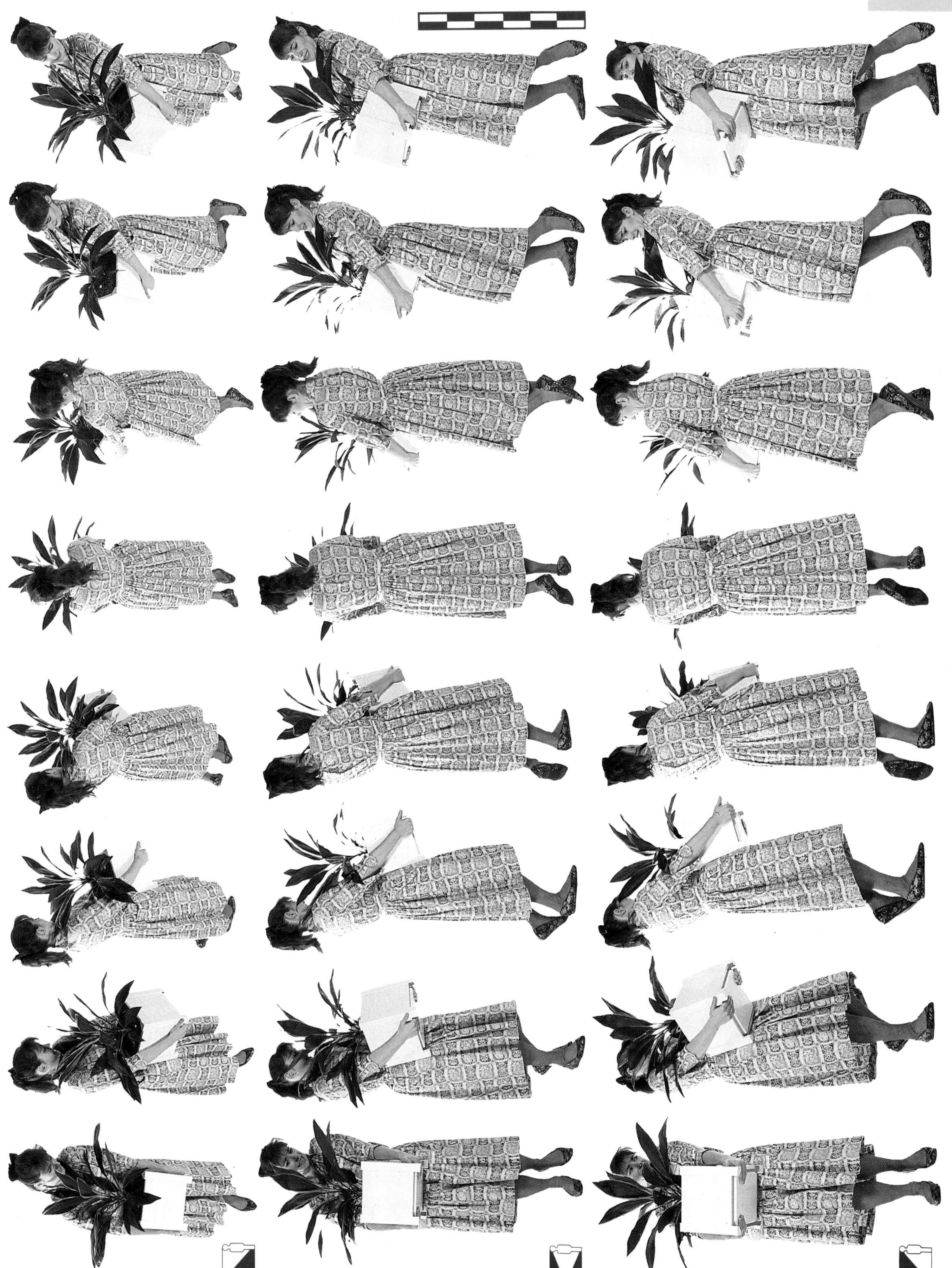

Step-ladder

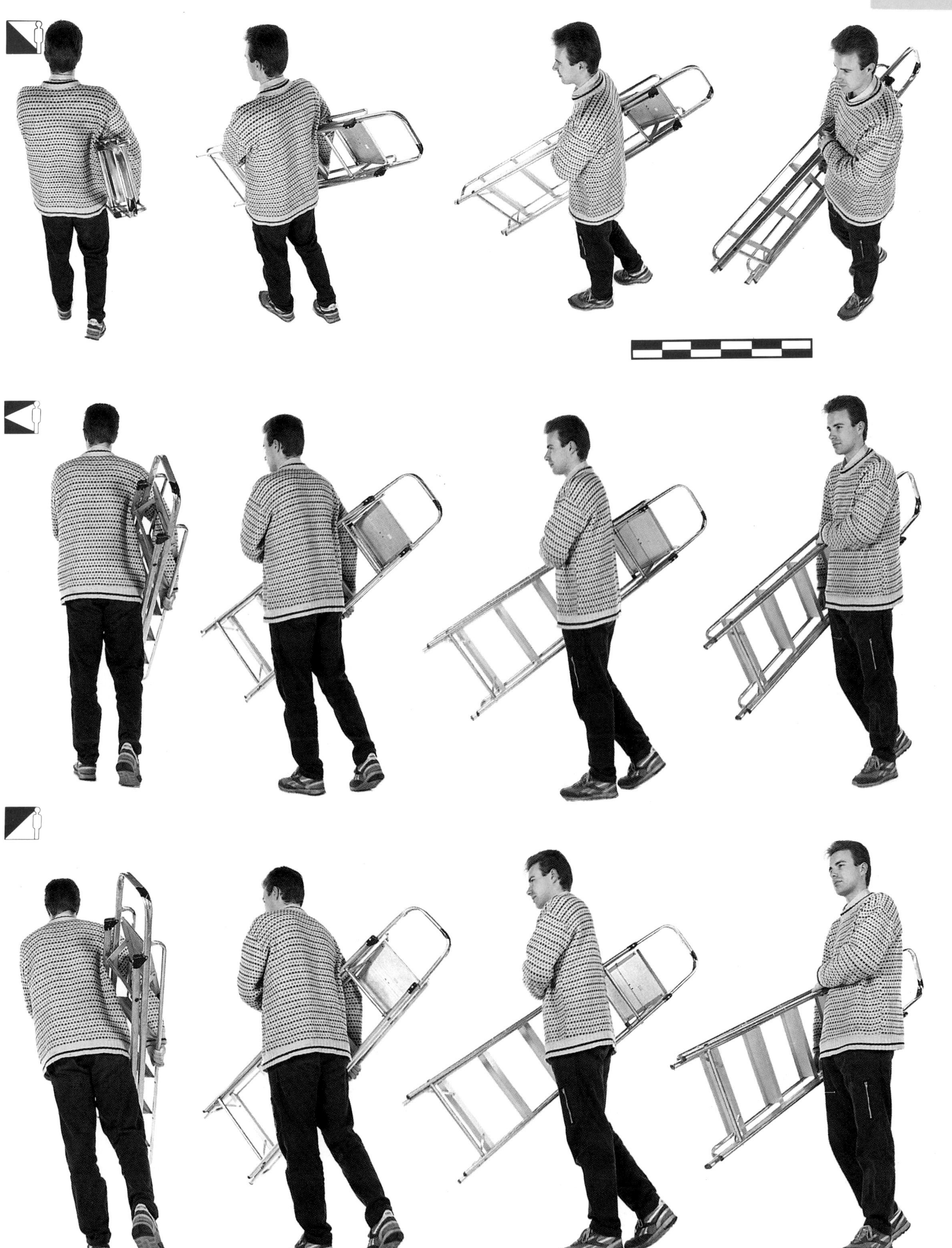

“Smelly socks”

Shoulder bag and carrier bag

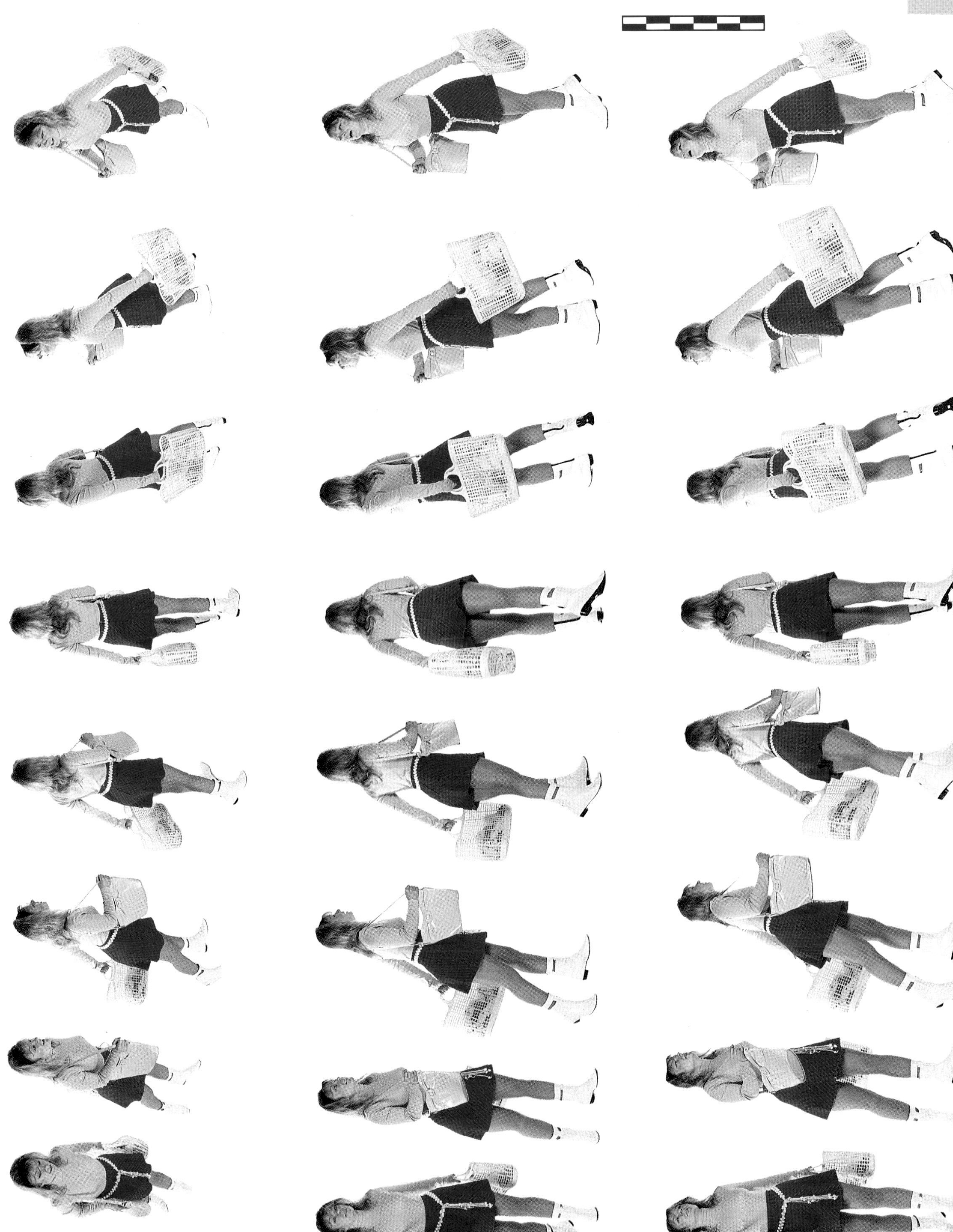

Sewing

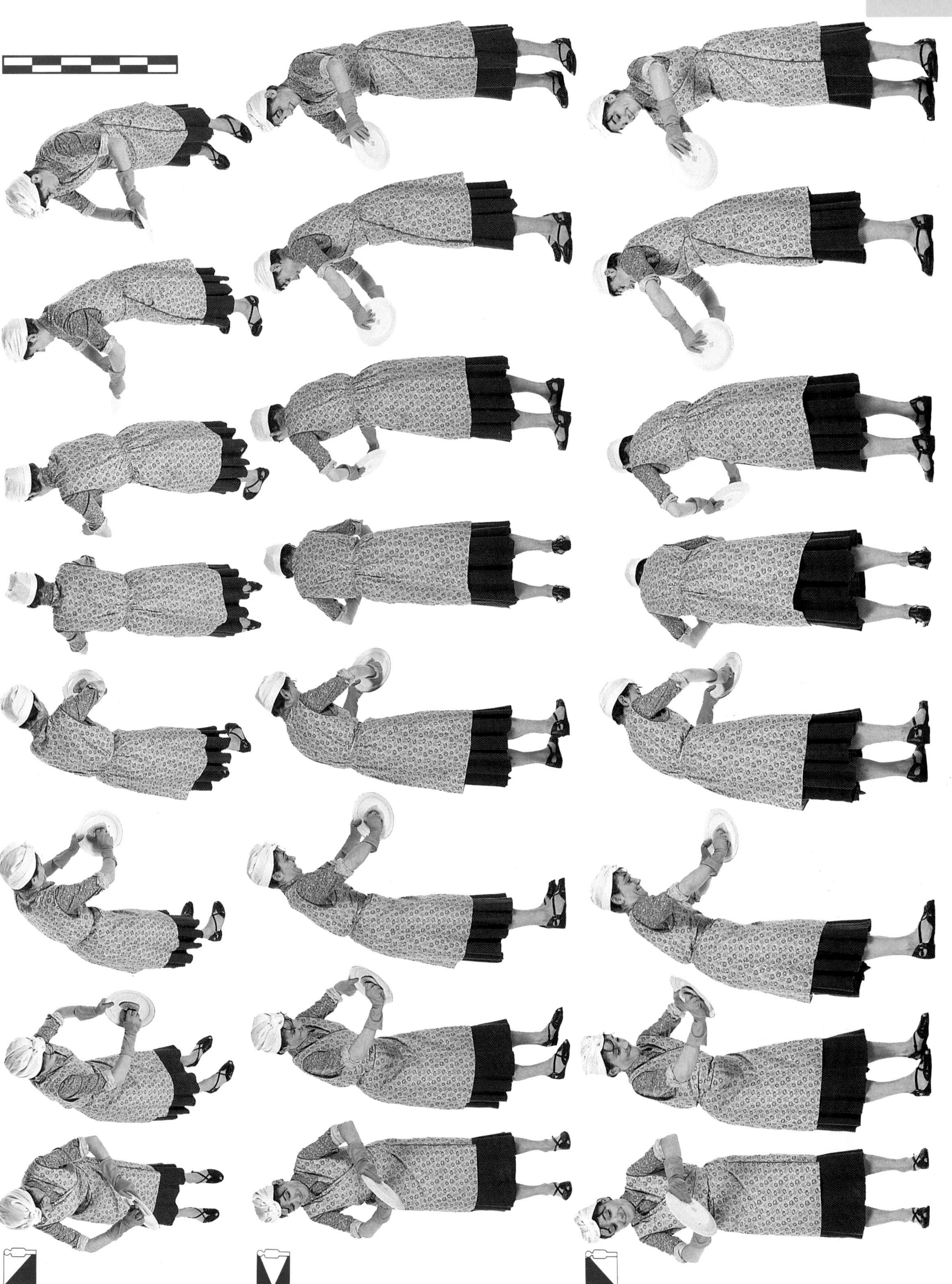

10·03 French maid dusting

Sweeping up

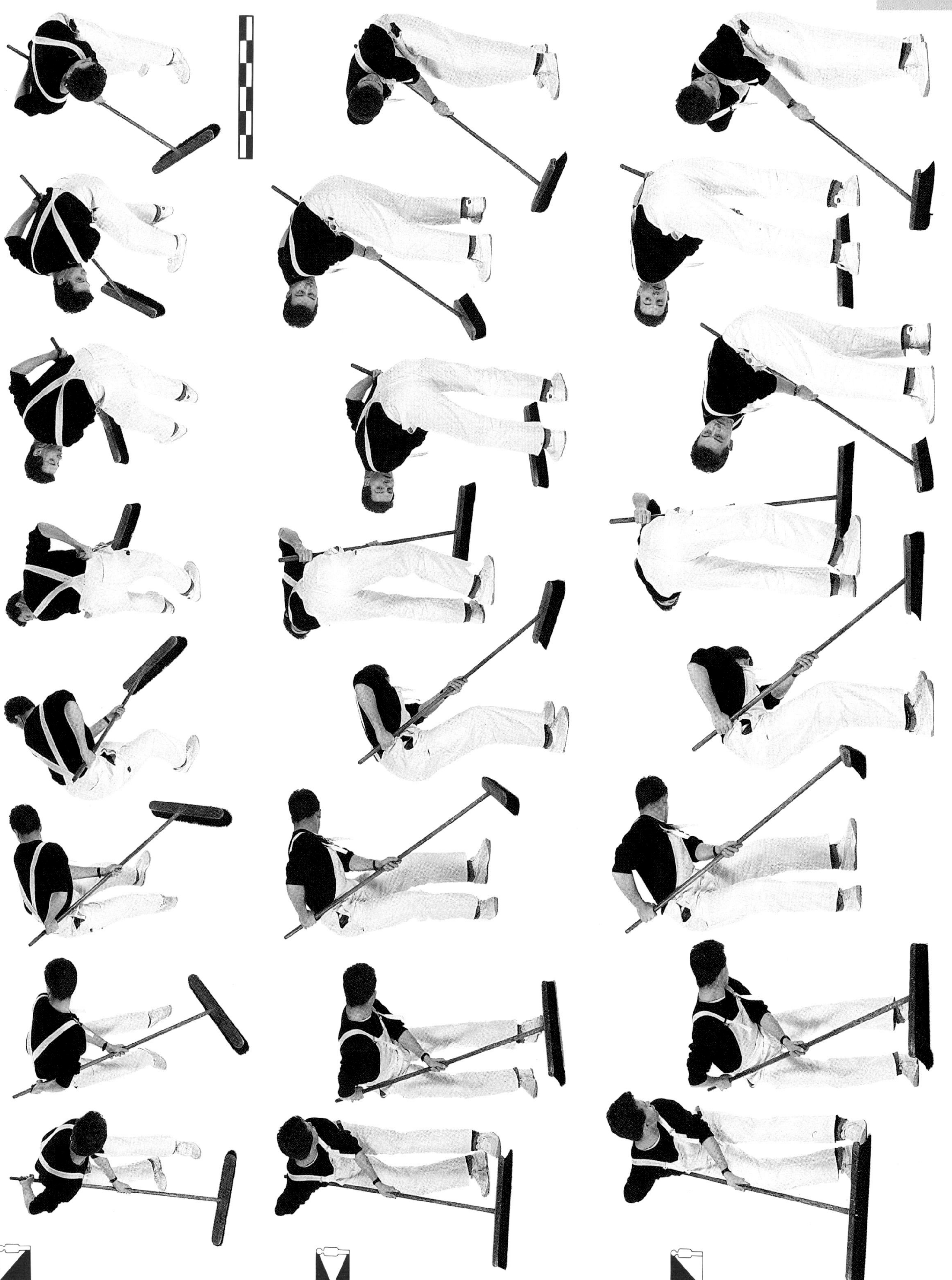

Vacuuming

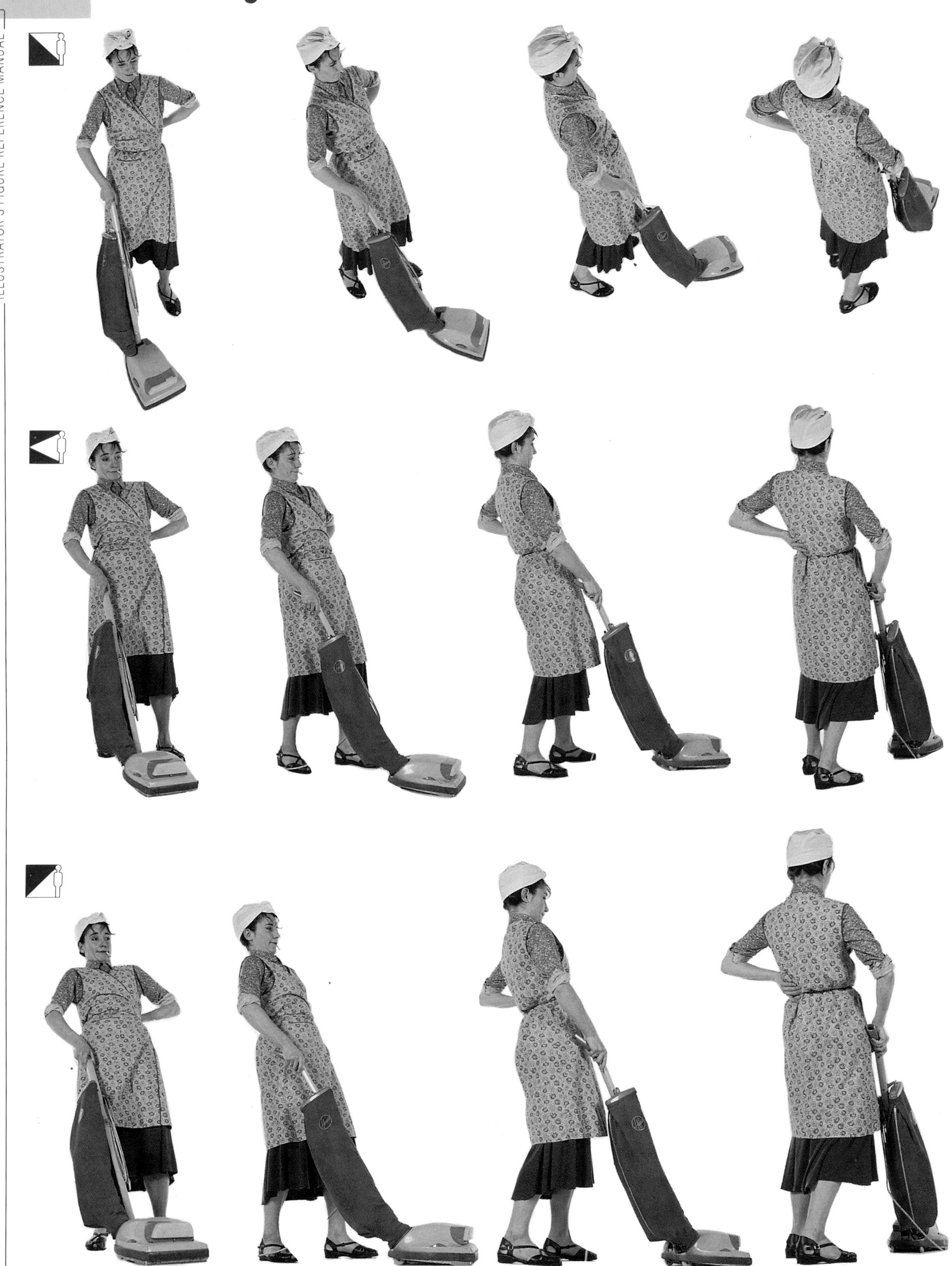

10·06 Knitting in rocking chair

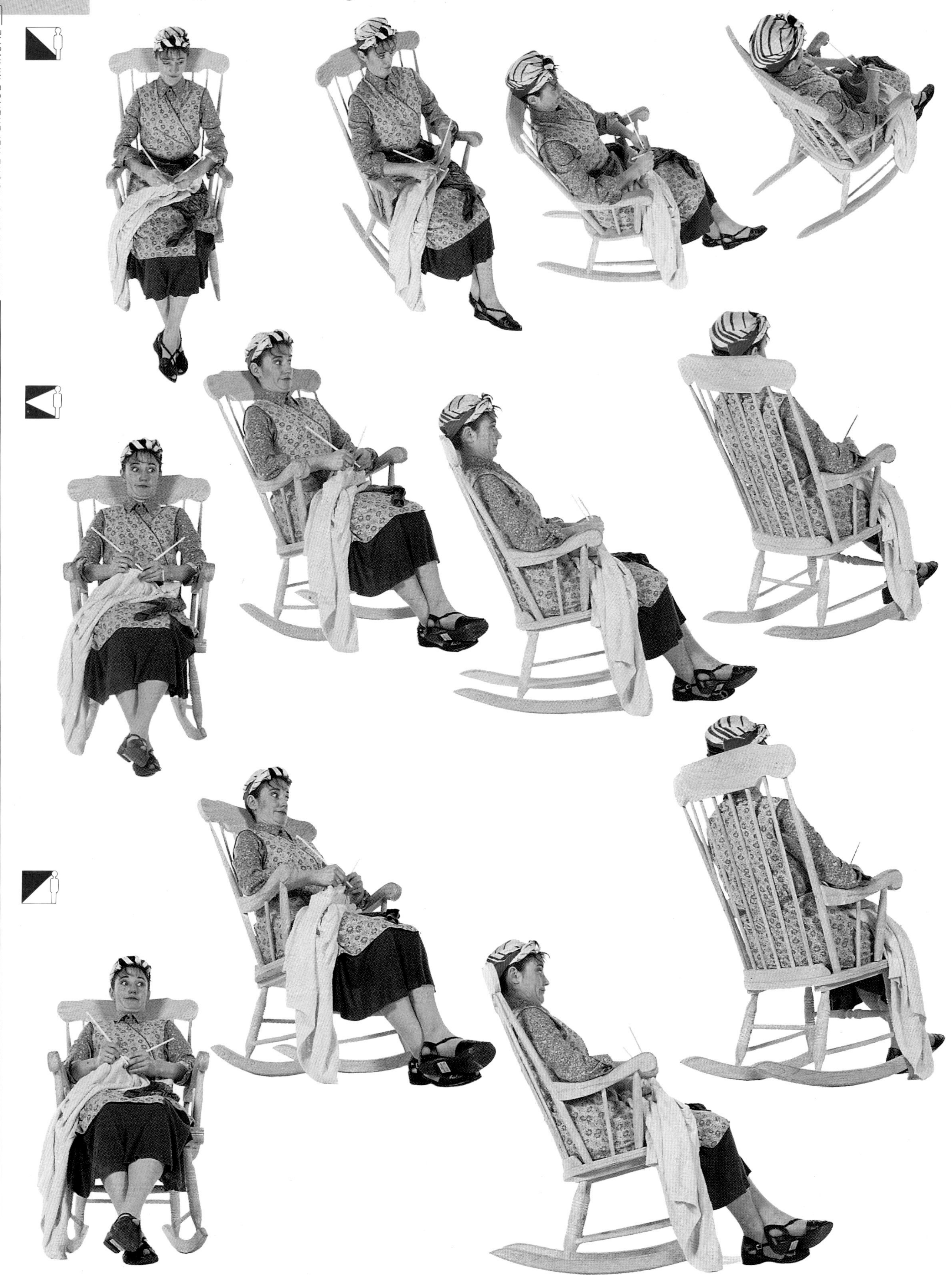

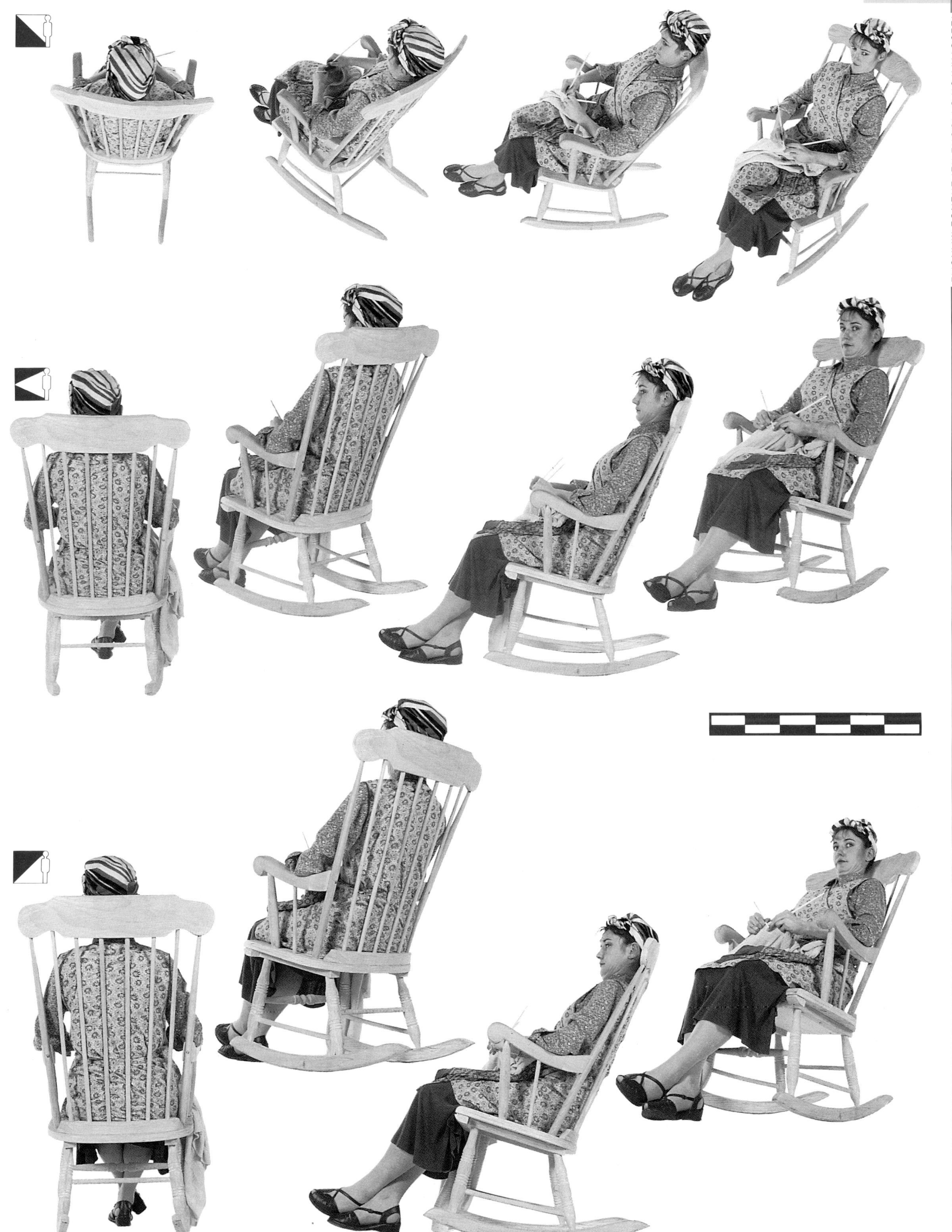

Painting with a roller

ILLUSTRATOR'S FIGURE REFERENCE MANUAL

10·08 Leaning on broom

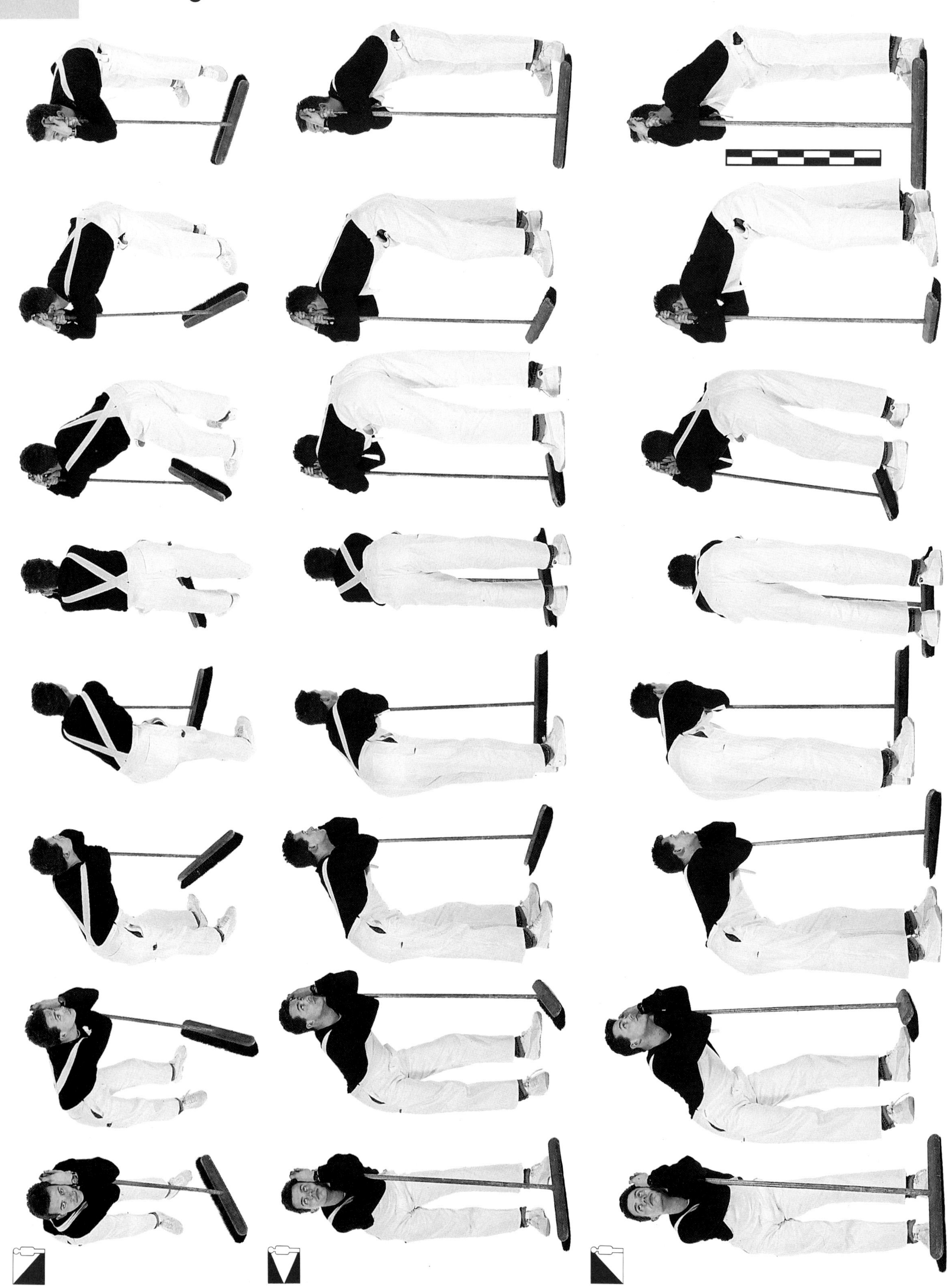

Sawing

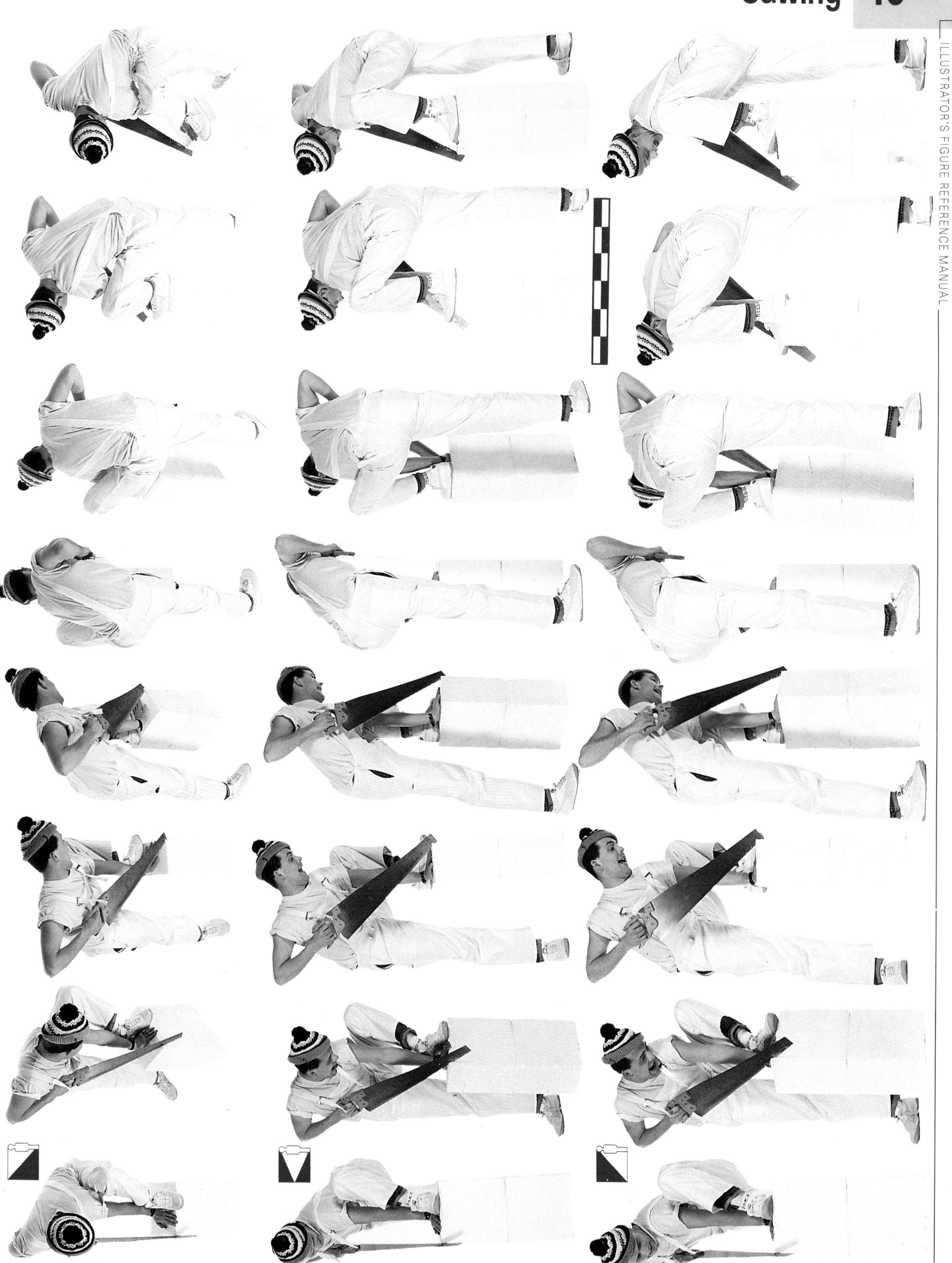

10·10 Hammering in a nail

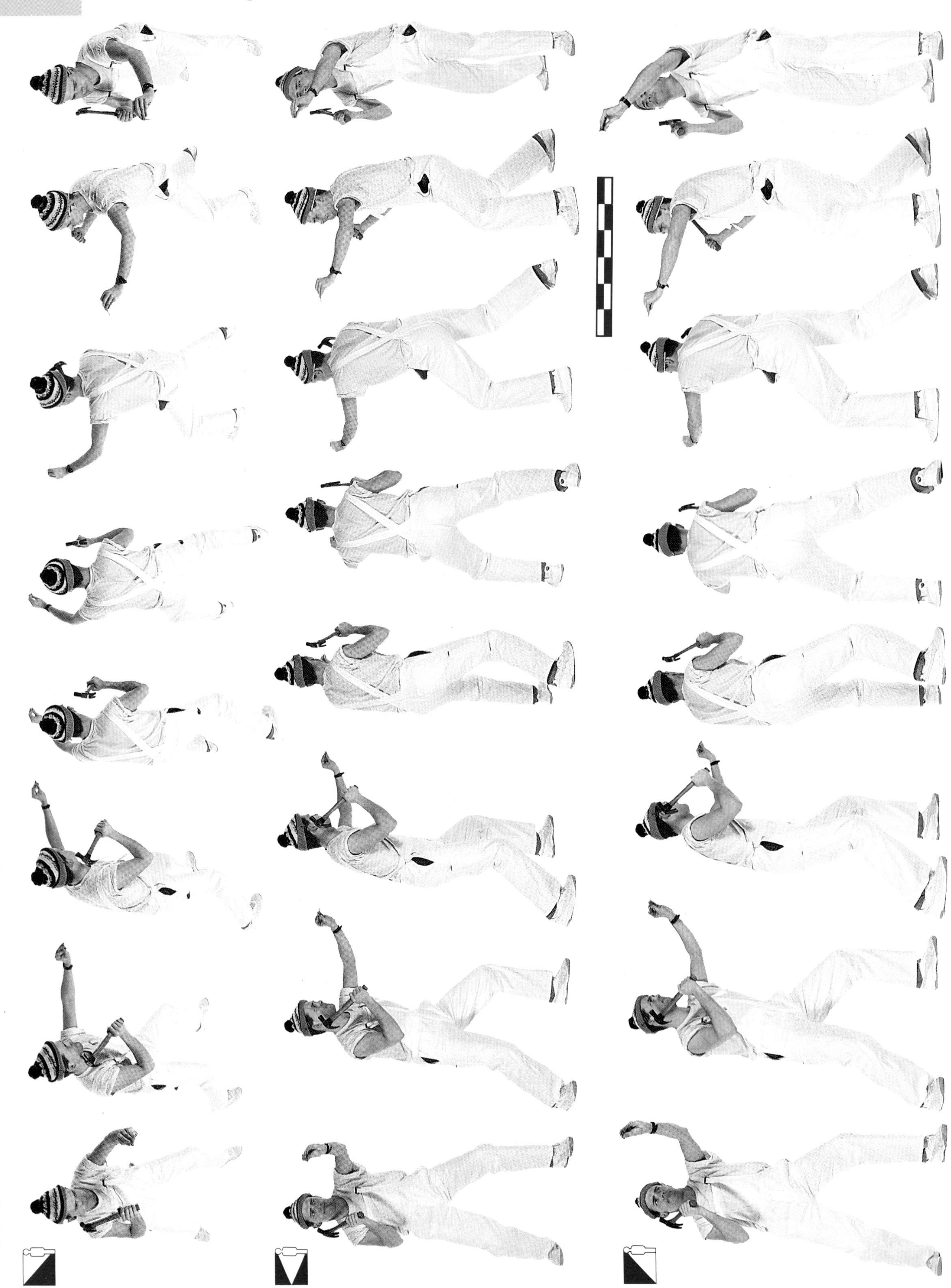

Hitting thumb with hammer

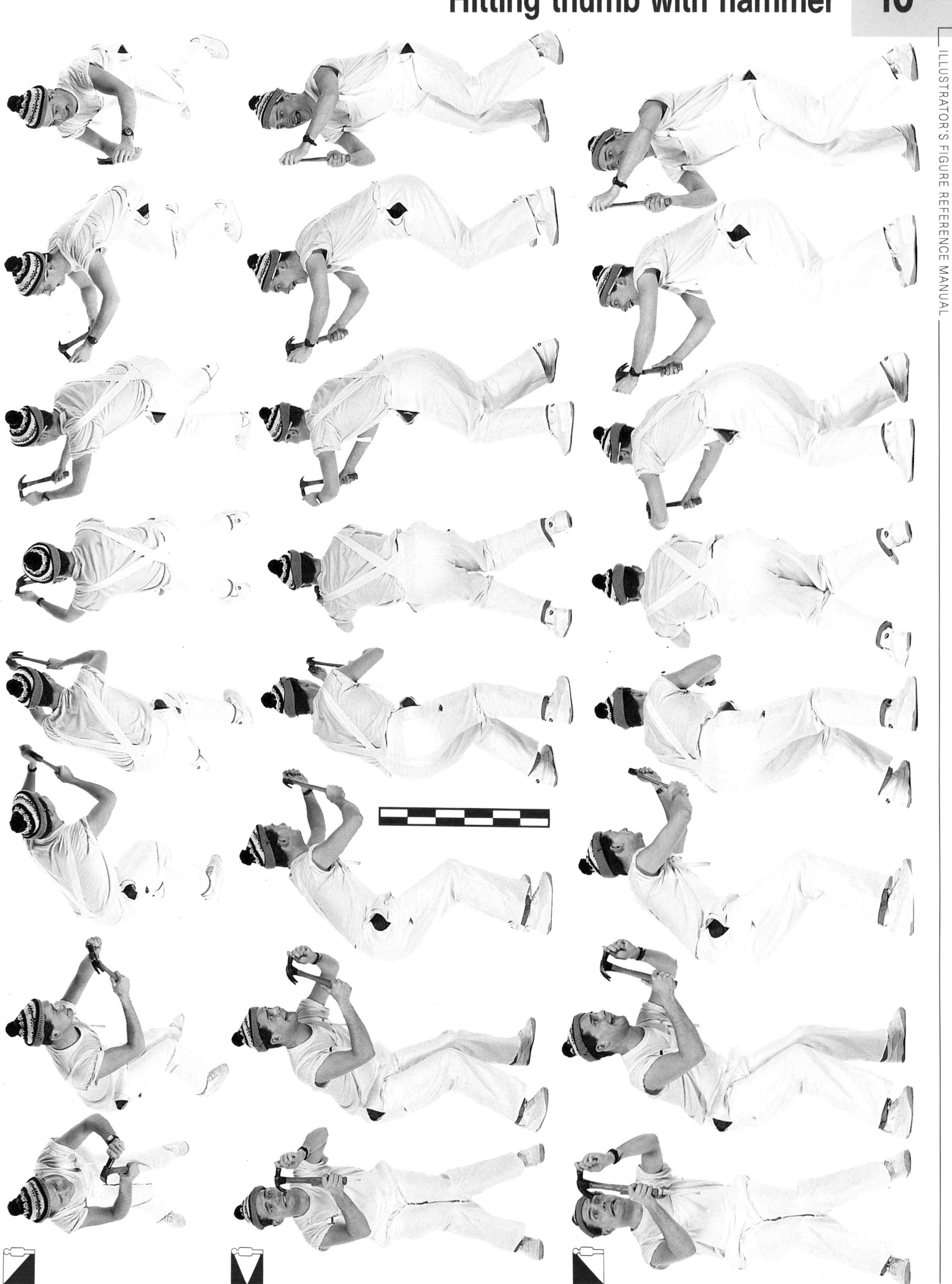

Ironing

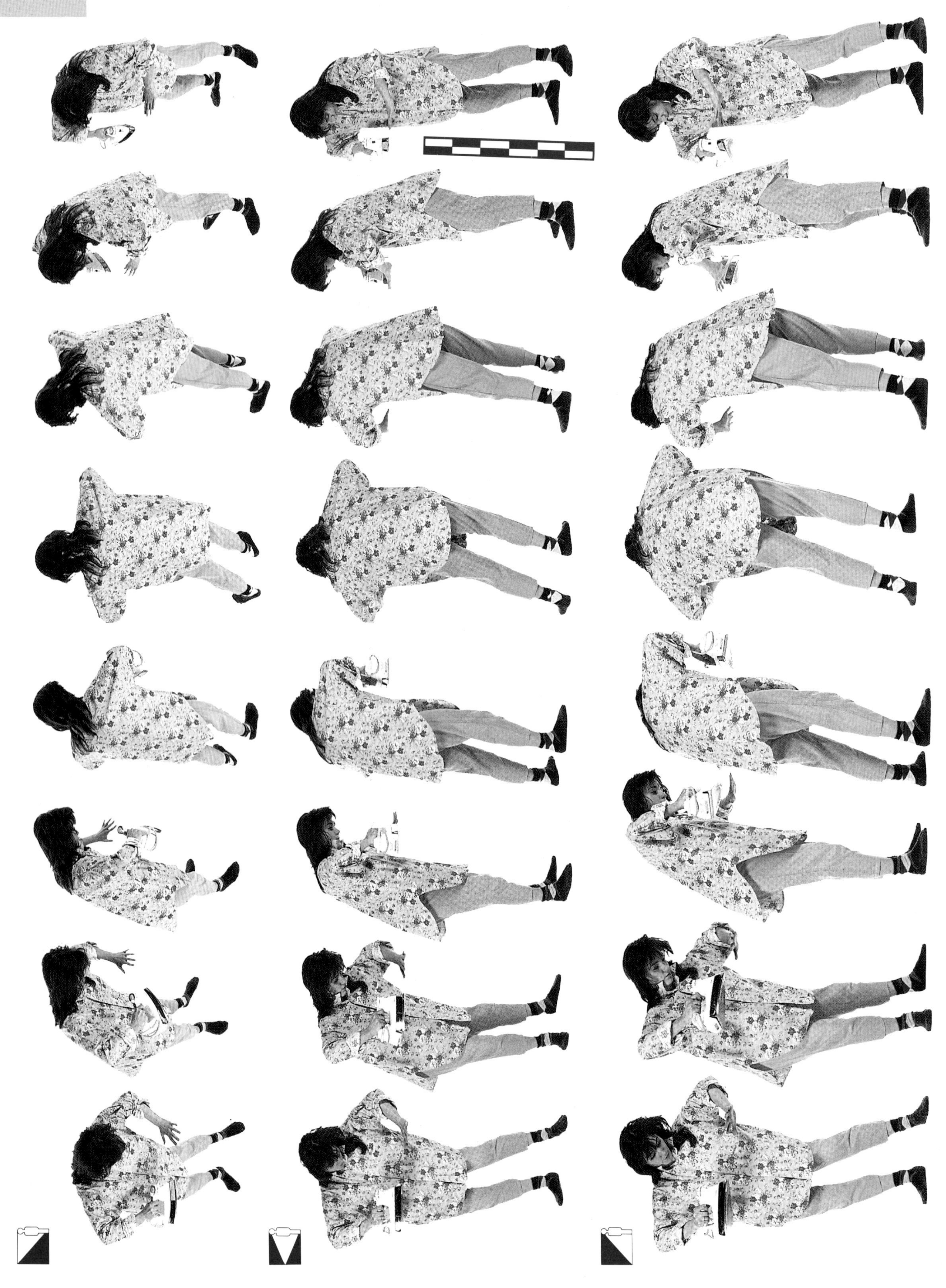

Painting with a brush

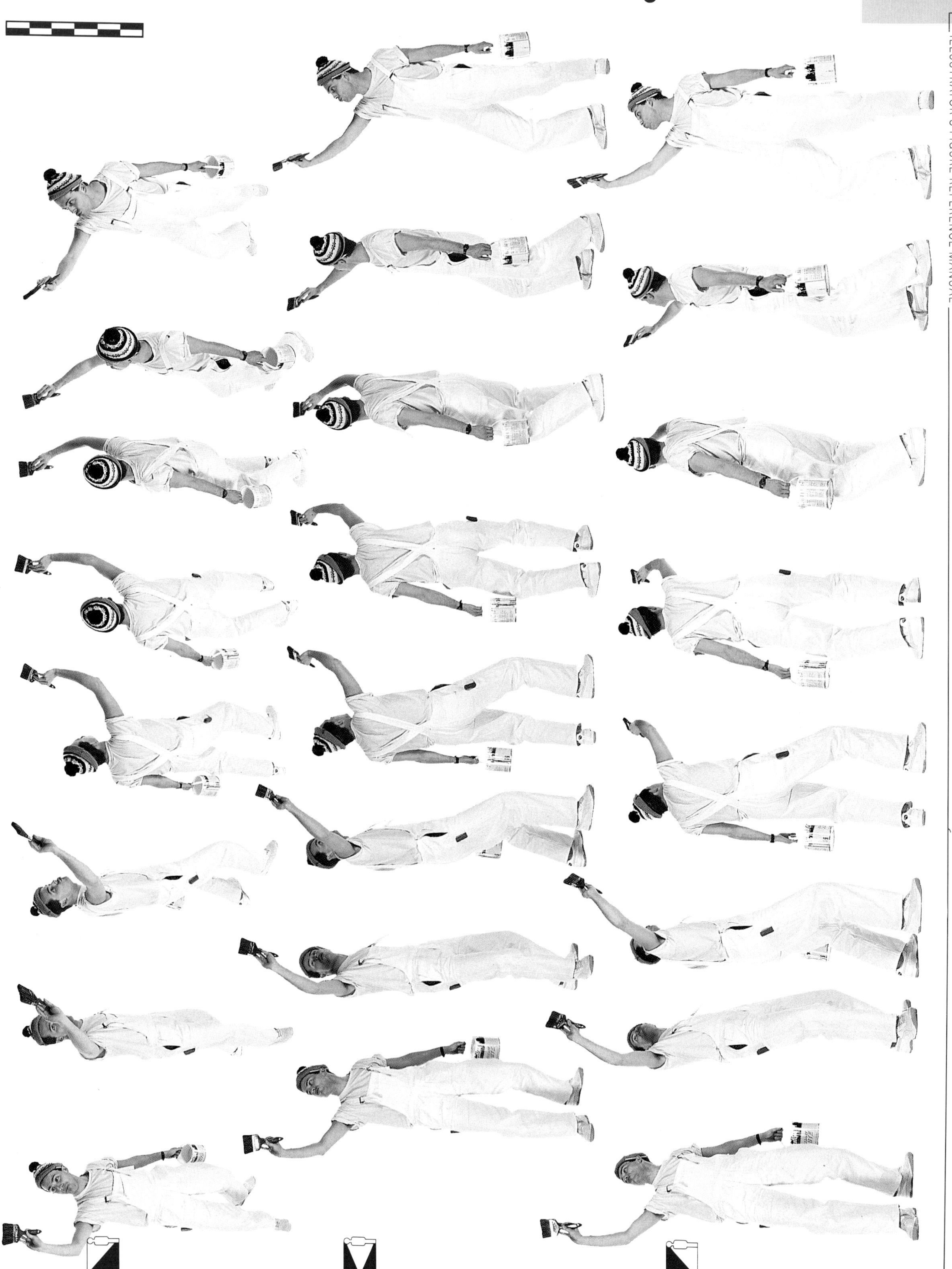

Eating sandwiches and drinking tea

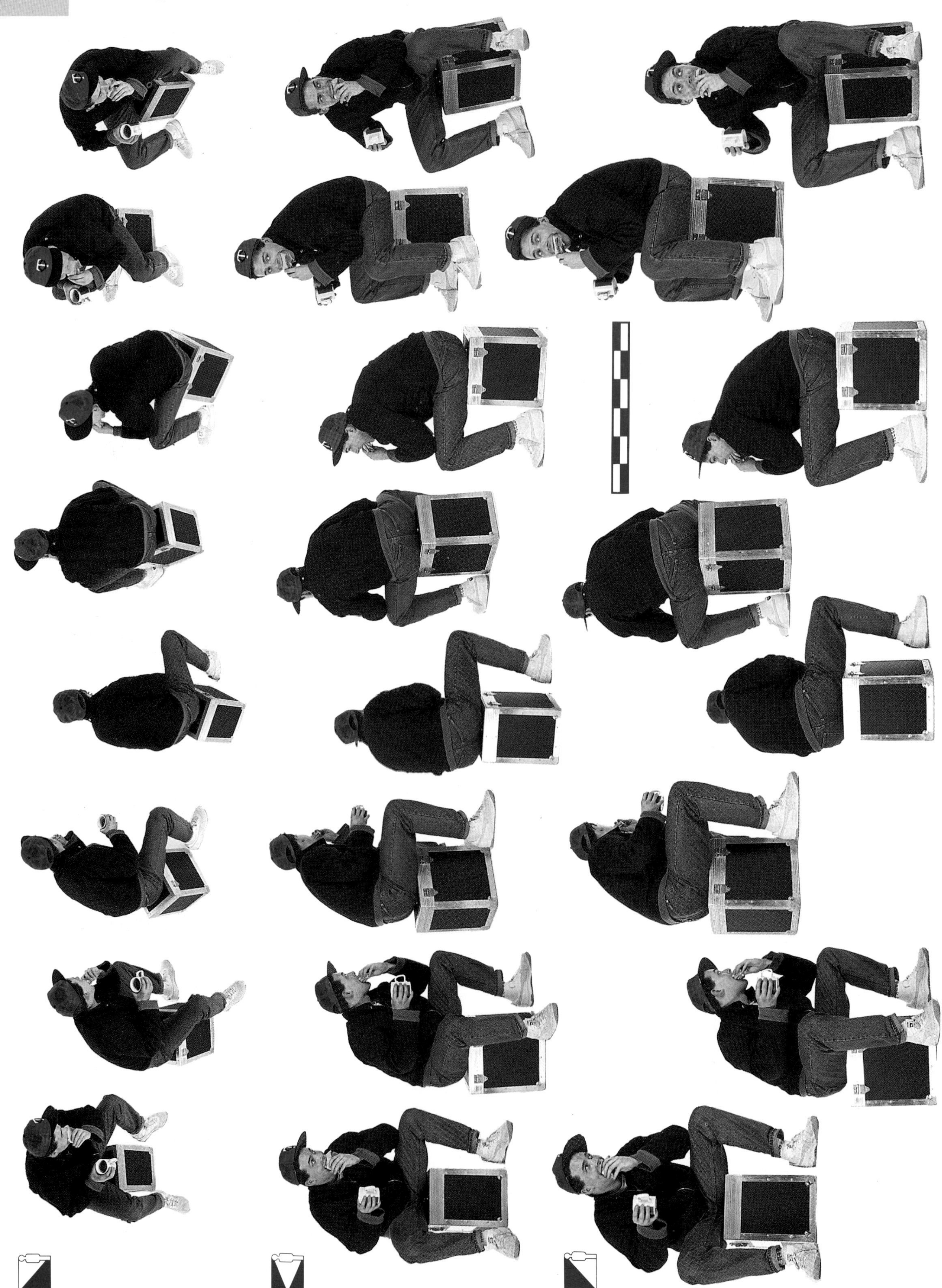

Drinking from a can

11·03 Eating pizza with hands

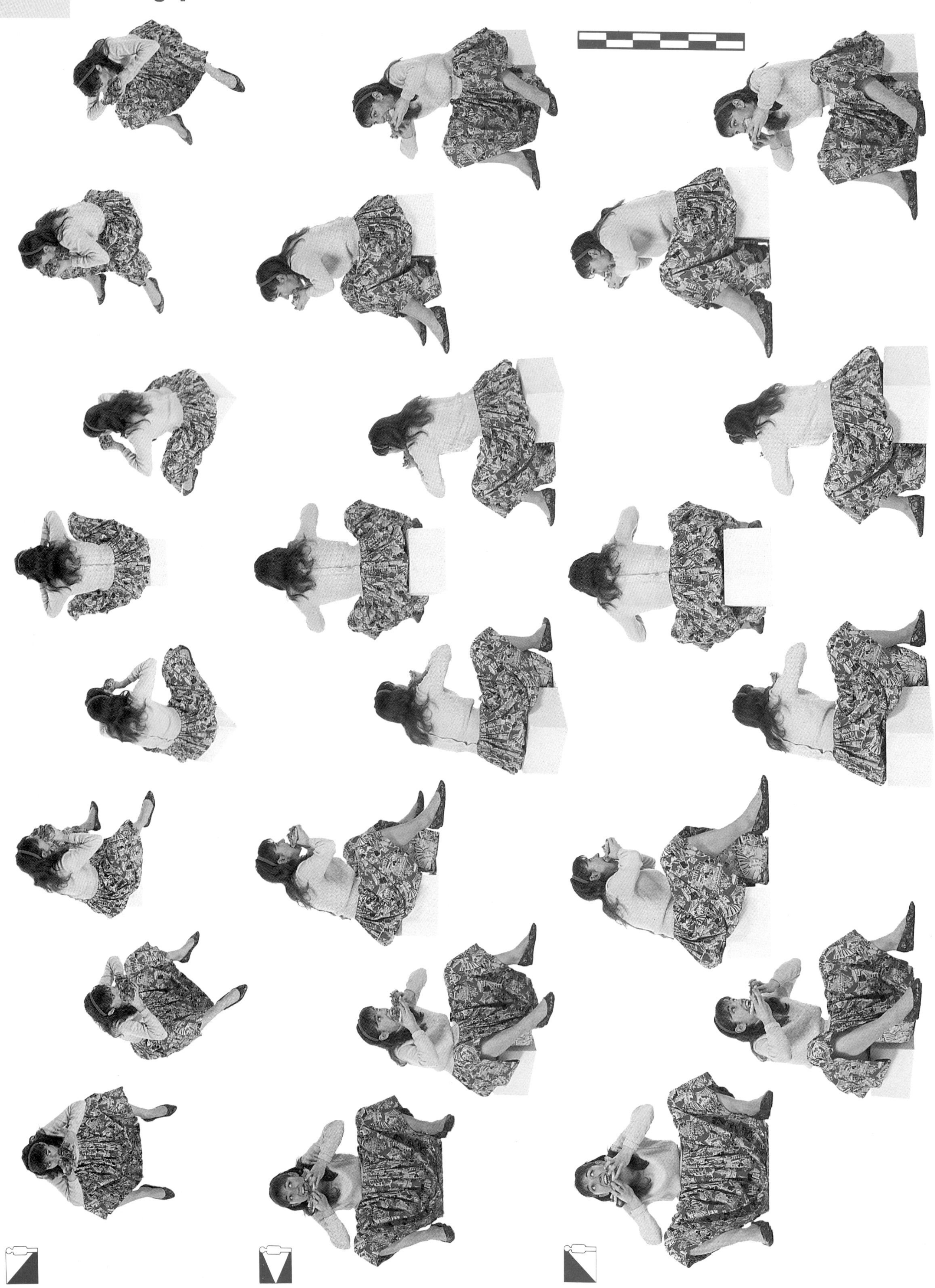

Eating with chopsticks

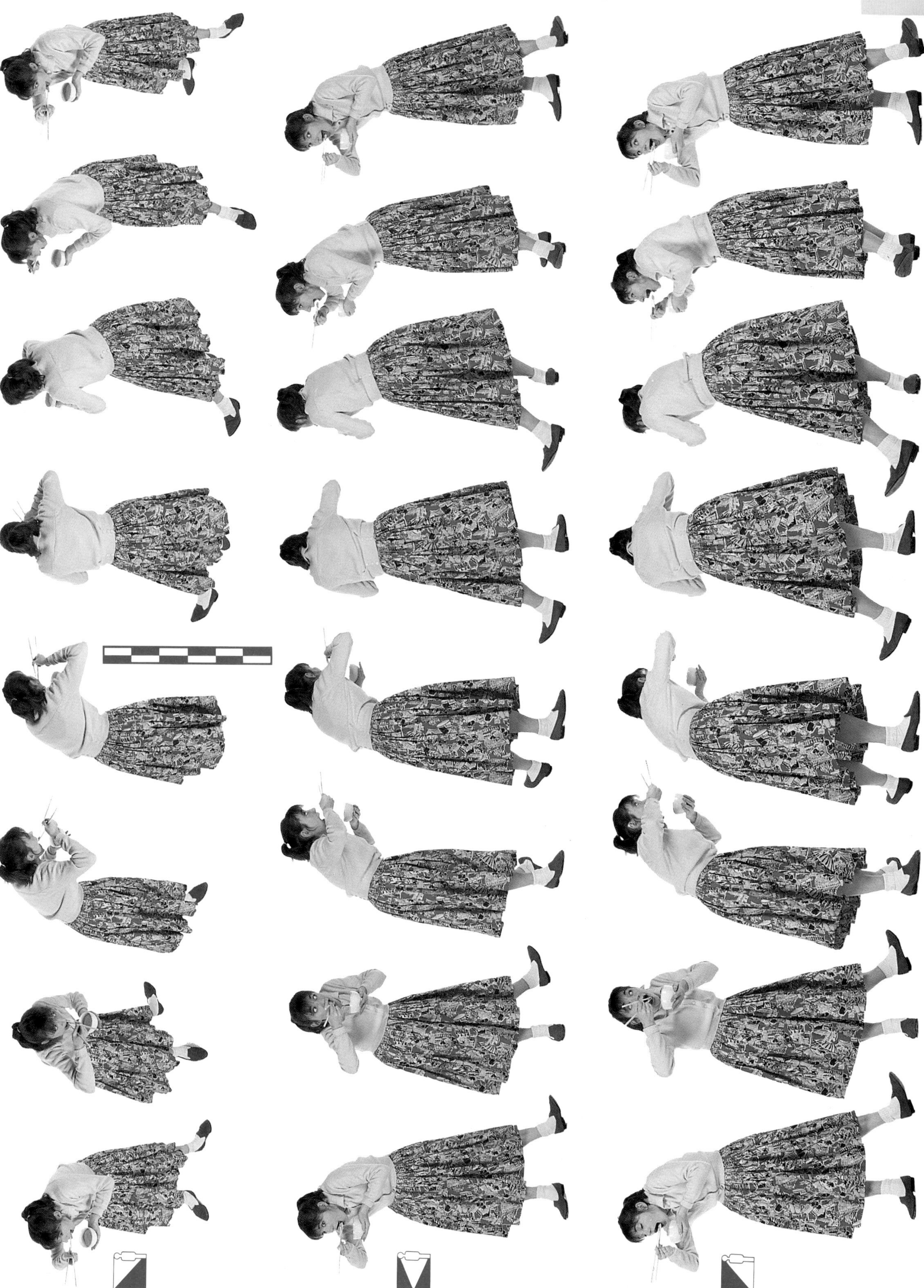

Secretary drinking from teacup and saucer

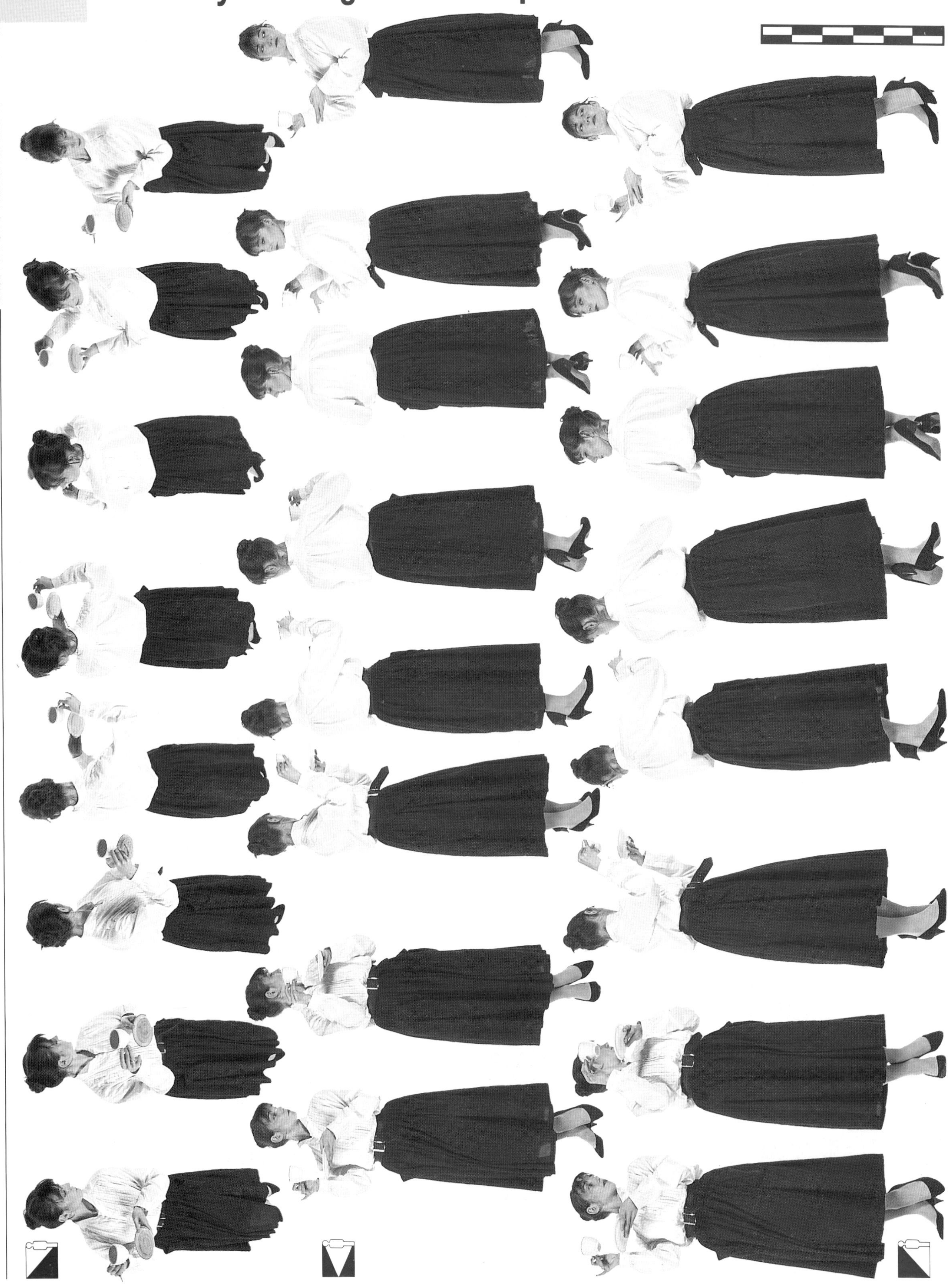

Vicar drinking tea and biscuits

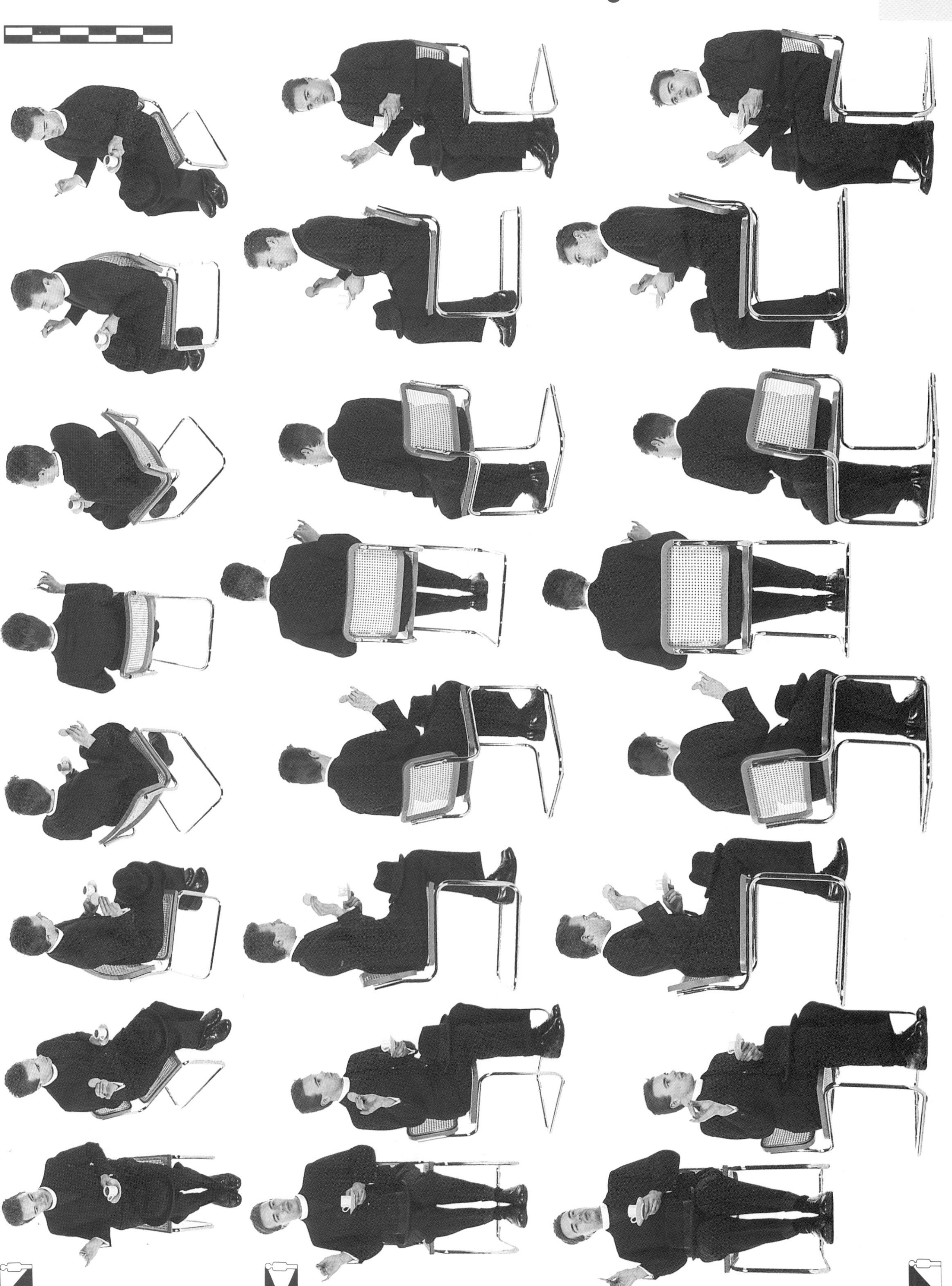

11·07 Drinking wine and smoking

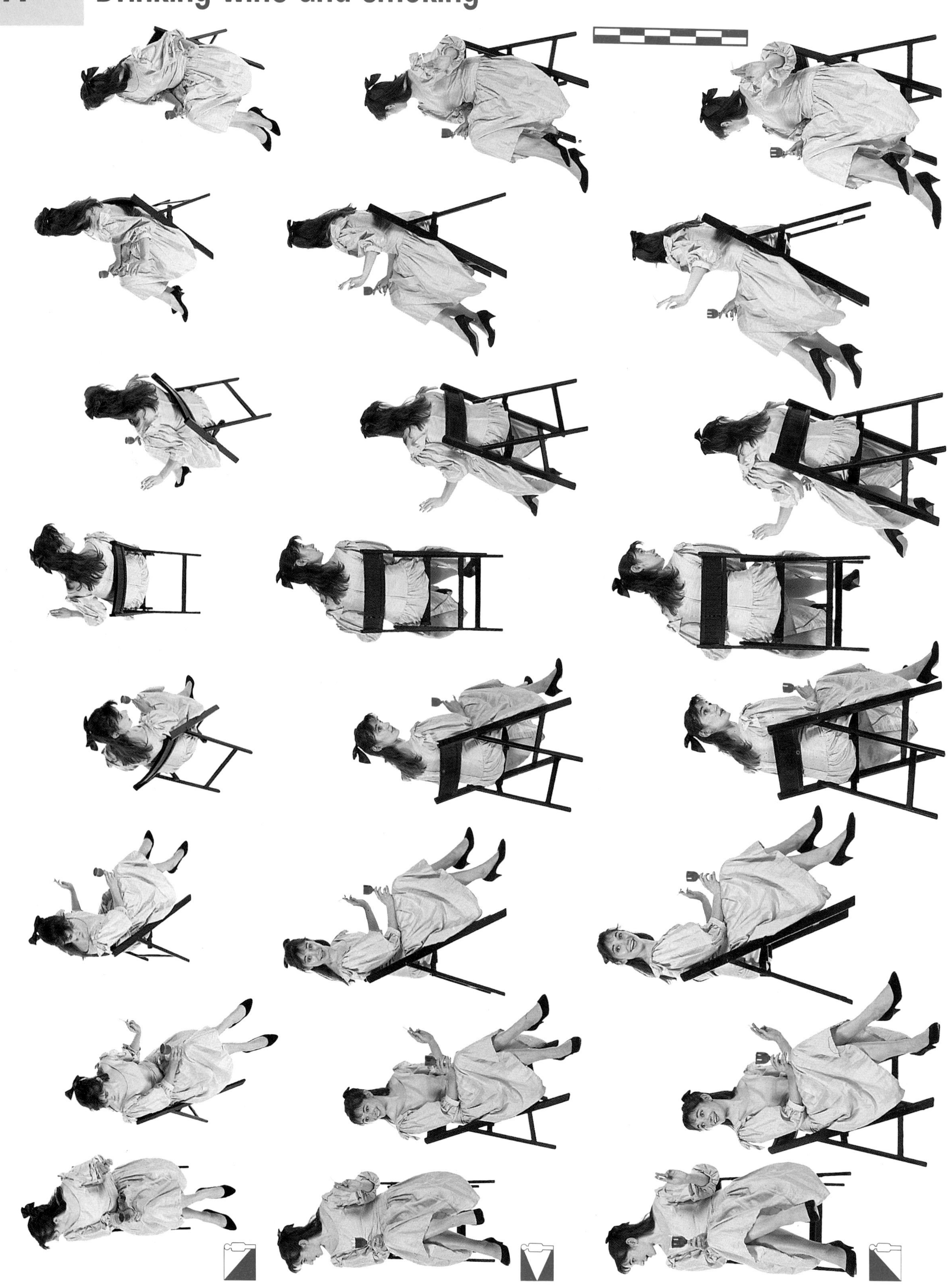

Drinking wine at cocktail party

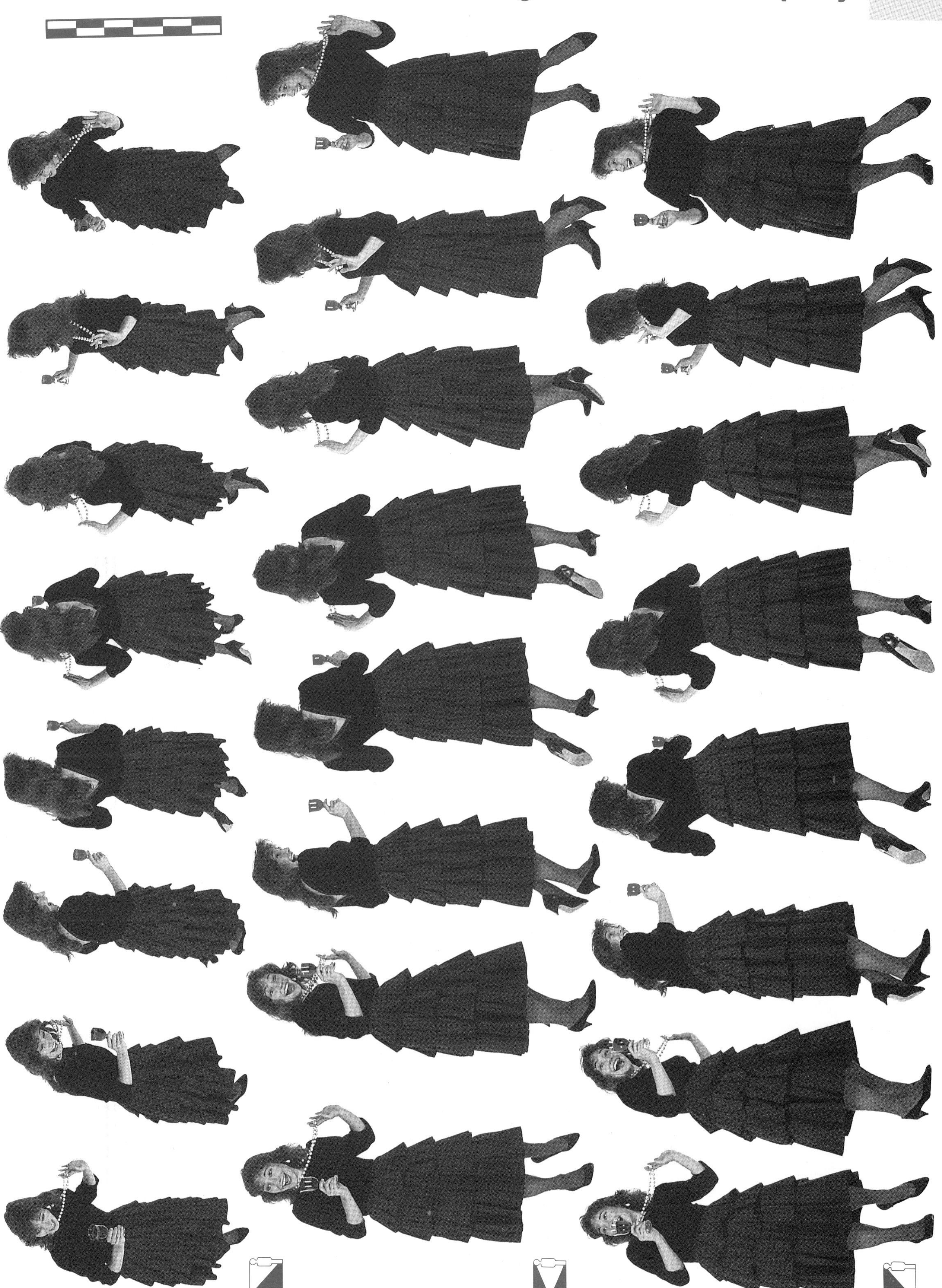

Waiter serving wine

ILLUSTRATOR'S FIGURE REFERENCE MANUAL

11.10 Waitress with tray

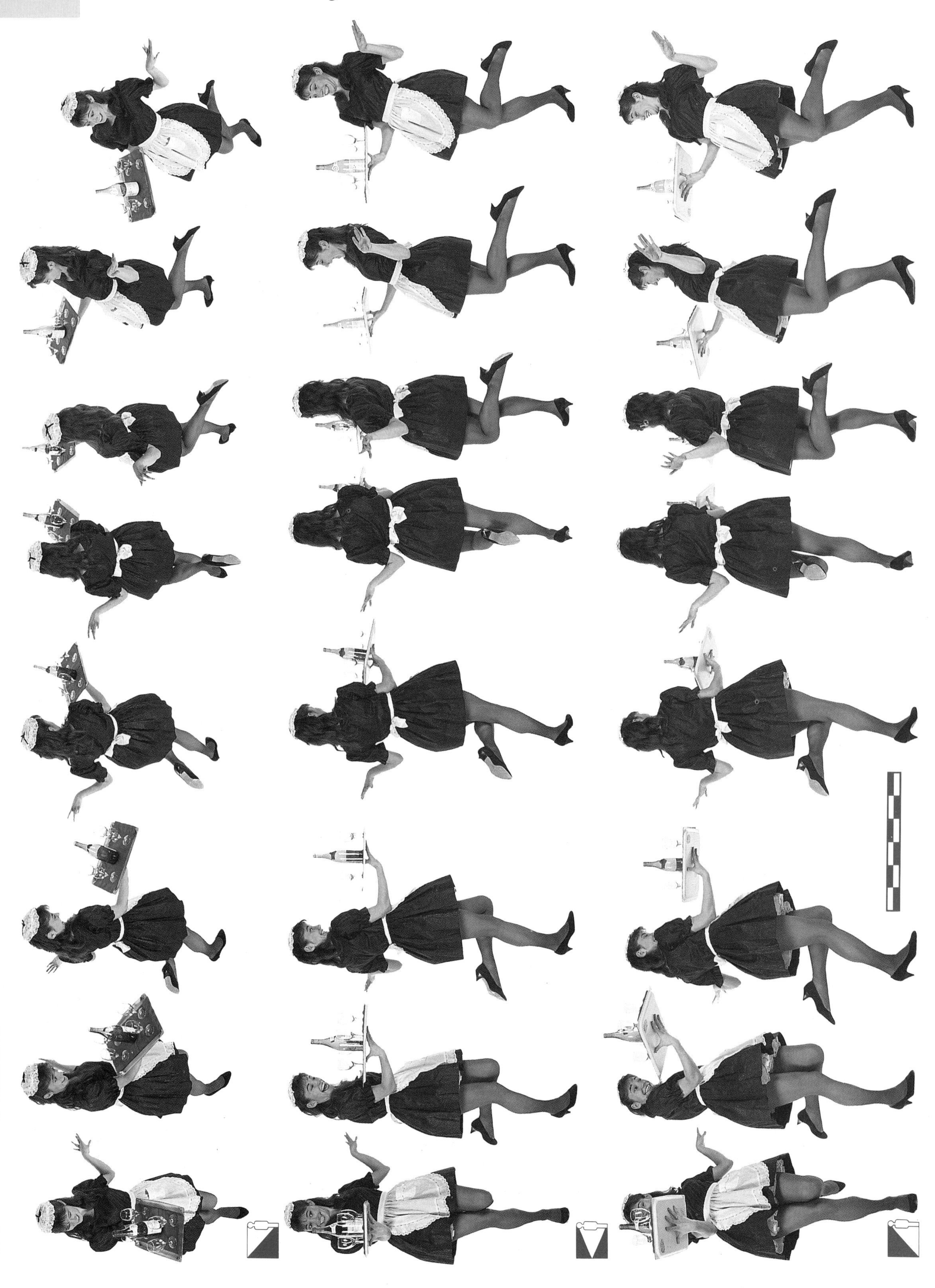

Disco dancing

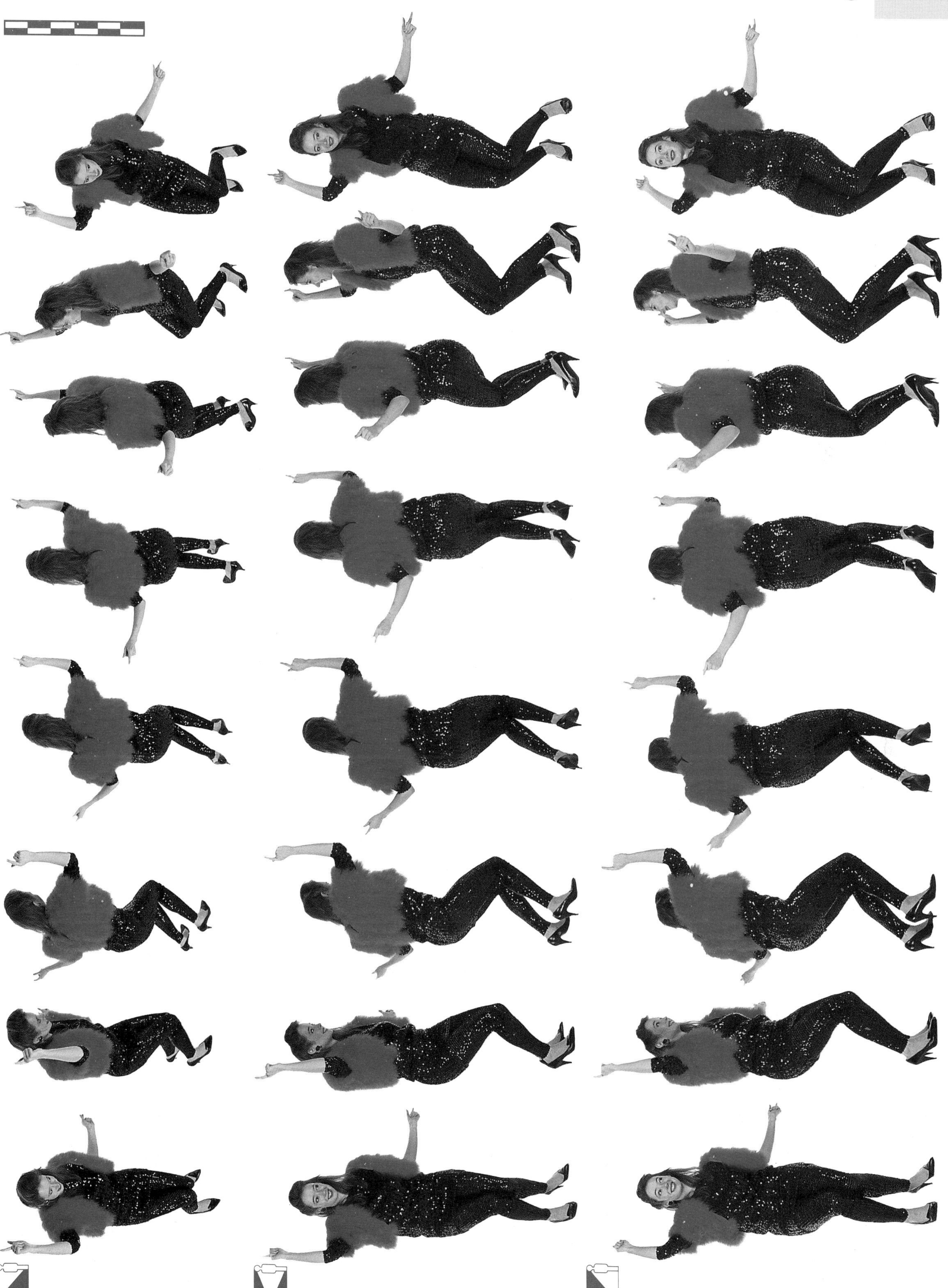

12·02 Rock and roll dancing

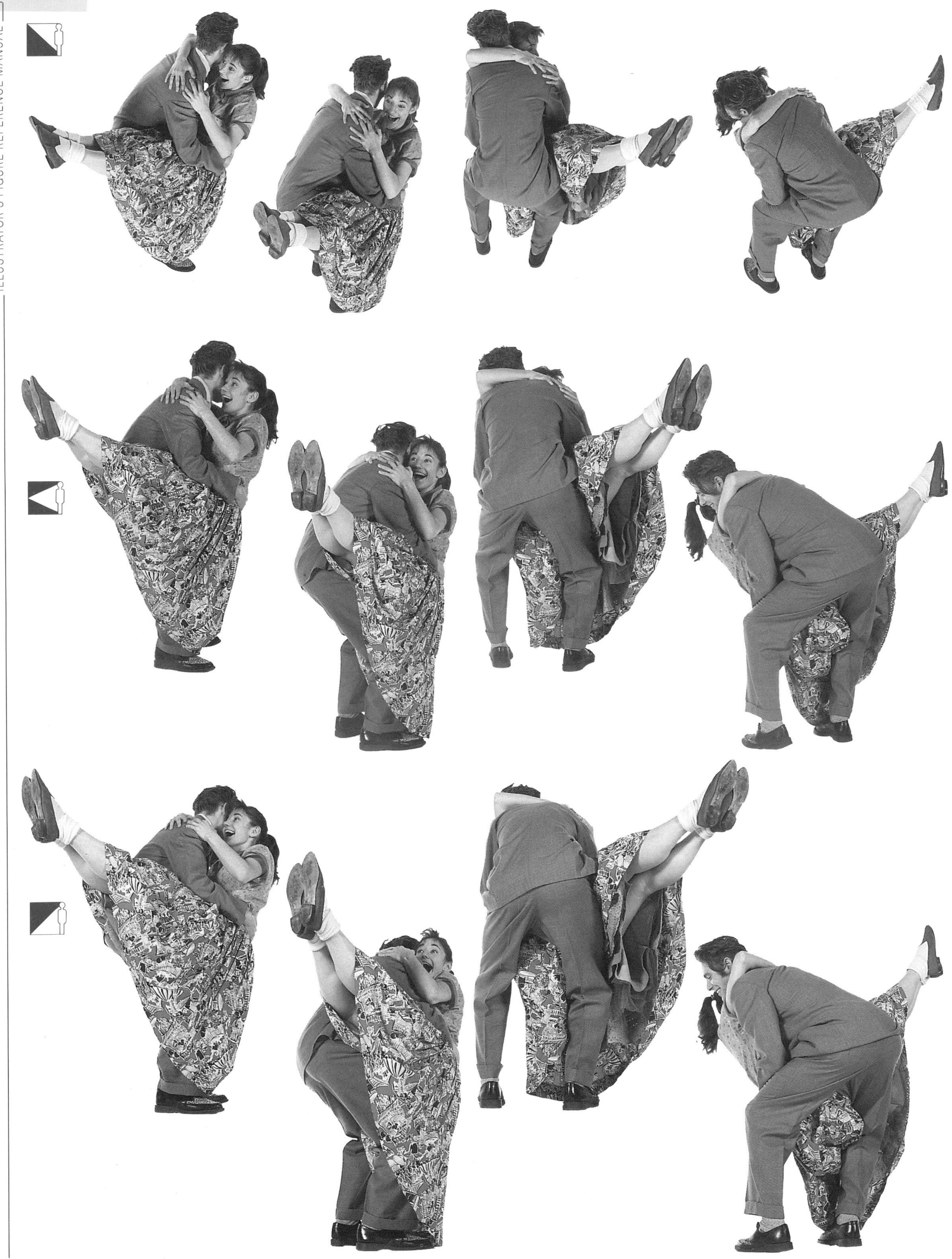

12·03 Ballroom dancing – quickstep

12·04 Ballroom dancing – waltz

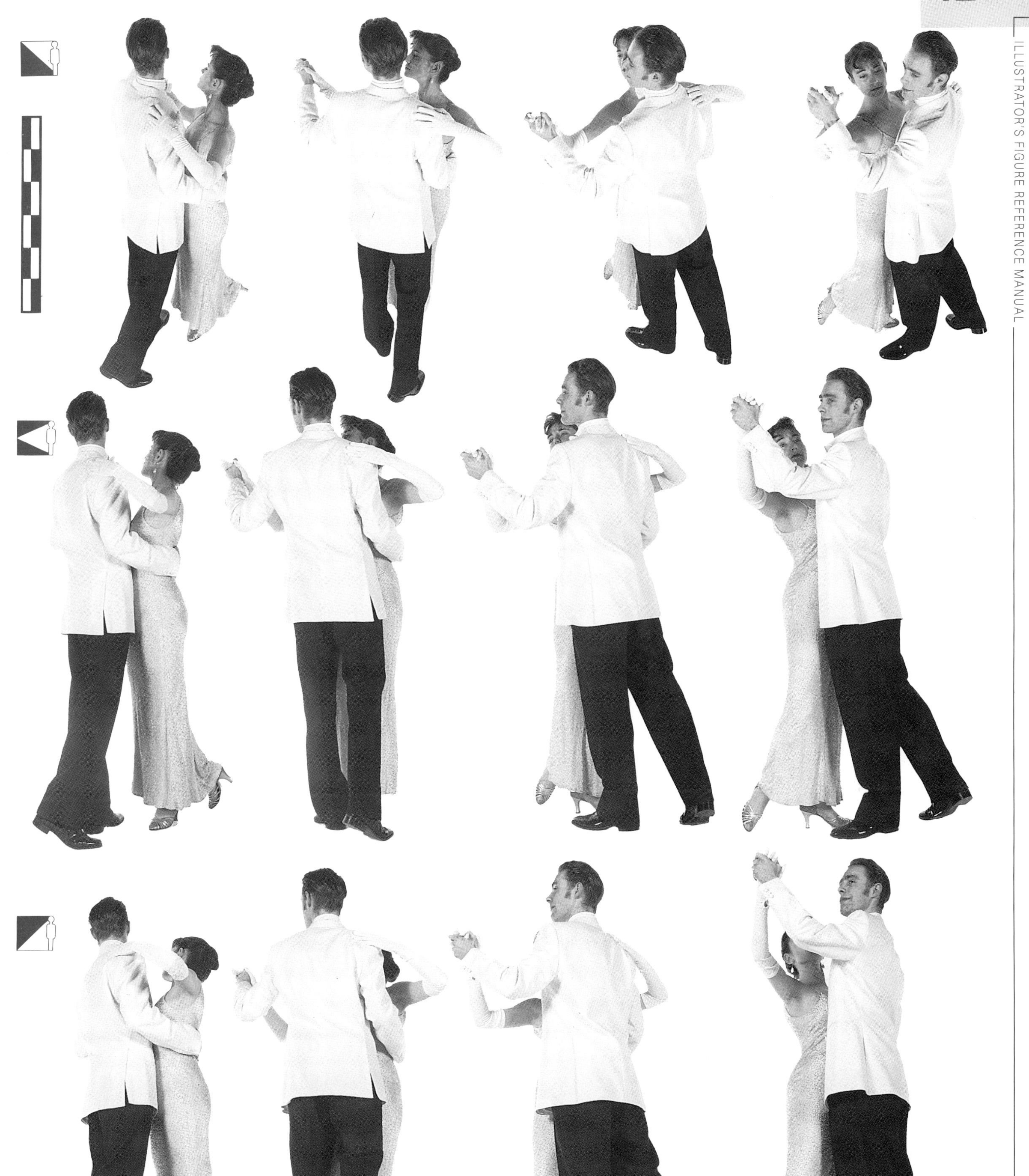

12·05 Ballroom dancing – tango

12·06 Conducting – vivace

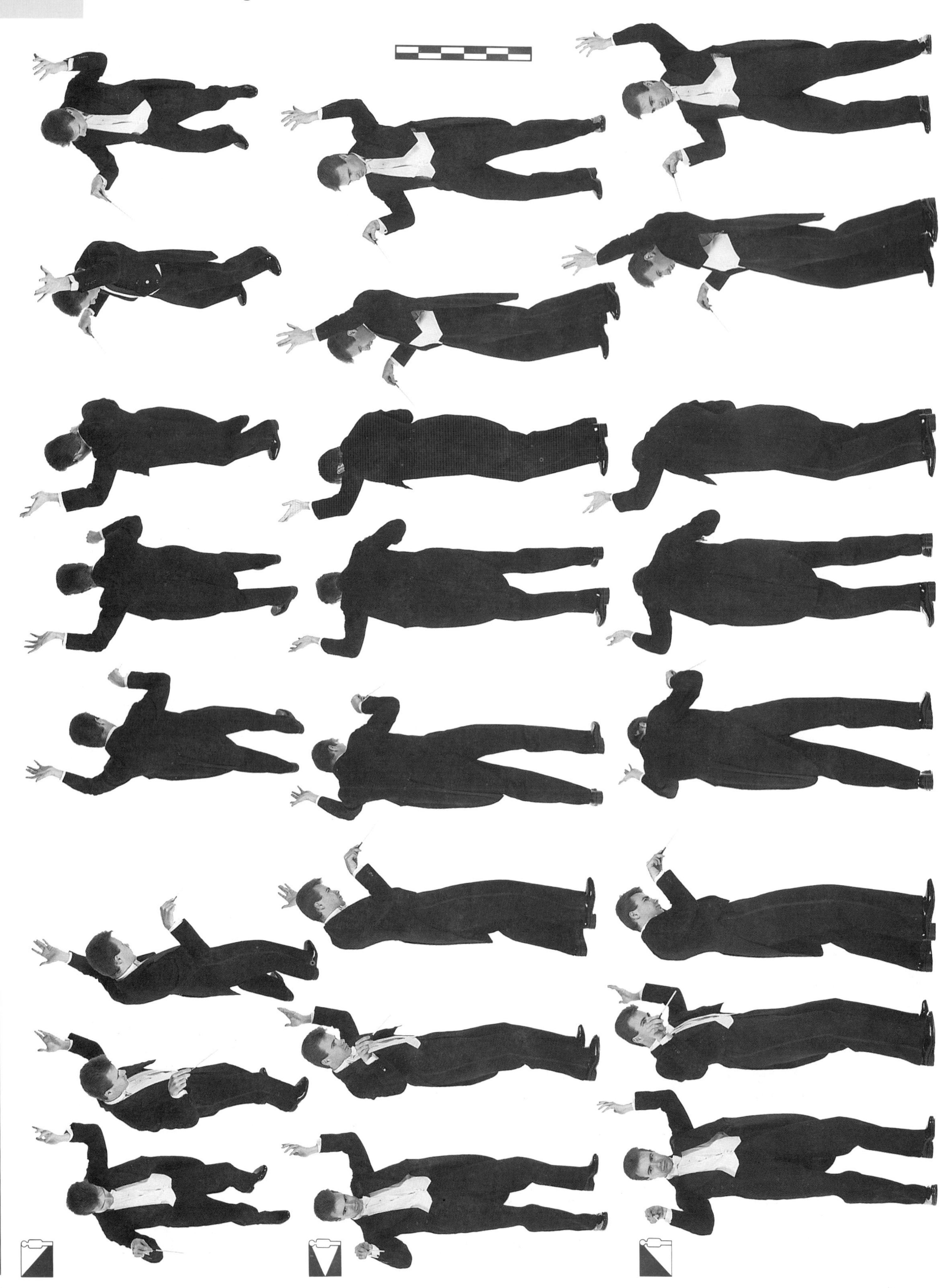

Conducting – adagio

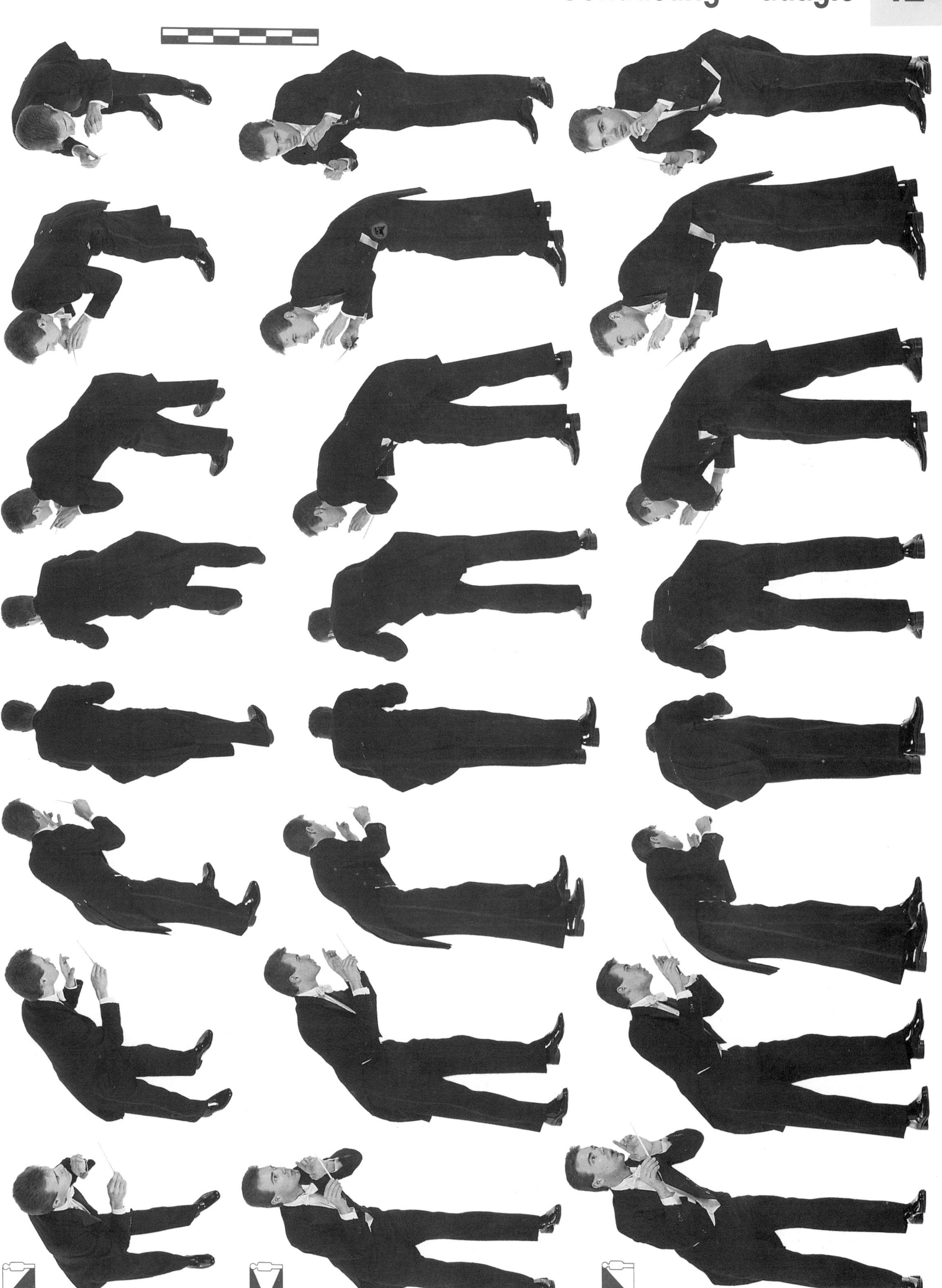

12·08 Playing the clarinet

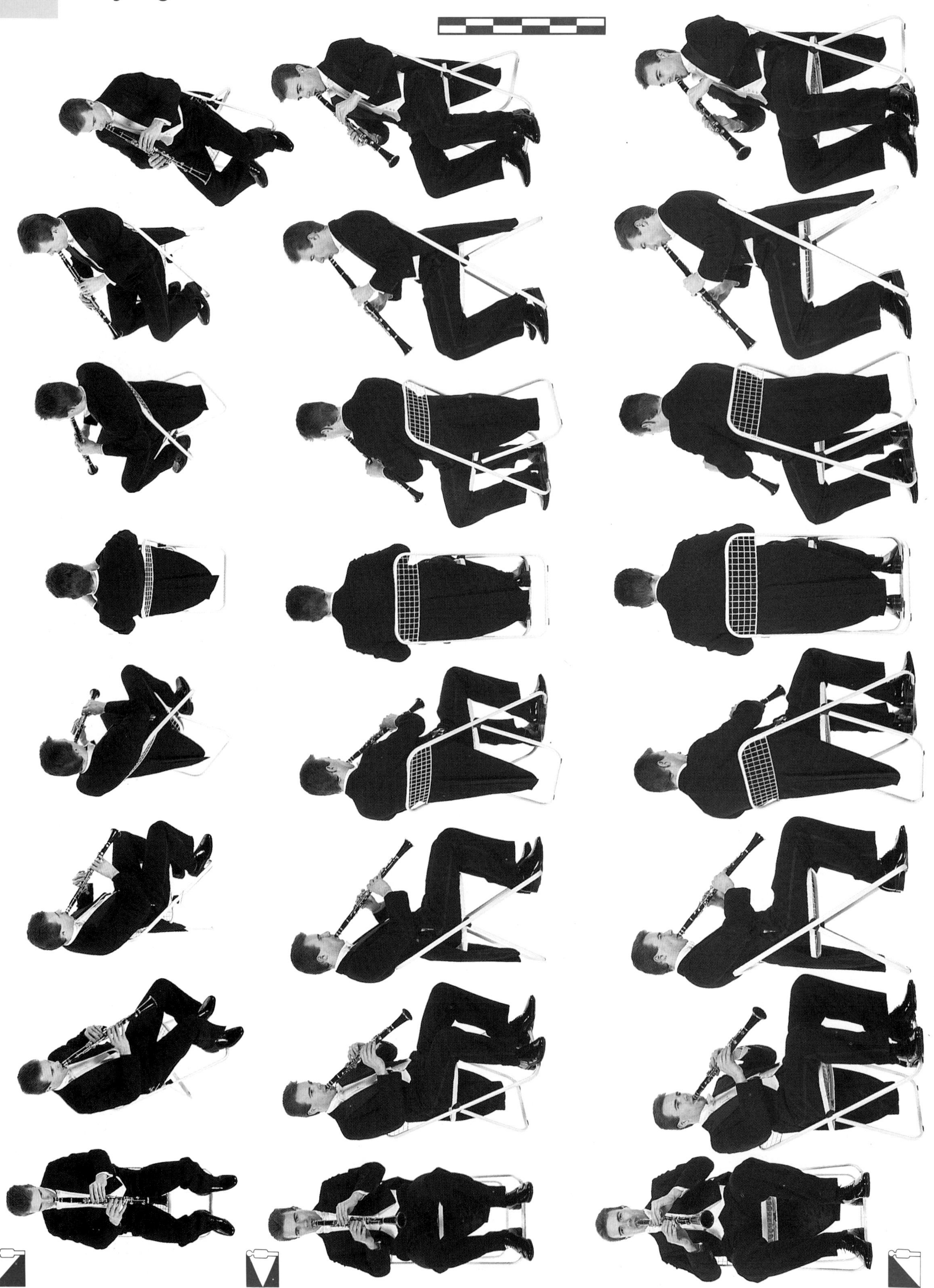

Playing the violin

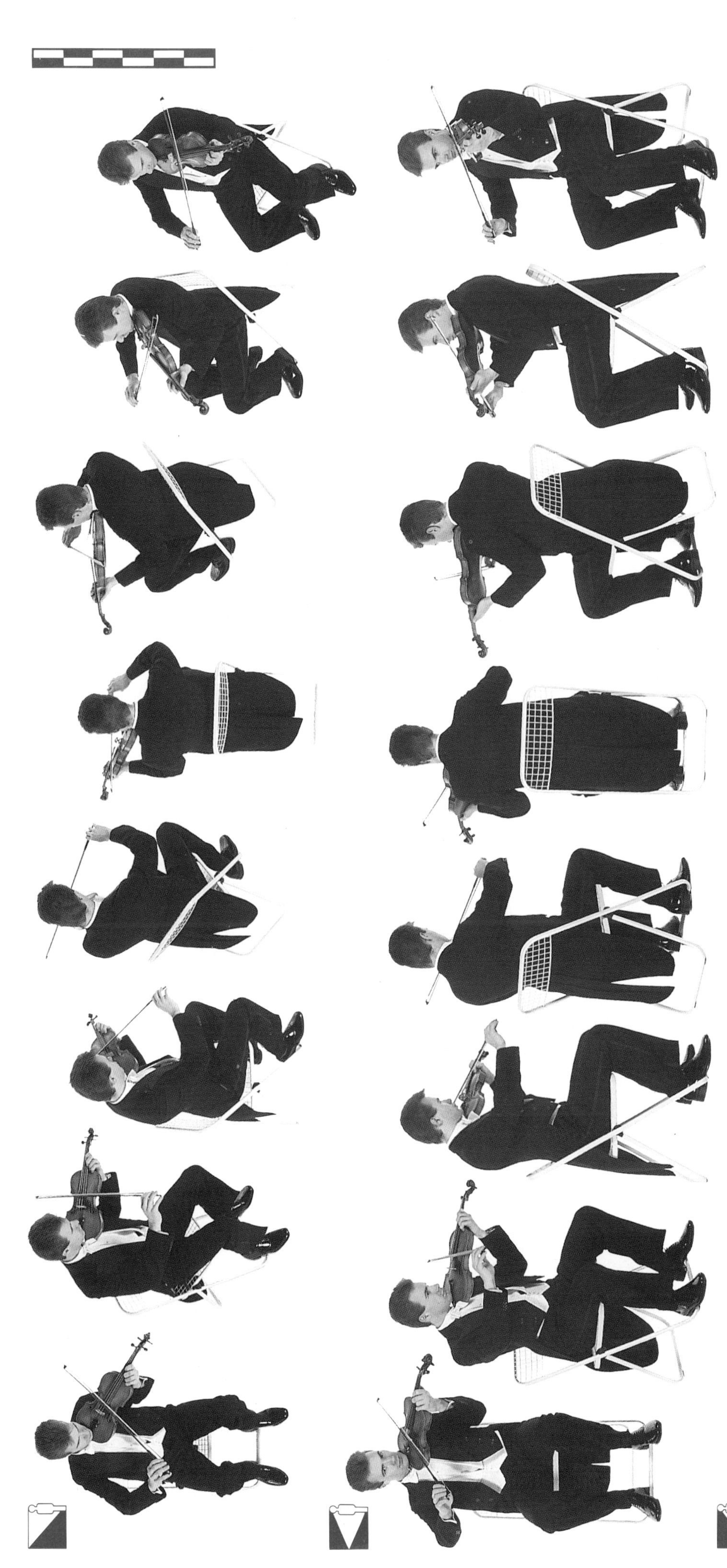

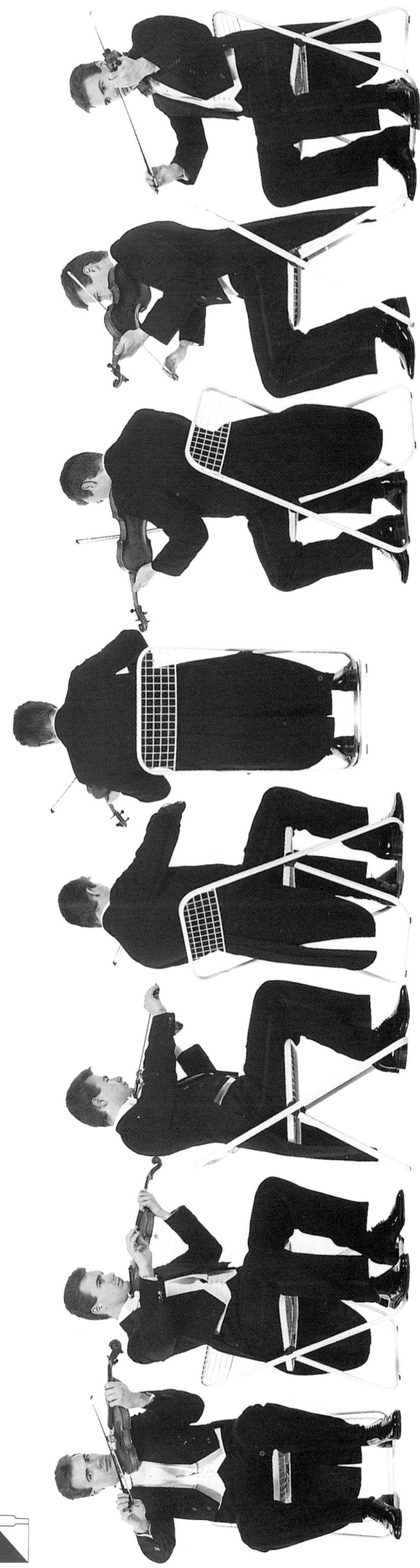

12·10 Playing the double bass

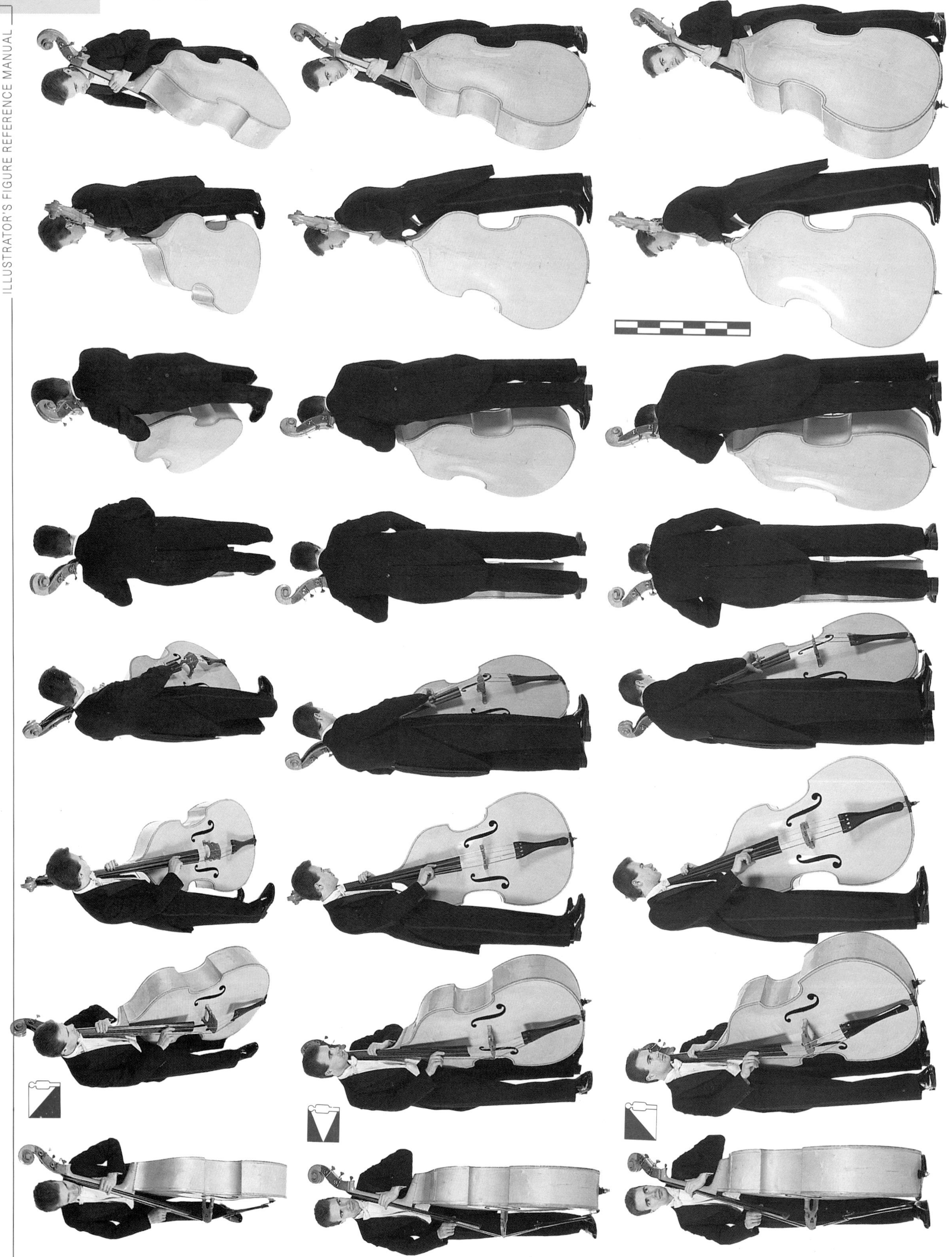

Opera singer

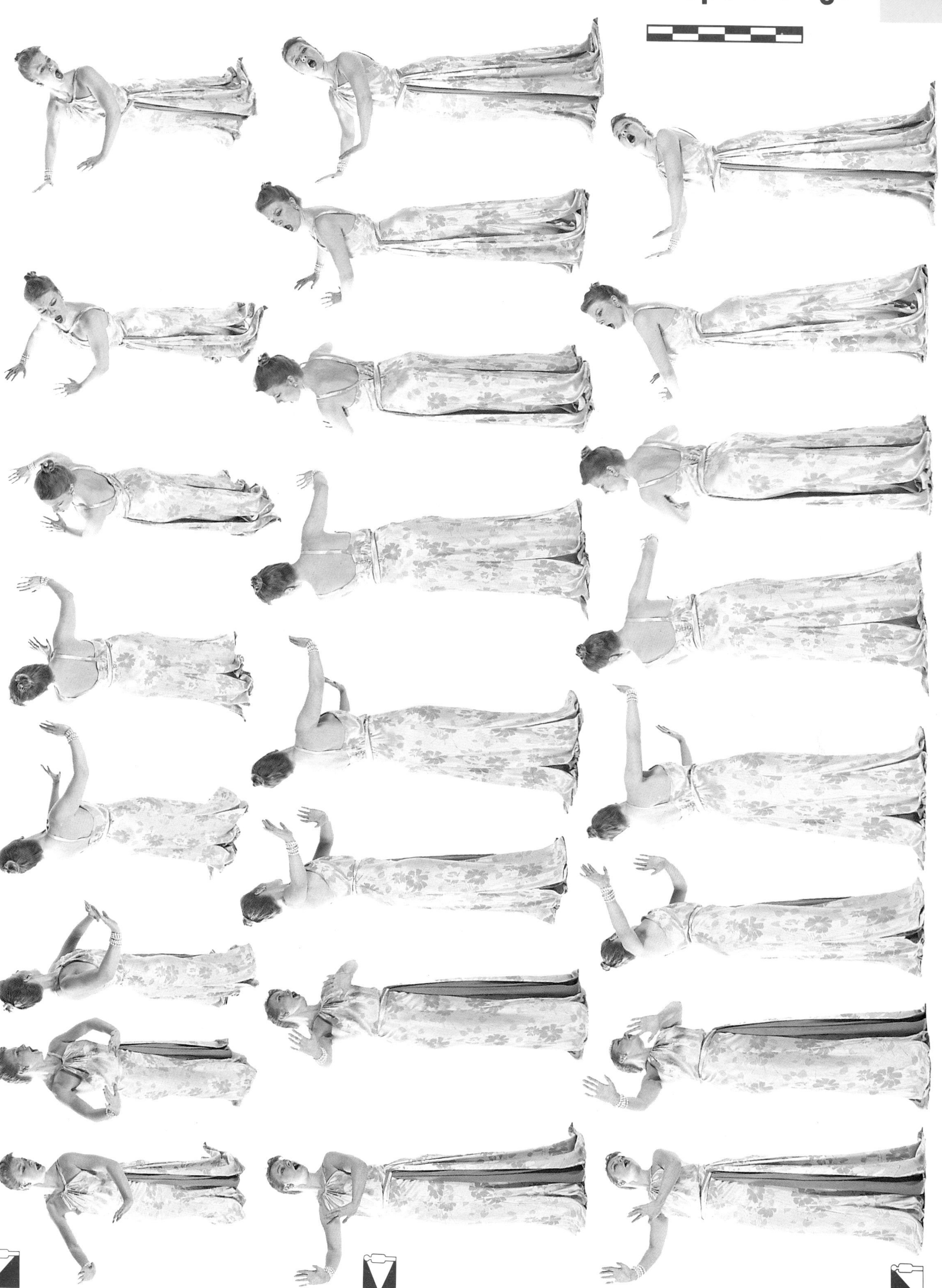

12·12 Country and western singer

Rock singer

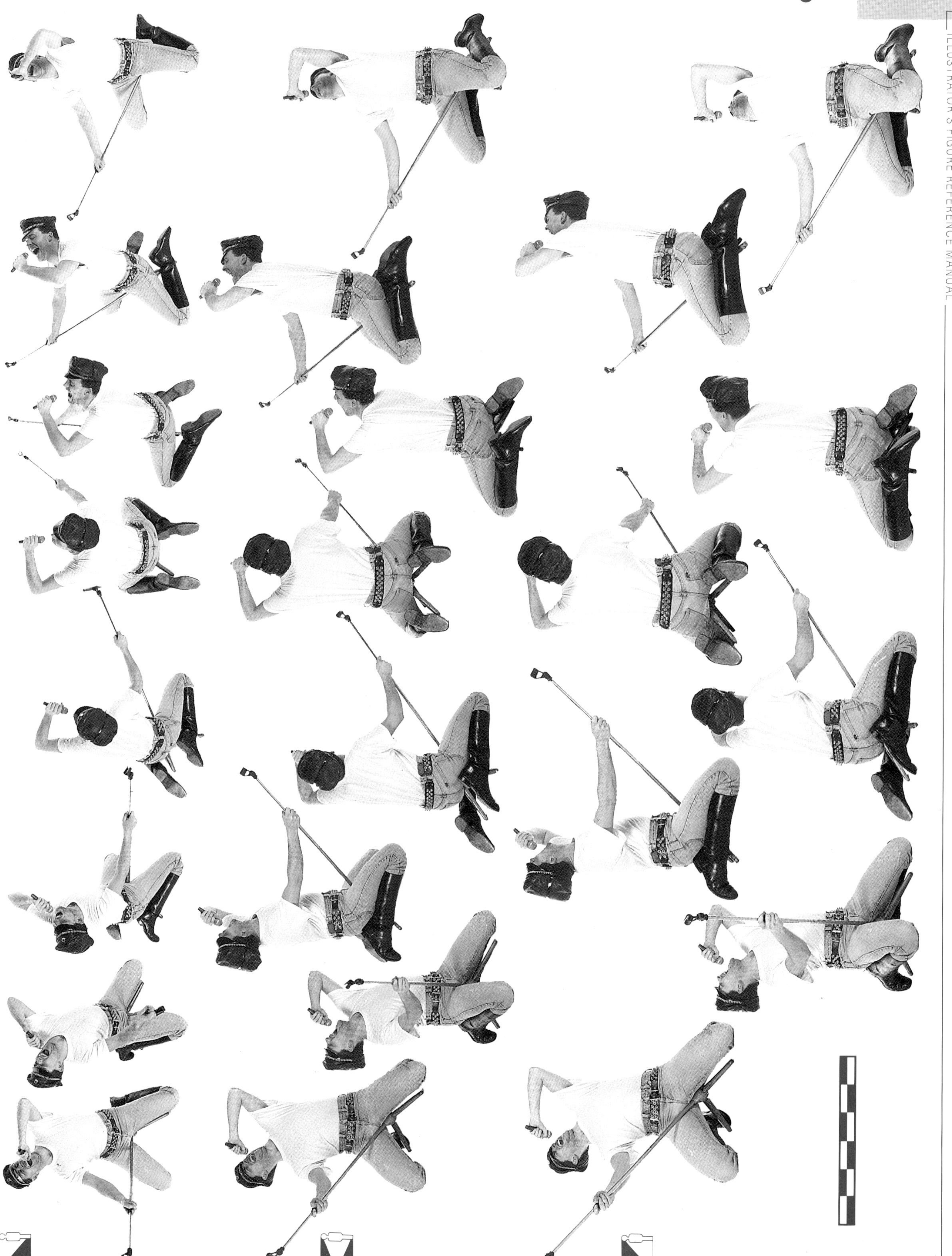

Playing an acoustic guitar

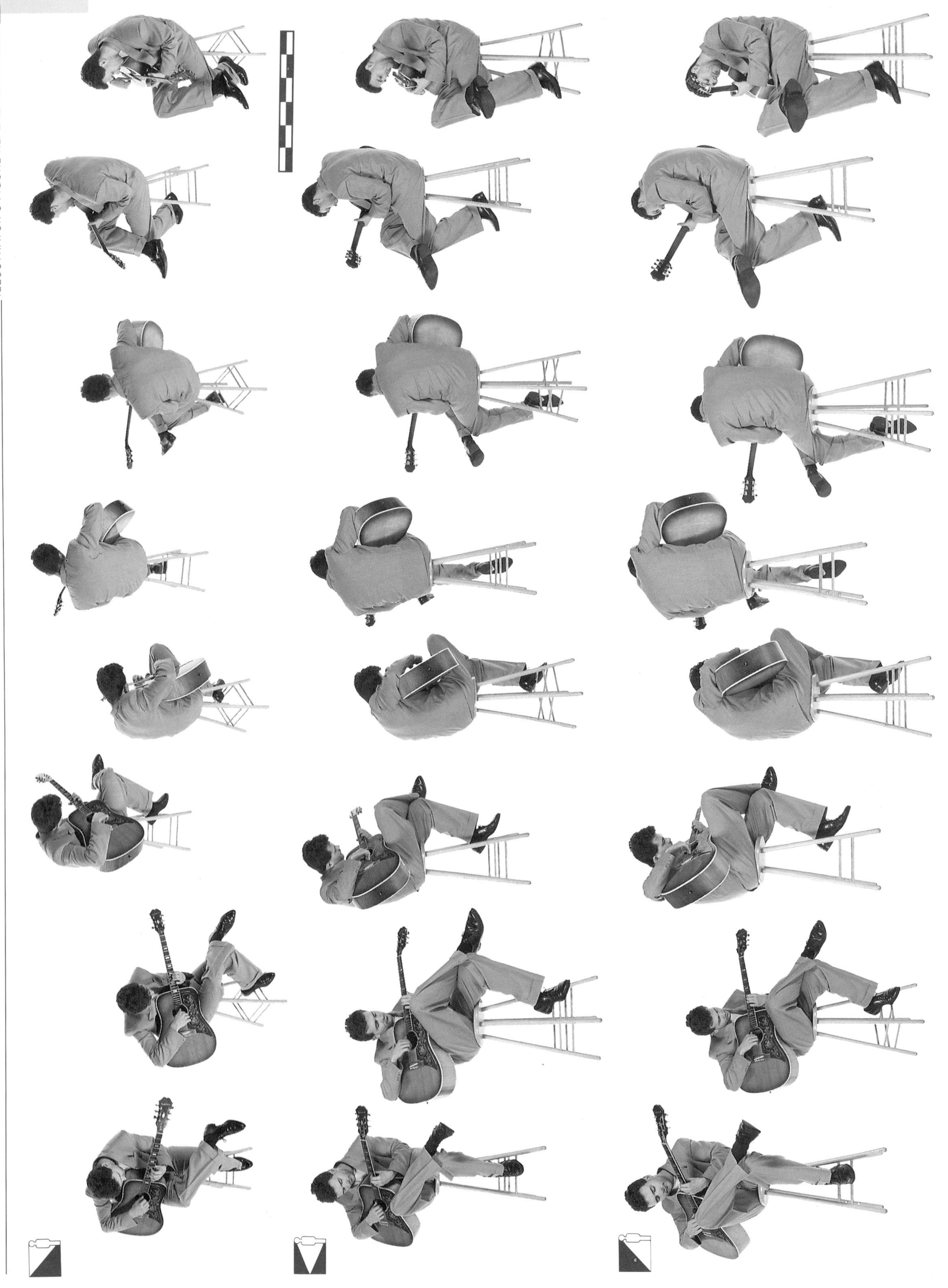

Playing an electric guitar

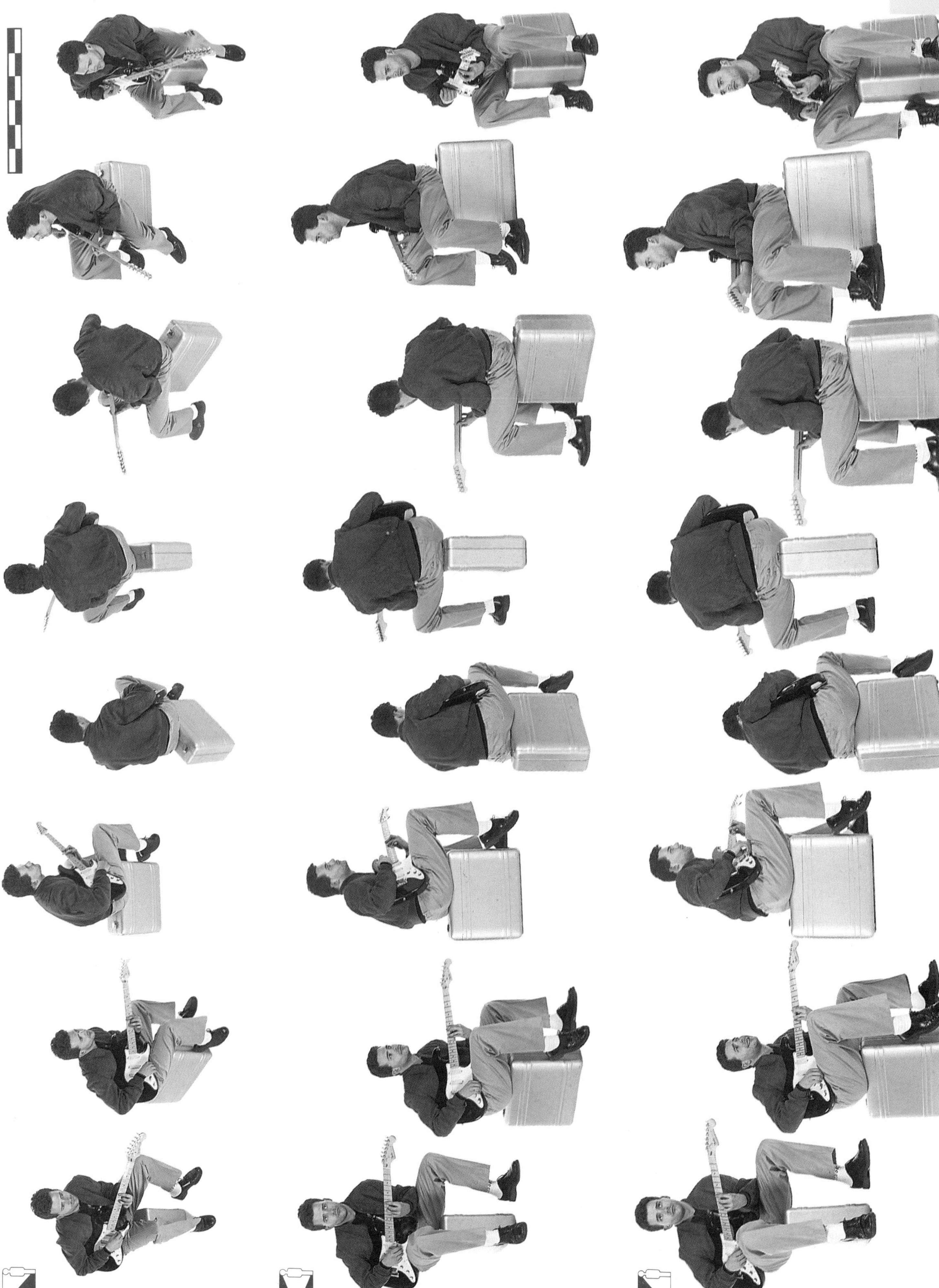

12·16 Playing an electric piano

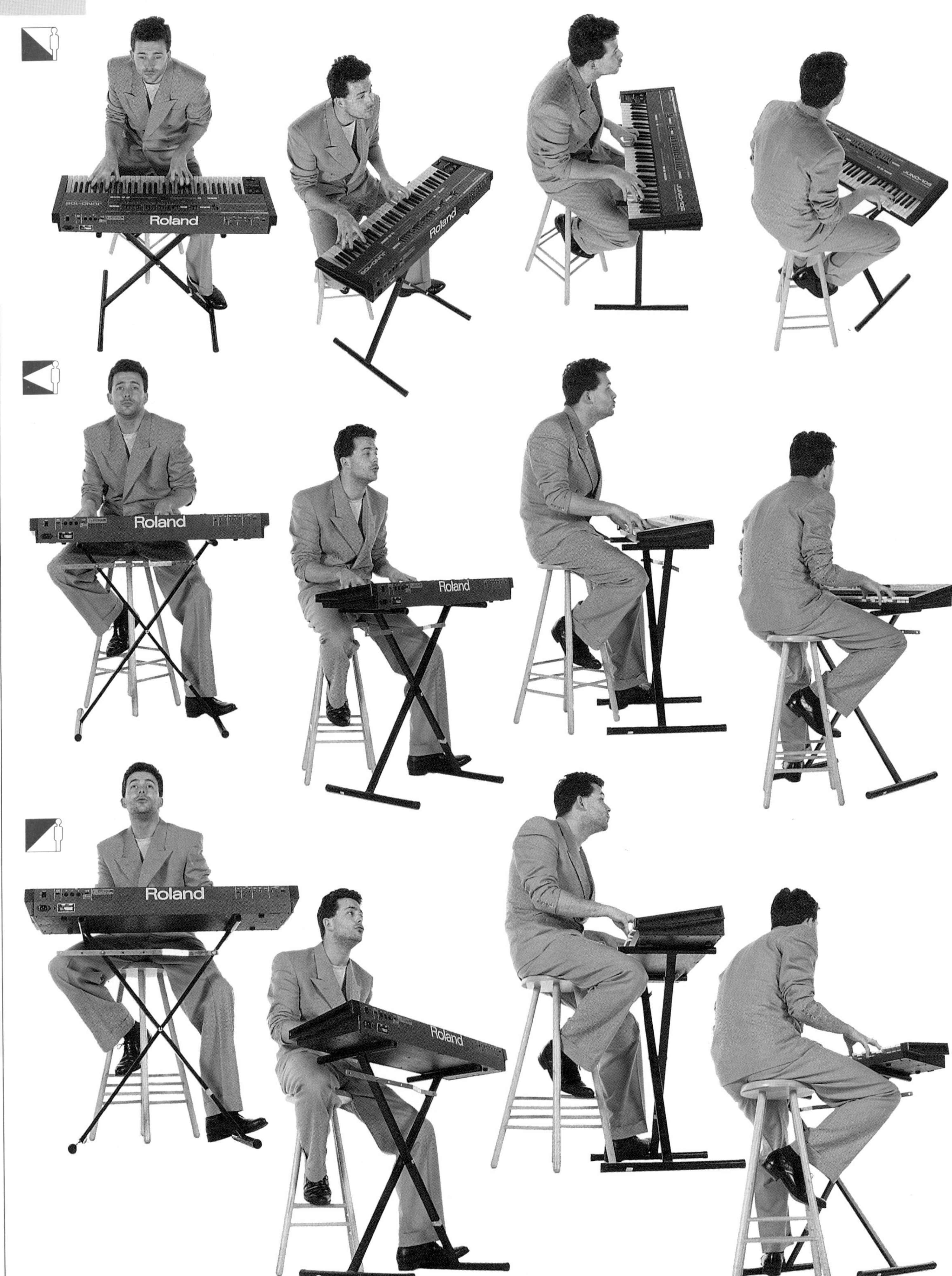

Roland
Roland
Roland

12·17 Jazz trumpeter

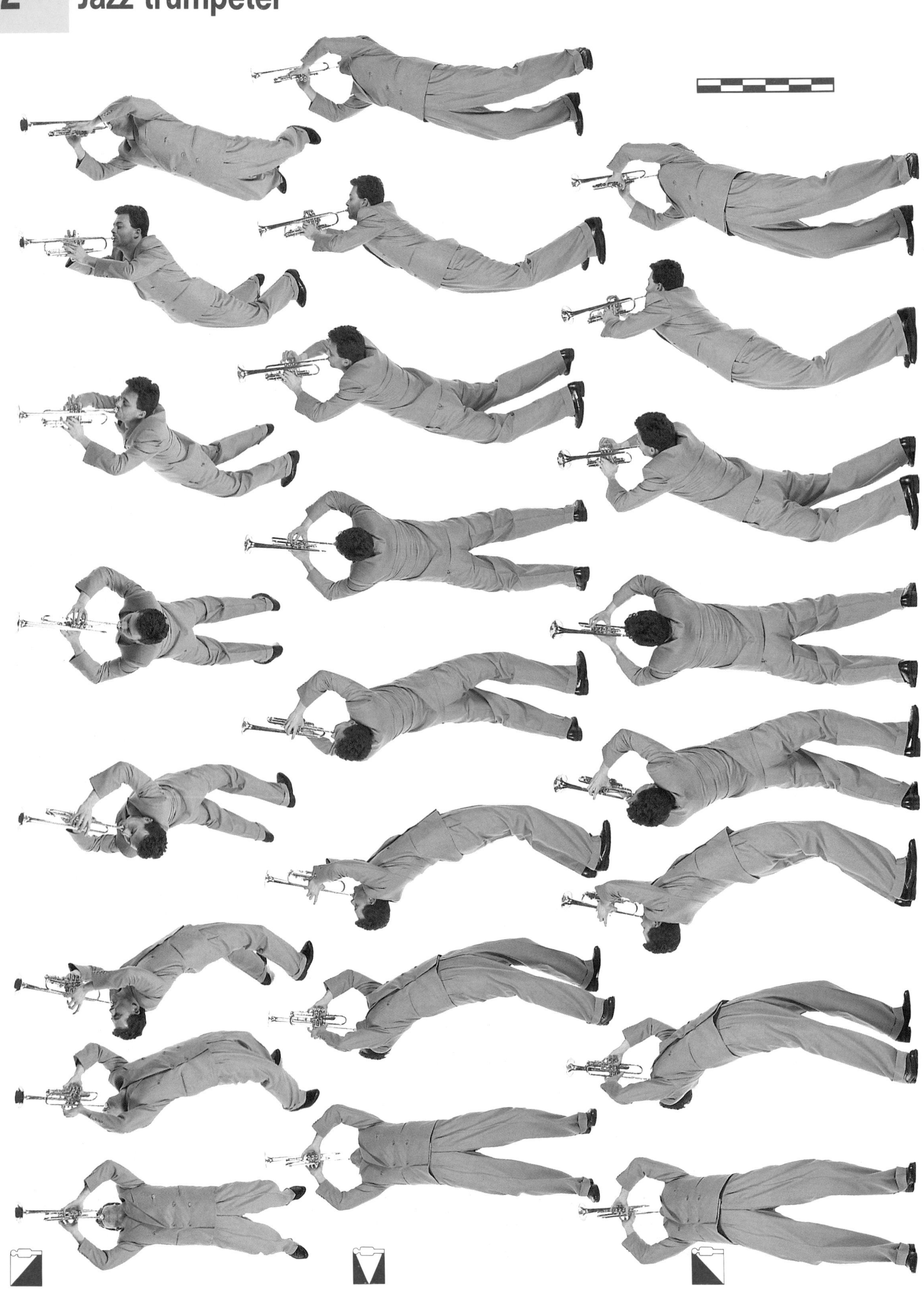

Putting hat on

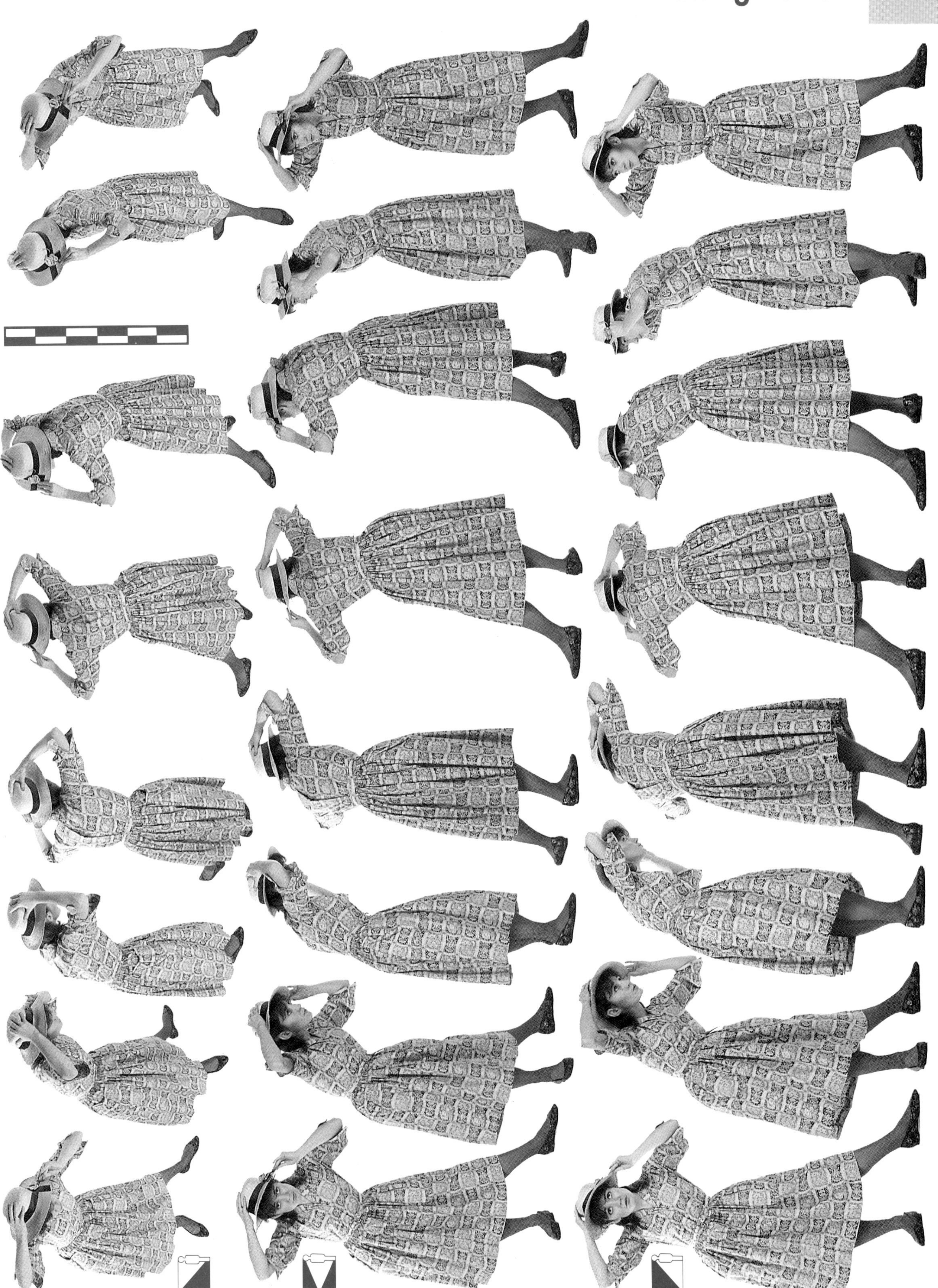

13·02 Putting jacket on

Clipping suspenders

13·04 Putting skirt on

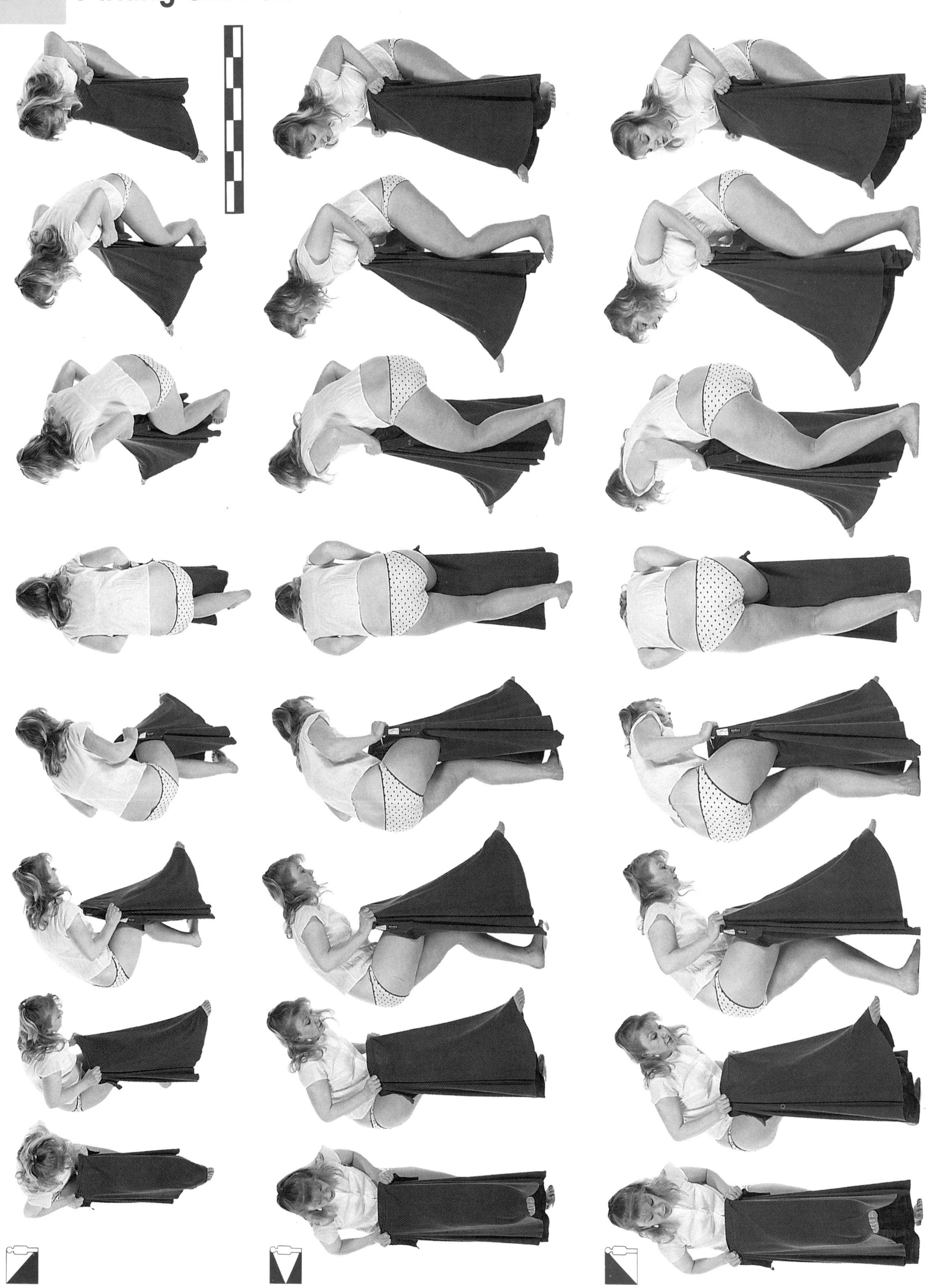

Putting trousers on

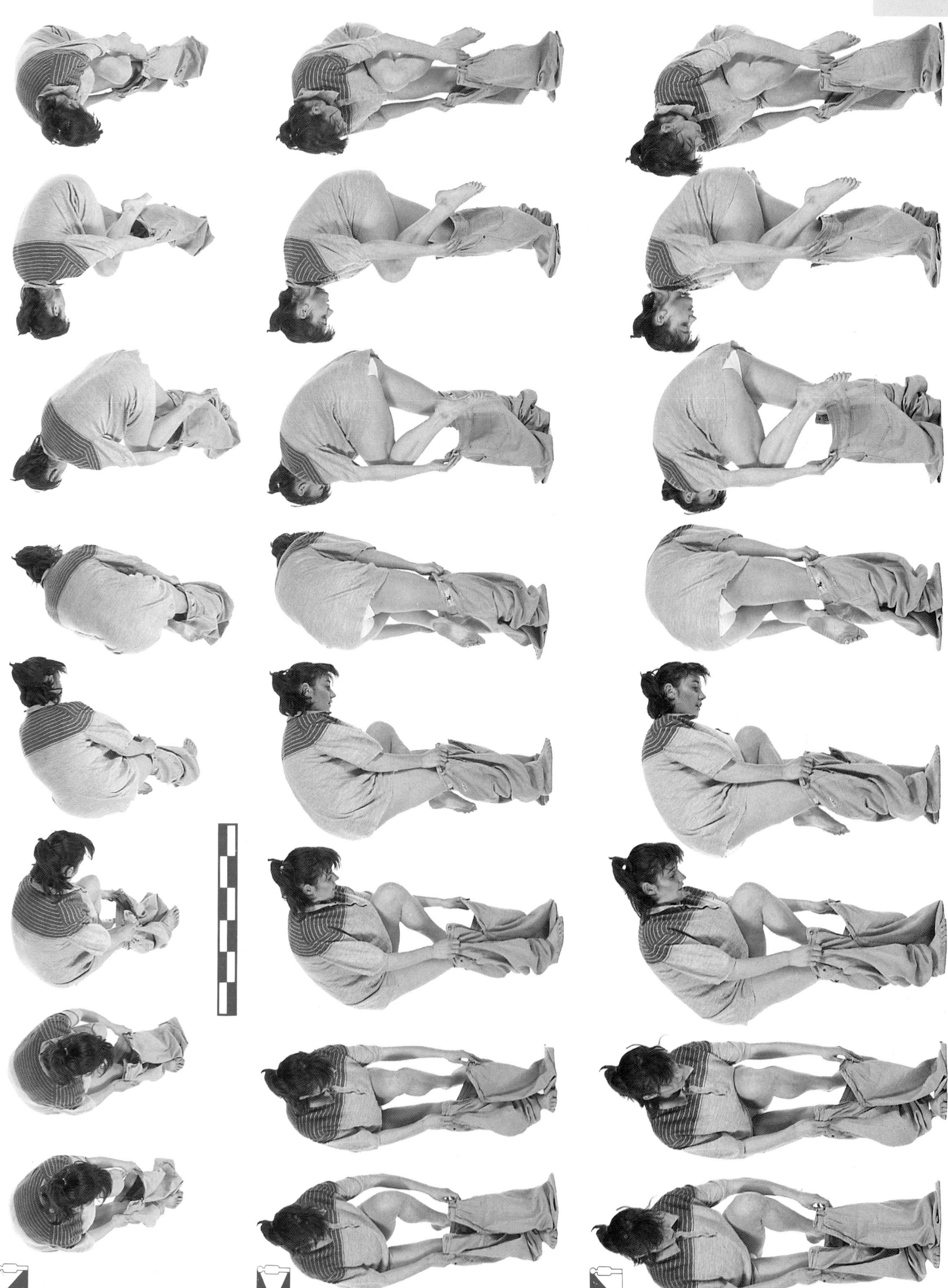

13·06 Putting socks on

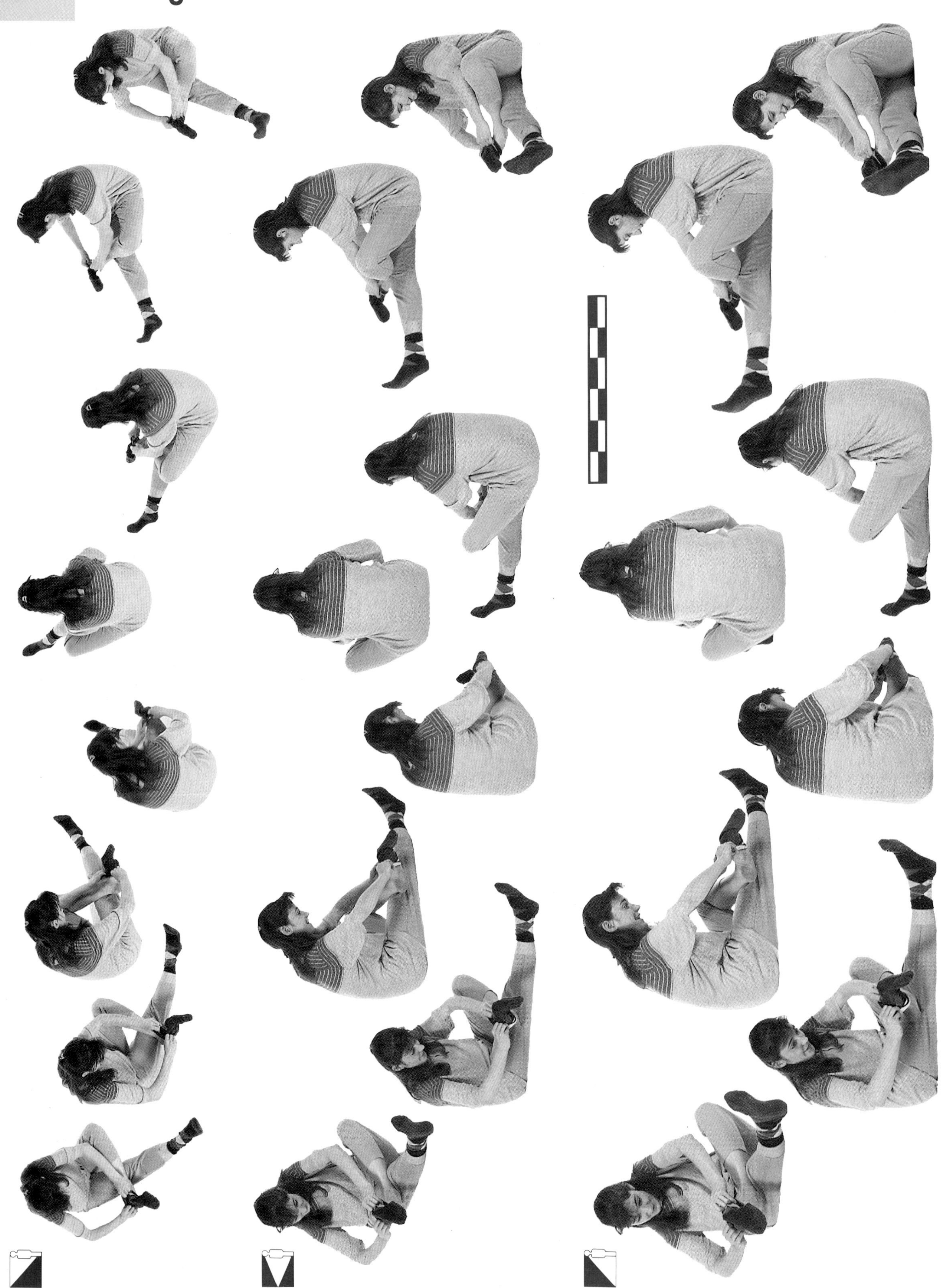

Putting shoes on

13·08 Taking boots off

Taking jumper off

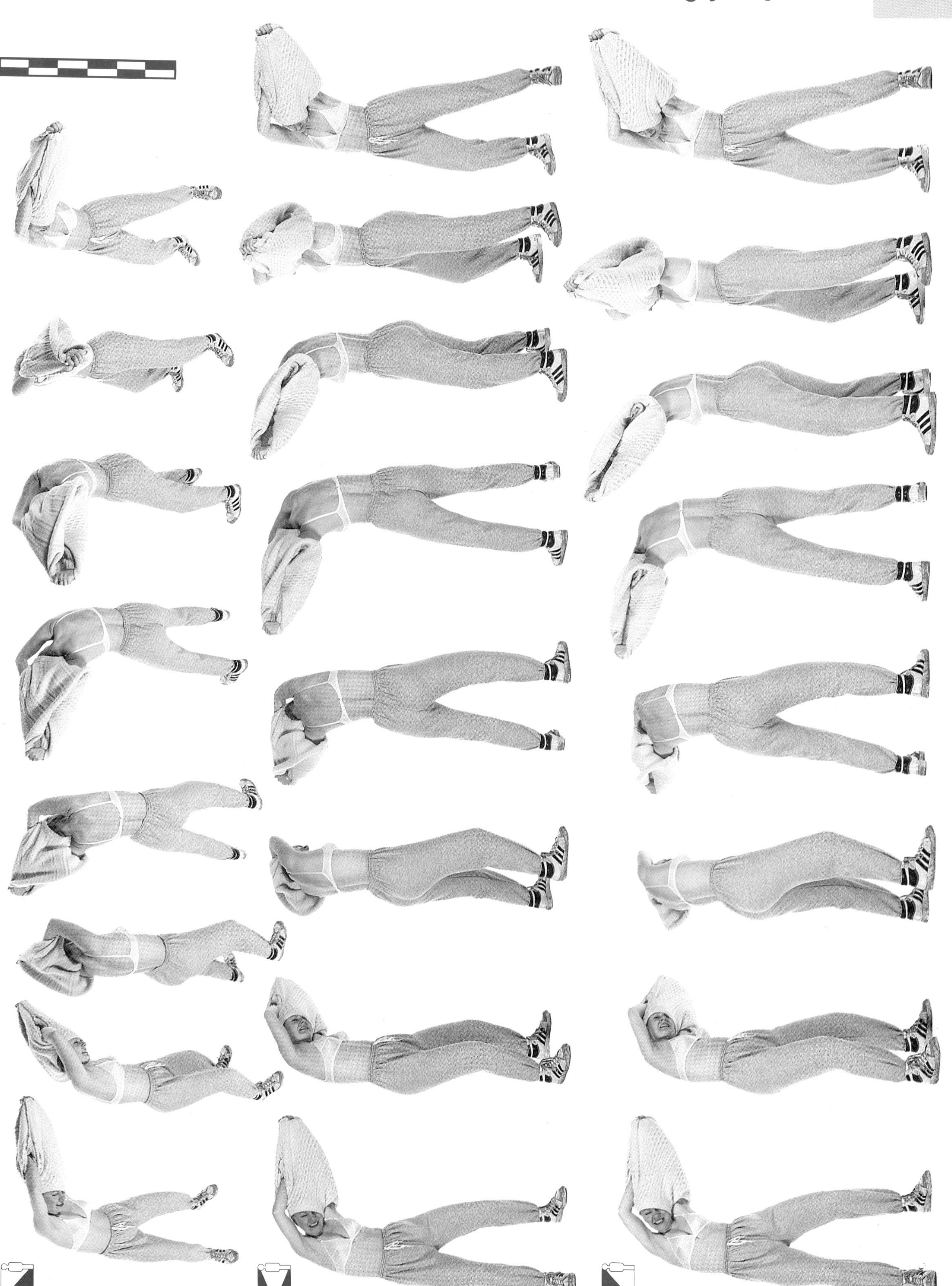

13.10 Clipping brassiere

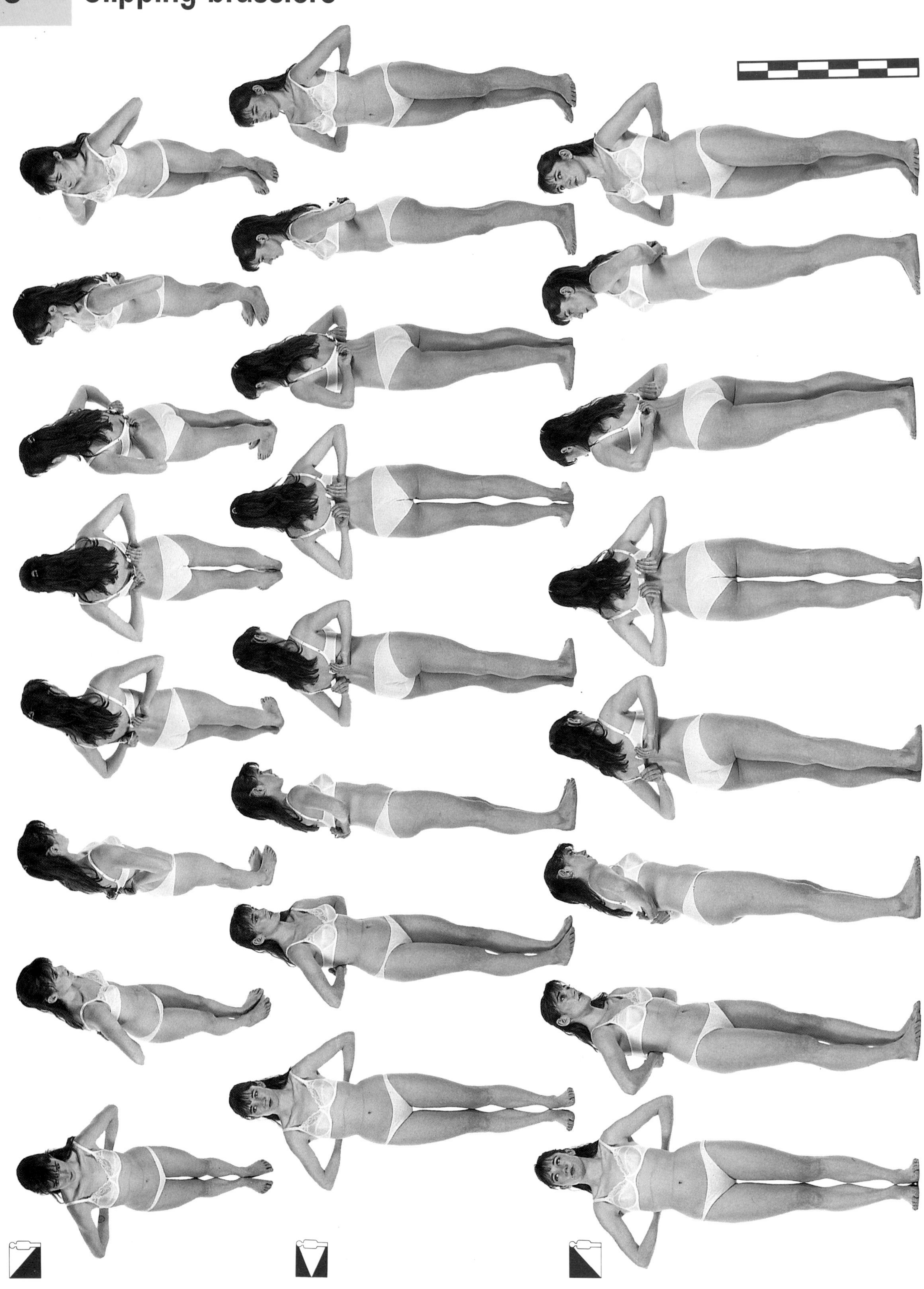

Putting shirt on

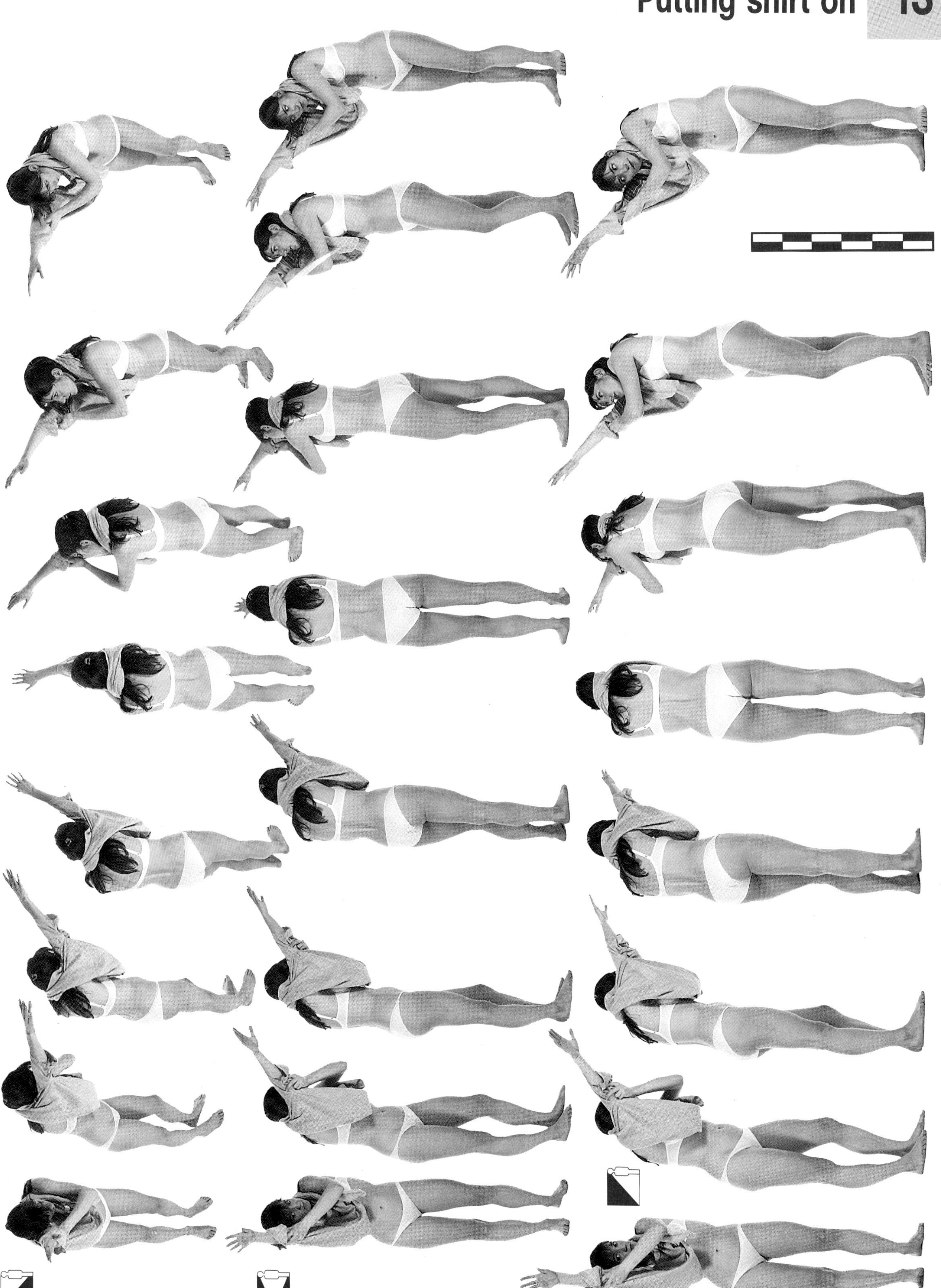

14·01 Drying hair with towel

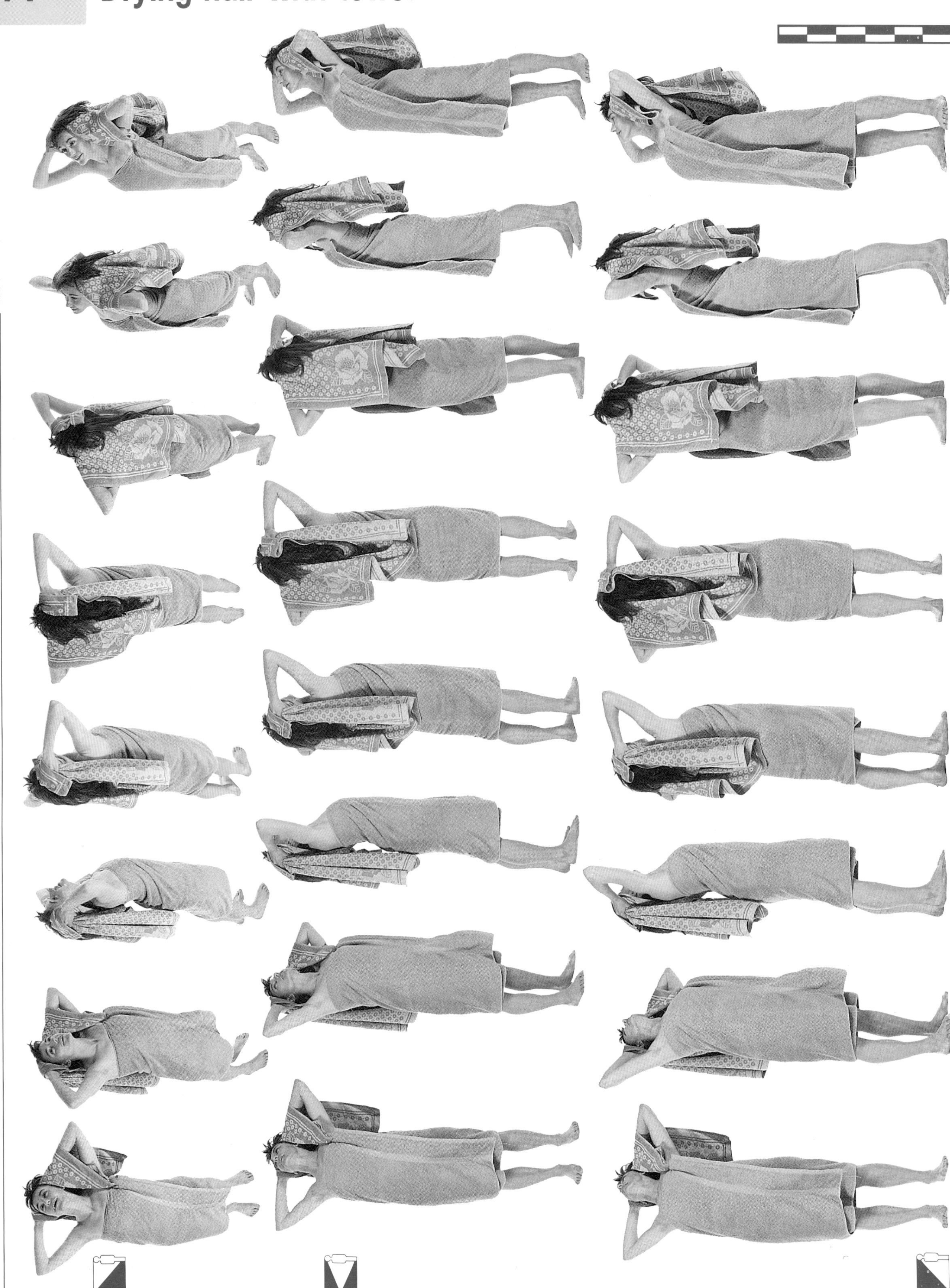

Brushing hair

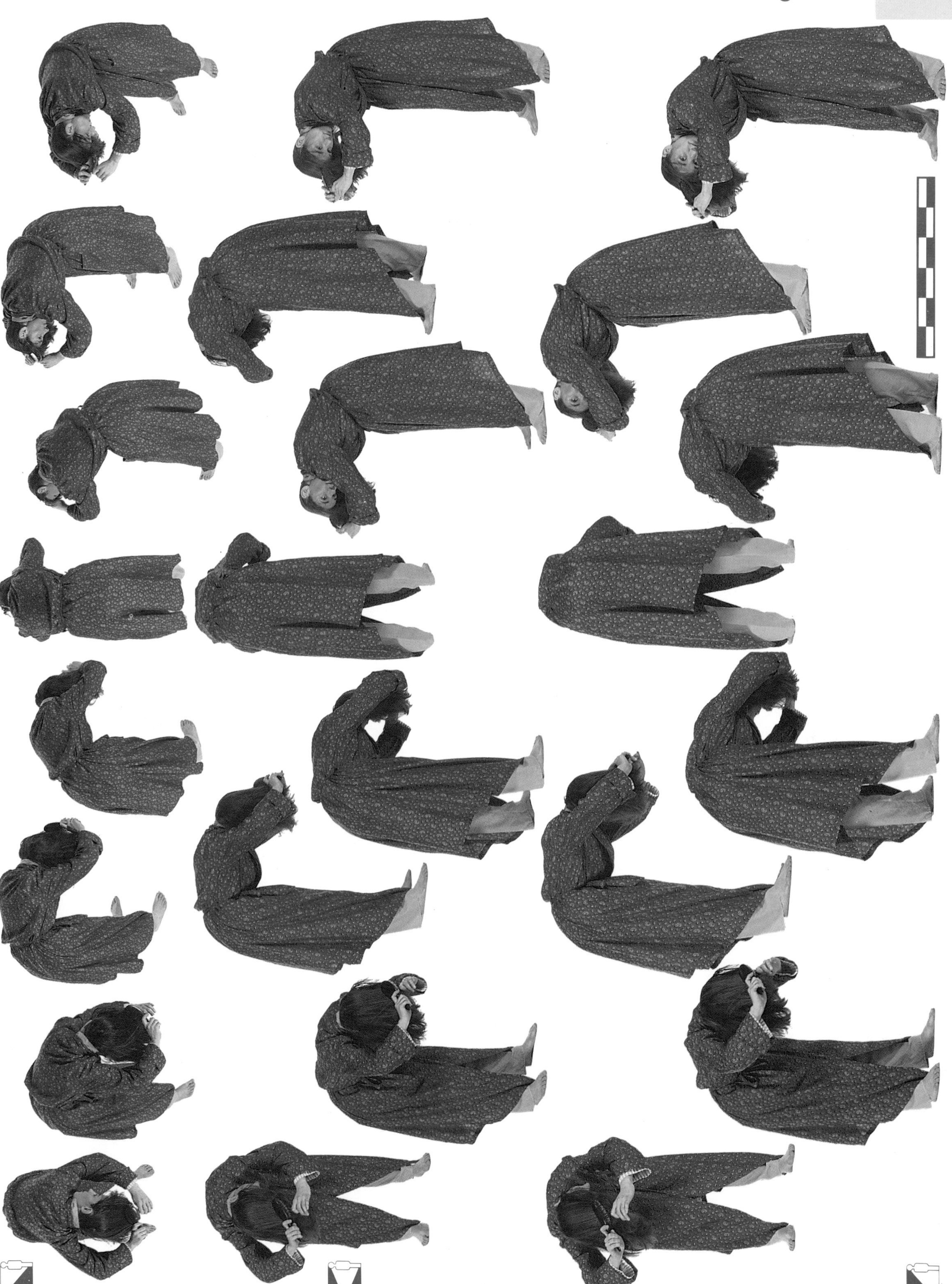

14·03 Brushing teeth

Filing nails

Touching up lipstick

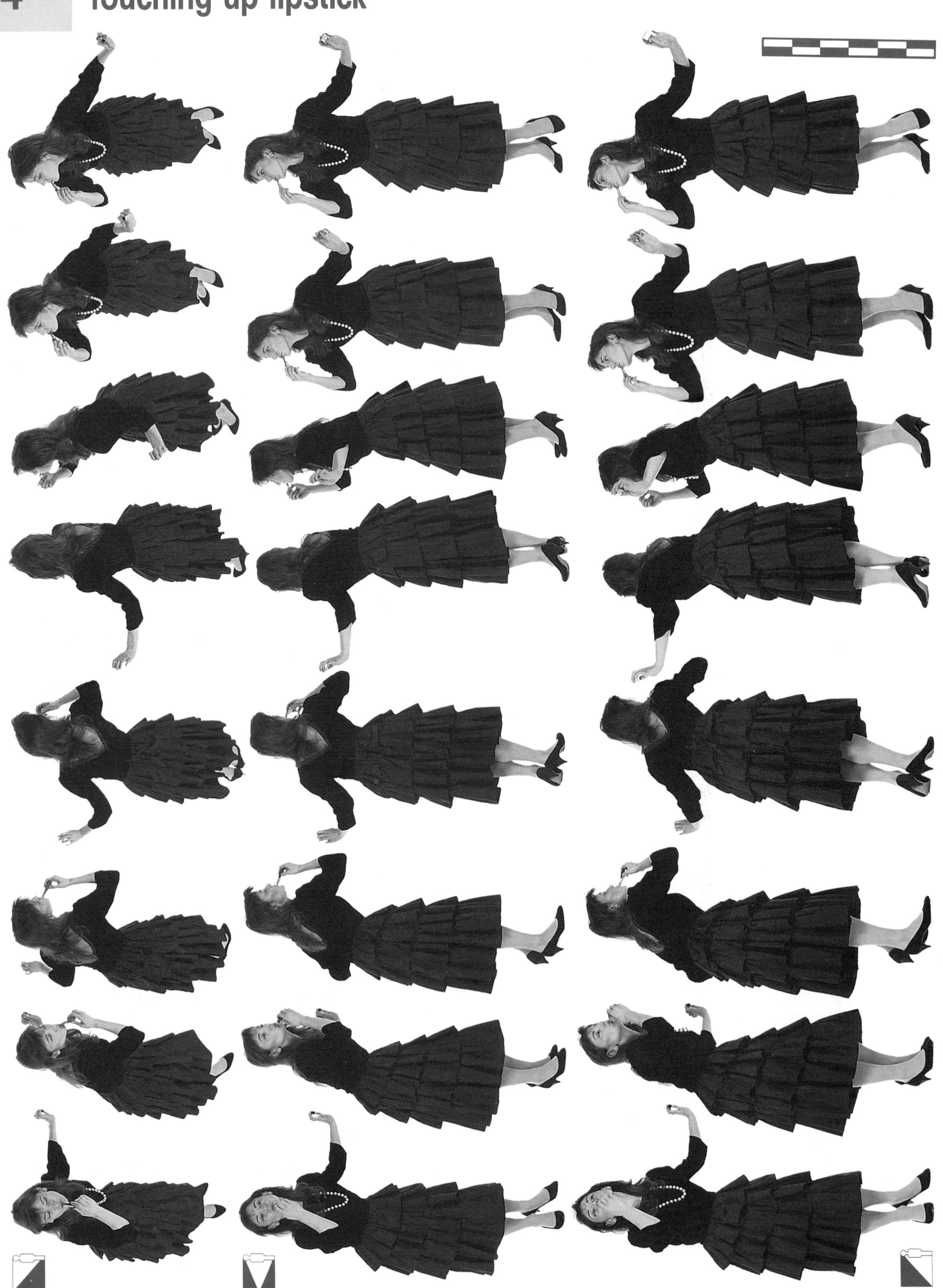

Shaving

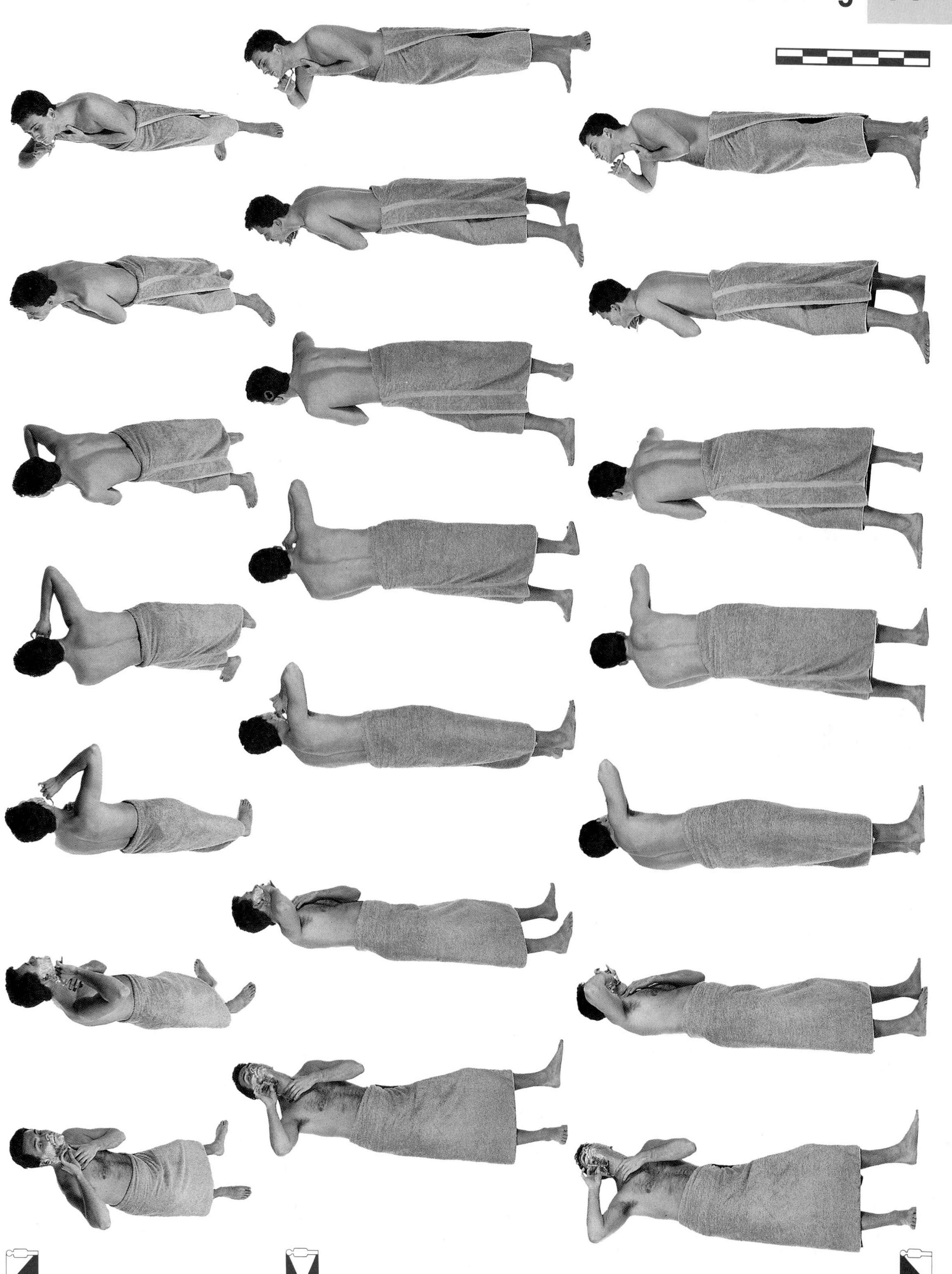

15·01 Cheesecake

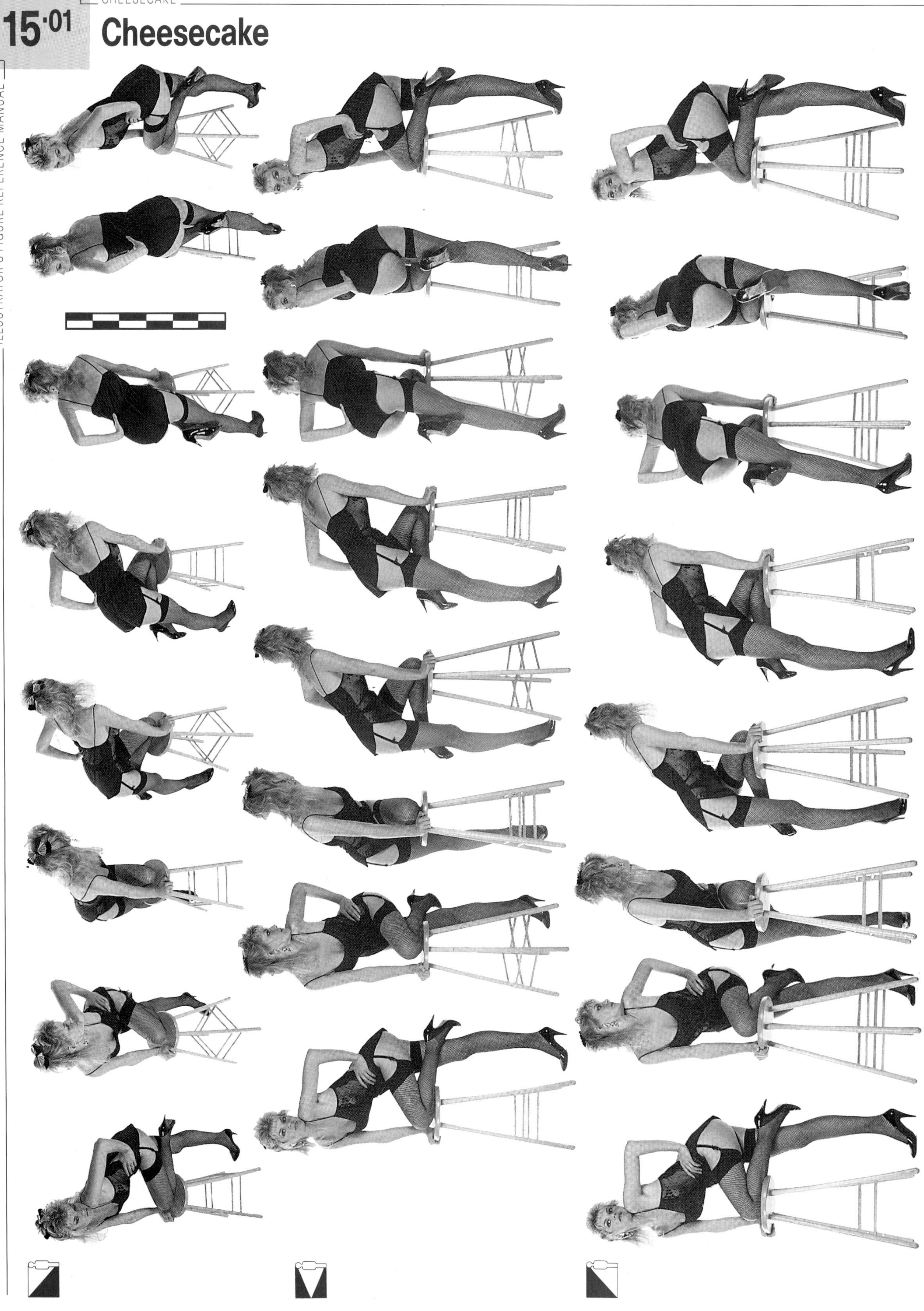

Cheesecake

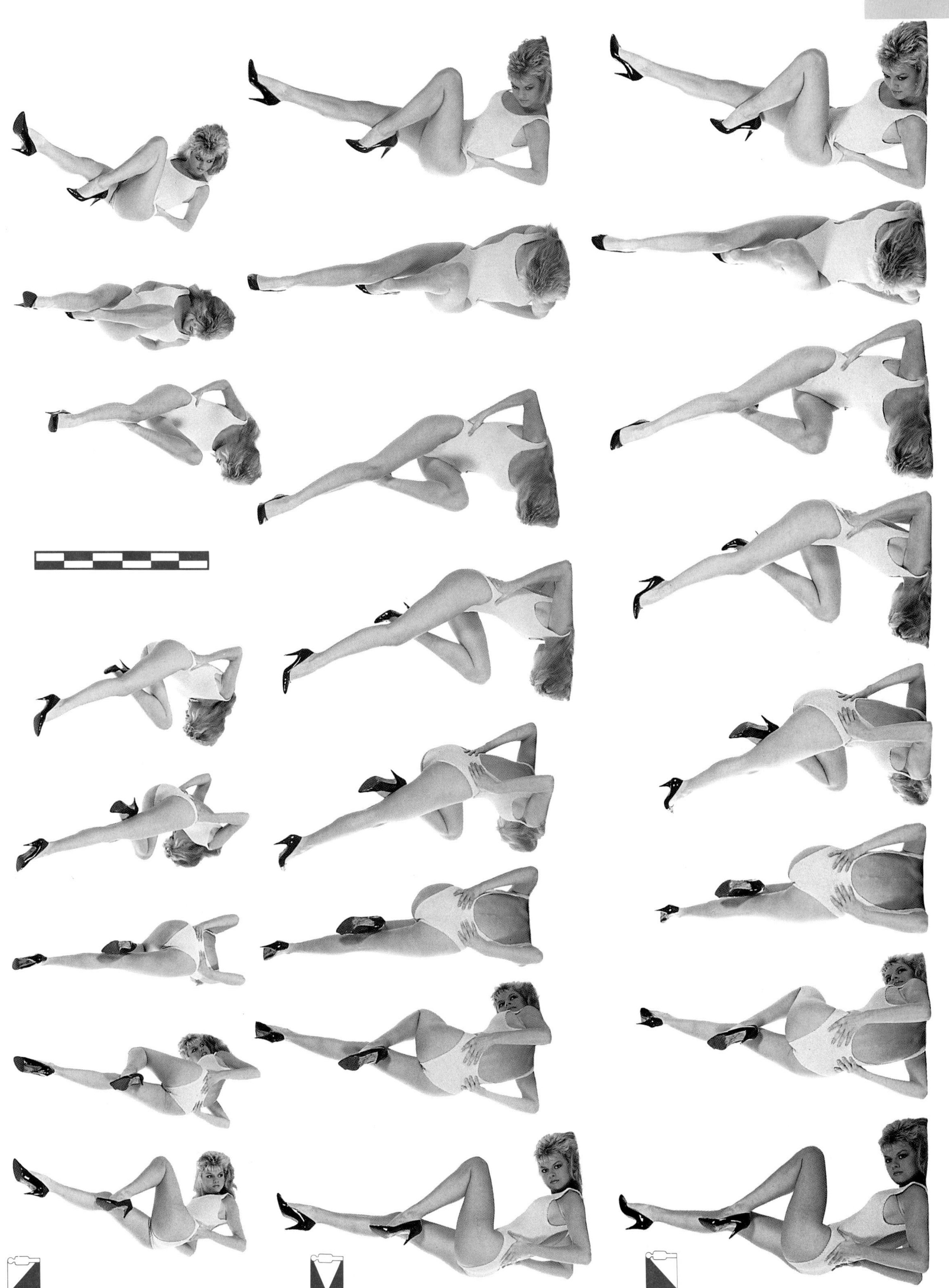

15·03 Cheesecake

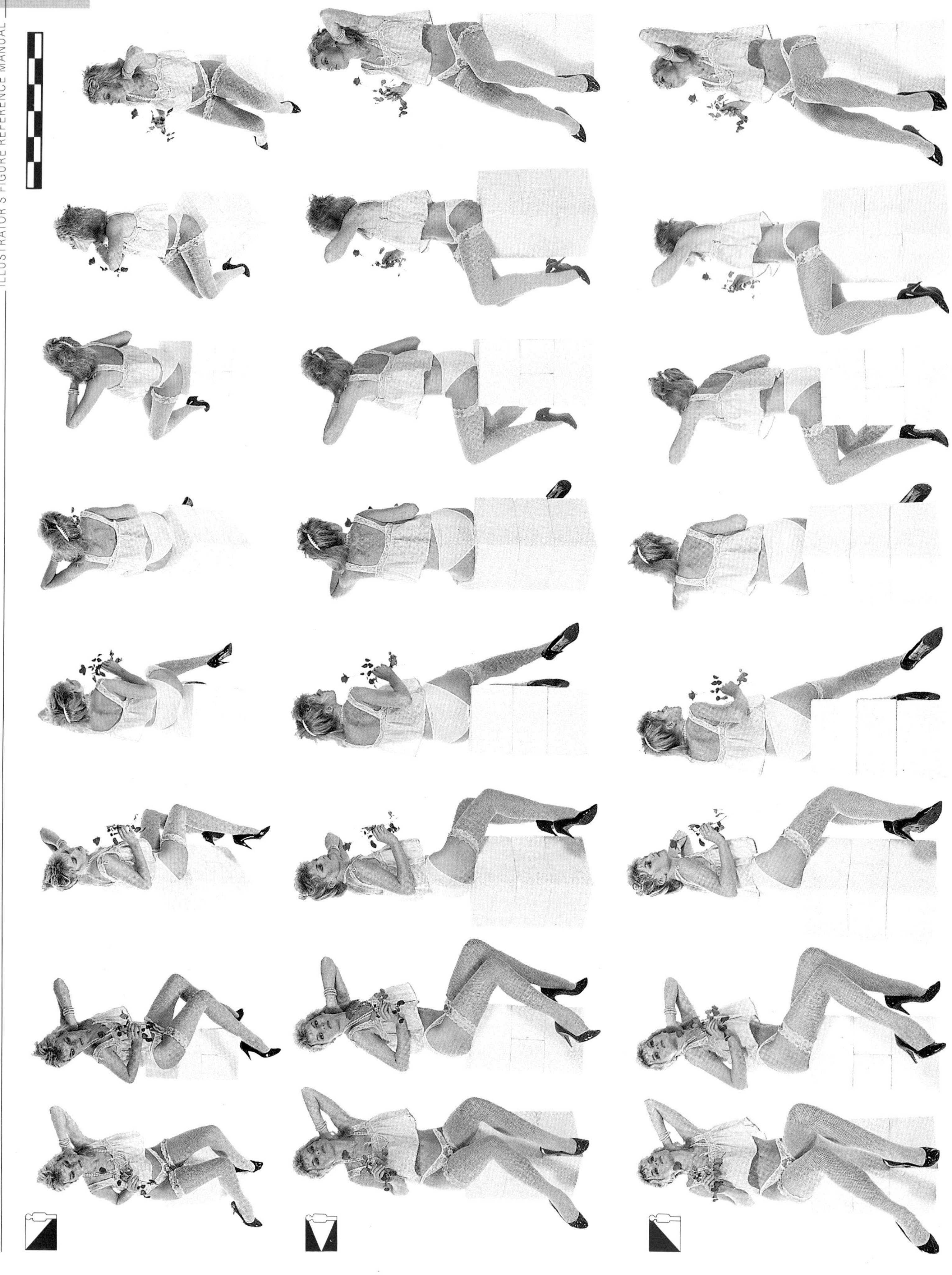

Cheesecake 15·04

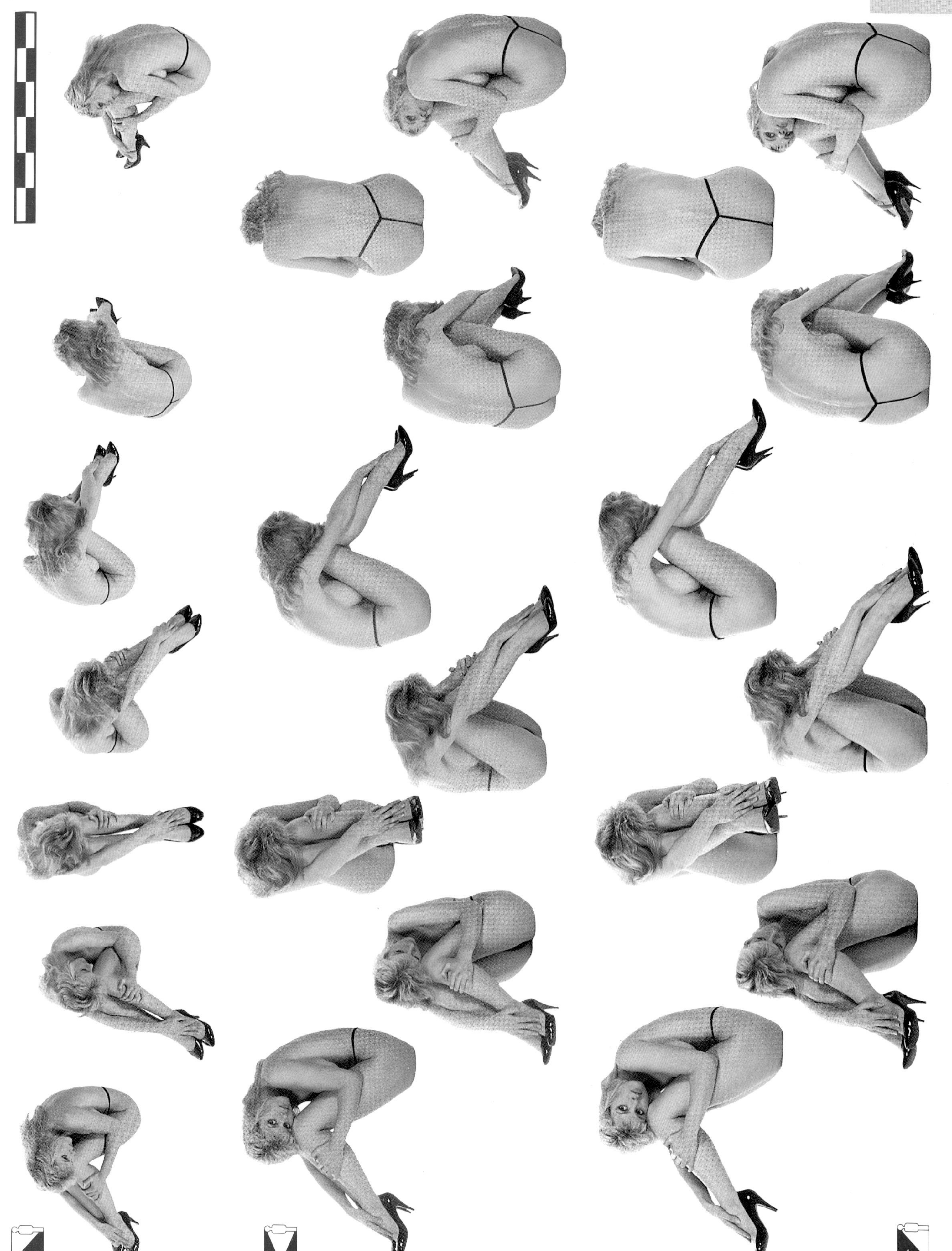

15·05 Cheesecake

15·07 Cheesecake

15·08 Cheesecake

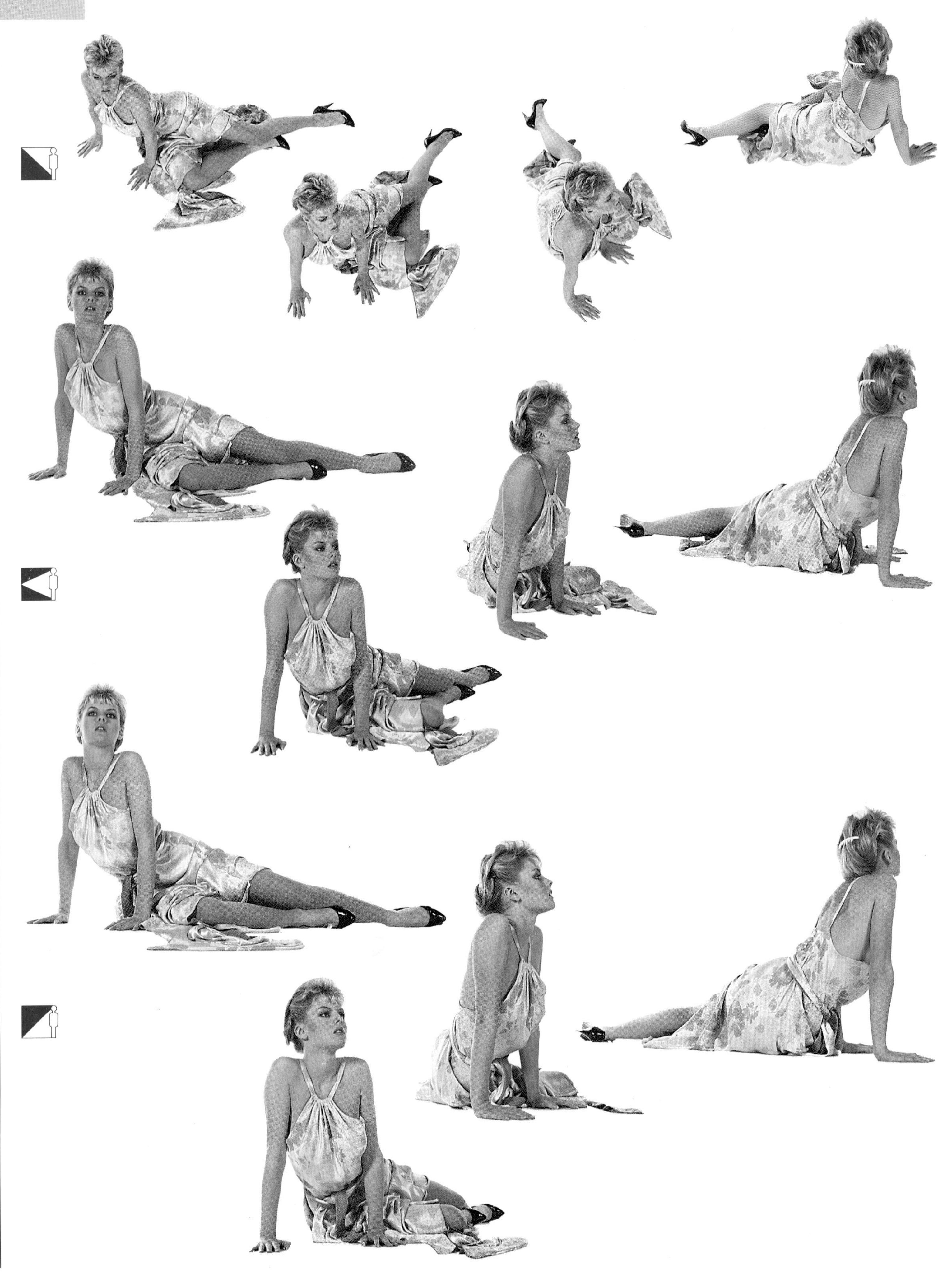

15.09 Cheesecake

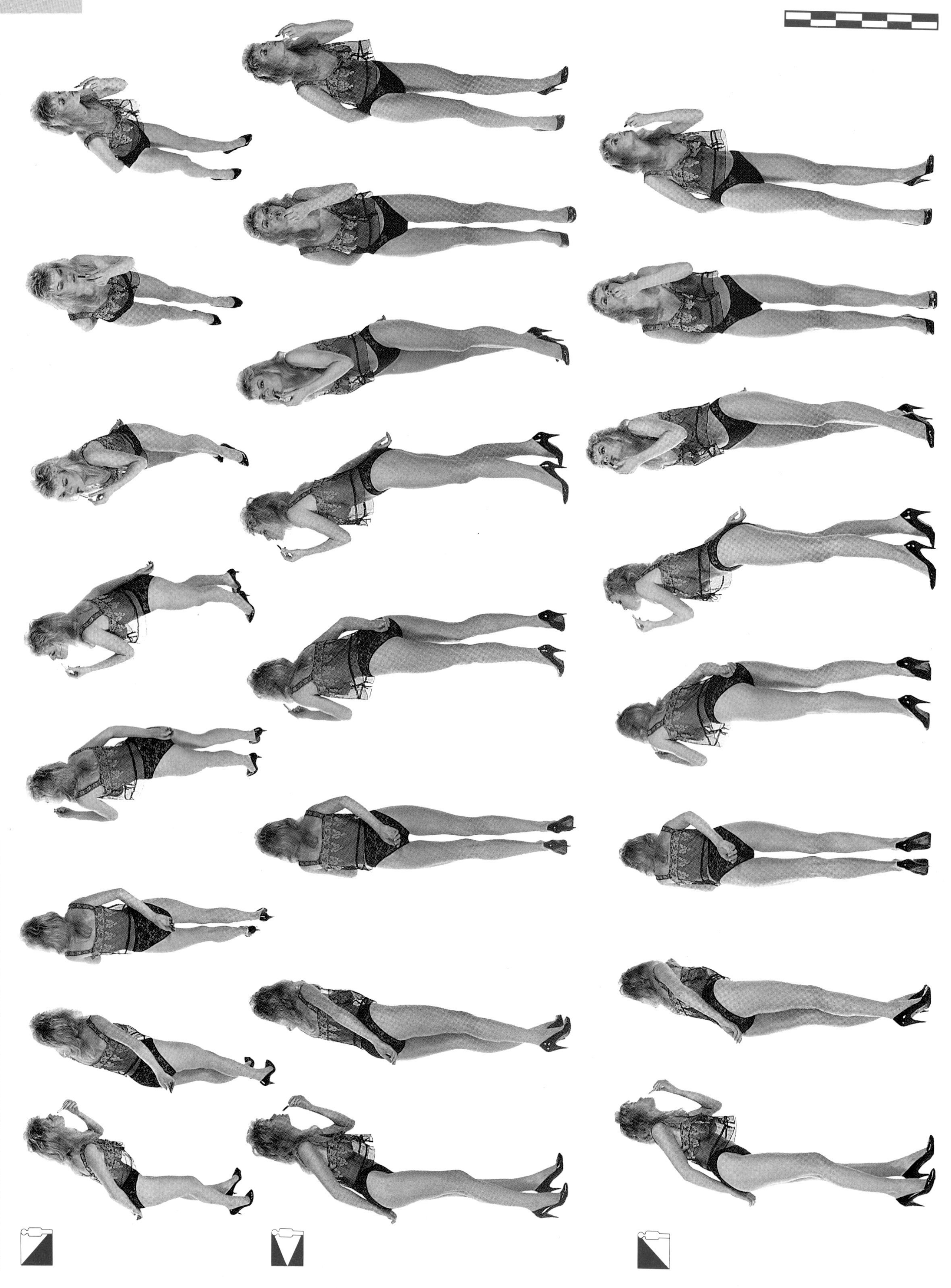

Cheesecake

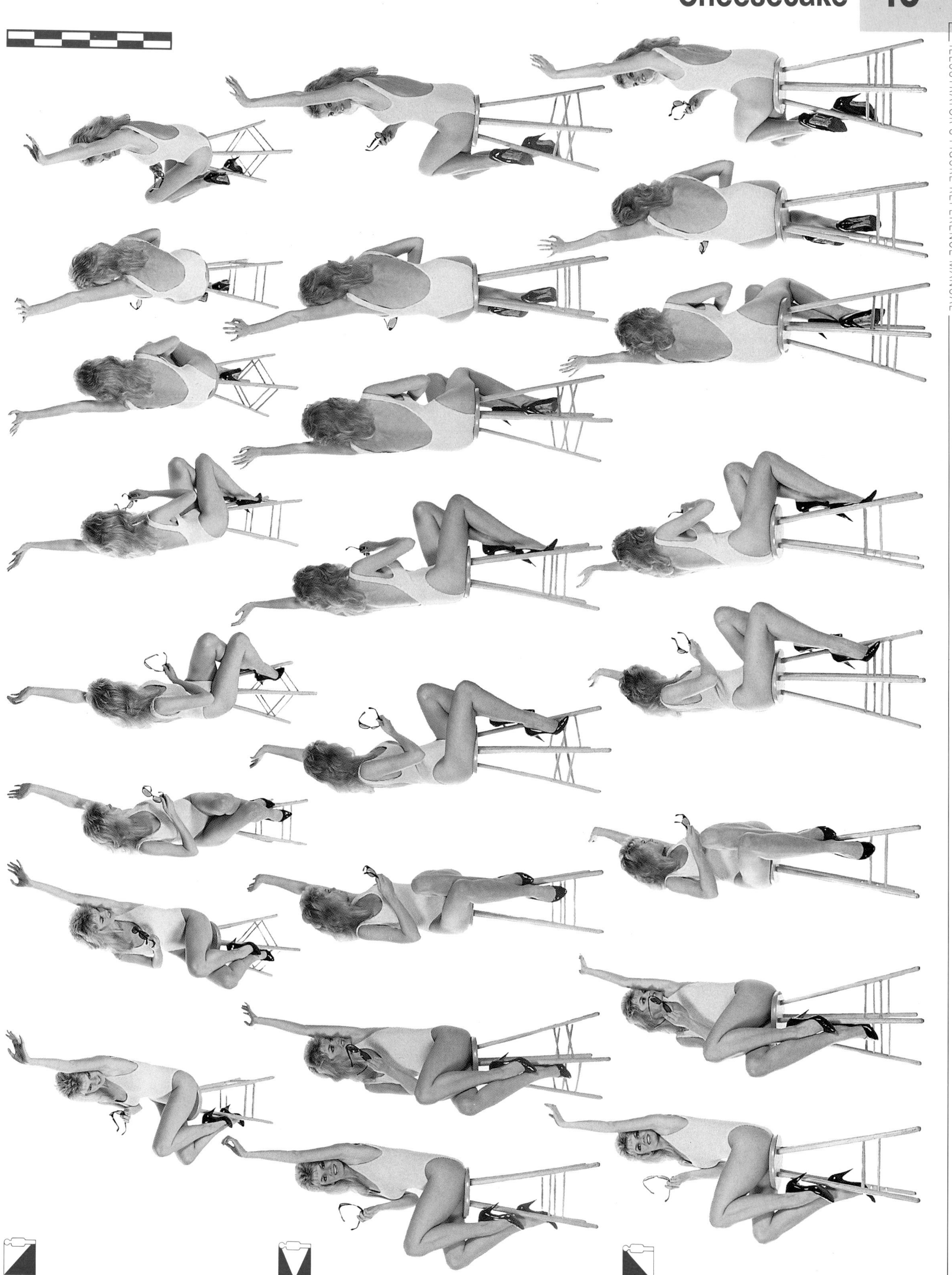

15·11 Cheesecake

Cheesecake

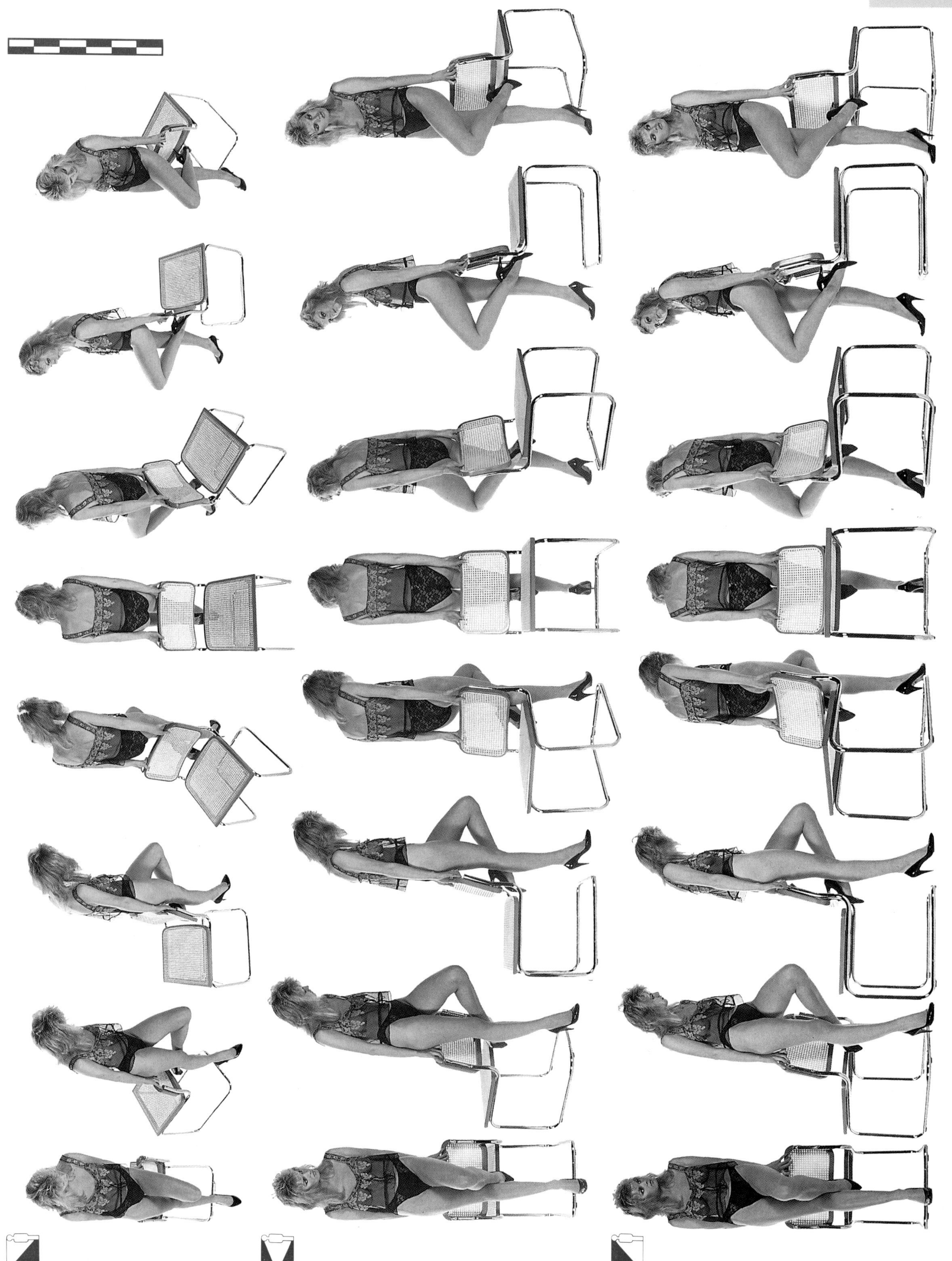

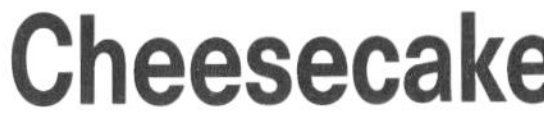

Acknowledgments

Quarto Publishing plc would like to thank the following for their assistance in the production of this book:

Alpine Sports Ltd
Bapty & Co. Ltd (weapons & militaria)
Estia Designs Ltd
Gordon Grose Sports
Lonsdale Sports Equipment Ltd
Mardi Gras (costumiers)
20th Century Props (costumiers)
Lee Robinson
Ben Smithies
Louise Talbot-Weiss

Credits

Quarto Publishing plc would like to thank the following actors, actresses and models for their highly professional work on this book:

Steve Beresford
Orla Brady
Matt Burton
Lucinda Galloway
Ruth Gordon
Simon Lambert
James Lumsden
Hannah Orthmann
John Sinnott
Carmen Stipetic

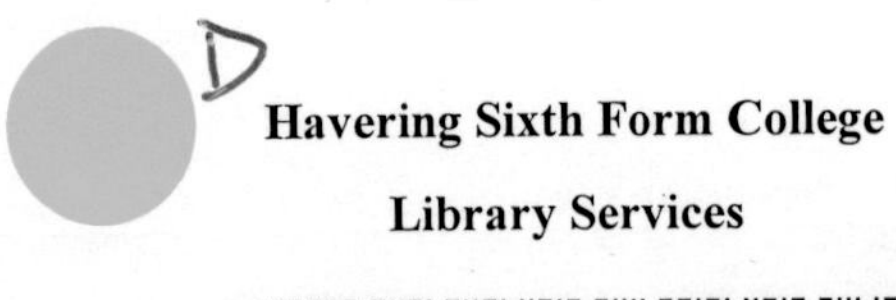

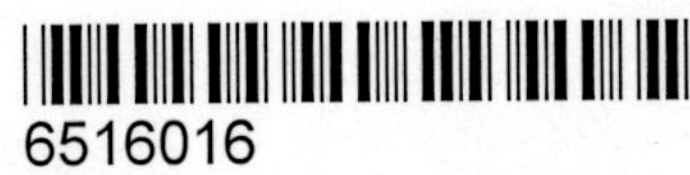